THE ART AND OF HEALTHY LIVING
I

SELECTED TOPICS:

LISTEN TO YOUR BODY AND SOUL
EXERCISE, BEAUTY AND MOVEMENT
FOOD: PSYCHOLOGY OF NUTRITION
THE HEALING POWER OF FORGIVENESS

George Kljajic, MD, M.Sc.
Vancouver–2011

AuthorHouse™
1663 Liberty Drive
Bloomington, IN 47403
www.authorhouse.com
Phone: 1-800-839-8640

© 2011 George J. Kljajic, MD, M.Sci. All Rights Reserved.

No part of this book may be reproduced, stored in a retrieval system,
or transmitted by any means without the written permission of the author.

First published by AuthorHouse 10/06/2011

ISBN: 978-1-4670-3313-8 (sc)

Library of Congress Control Number: 2011916481

Printed in the United States of America

Any people depicted in stock imagery provided by Thinkstock are models,
and such images are being used for illustrative purposes only.
Certain stock imagery © Thinkstock.

This book is printed on acid-free paper.

Because of the dynamic nature of the Internet, any web addresses or links contained in this book may have changed
since publication and may no longer be valid. The views expressed in this work are solely those of the author and do not
necessarily reflect the views of the publisher, and the publisher hereby disclaims any responsibility for them.

Design: K-Art, Vancouver, Canada

Tehnical support: Come2Fix, Bellingham, Wa, USA

Art editor: Dragica Kljajic

Editor in chief: Laurel Phelan

Printing:

All right reserved

No part of this book can be copied in written form, filmed or copied in electronic form or copied or transmitted in any other form without the written consent and approval of the author or publisher. These books contain a great deal of knowledge and information in fields of health and describe the course and nature of various illnesses. However, both the author and the publisher recommend that every reader should refer their health problems to their own physician. The author and publisher do not undertake responsibility for consequences of following health advice contained in these books. Health dysfunction or disease in each particular patient is very individual and requires specific, attention and approach.

Photography:

©www.shutterstock.com: 12, 13, 17, 20, 21, 24, 25, 27, 28, 31, 32, 36, 38, 39, 40, 41, 42, 43, 45, 46, 47, 48, 53, 54, 56, 58, 59, 61, 62, 63, 67, 69, 72, 73, 76, 77, 78, 81, 82, 83, 85, 86, 89, 90, 94, 95, 96, 98, 100, 101, 102, 103, 106, 108, 110, 111, 112, 113, 114, 117, 120, 121, 123, 124, 126, 127, 128, 129, 131, 132, 134, 137, 138, 139, 140, 142, 143, 144, 145, 146, 147, 151, 152, 153, 155, 156, 158, 159, 161, 163, 164, 167, 169, 171, 172, 173, 174, 175, 176, 177, 180, 182, 183, 184, 185, 186, 187.

©K-Art: 14, 15, 16, 18, 22, 35, 44, 50, 57, 64, 65, 68, 71, 72, 75, 76, 79, 80, 88, 89, 91, 92, 93, 97, 99, 103, 109, 116, 119, 122, 130, 138, 141, 148, 149, 162, 165, 166, 168, 170, 185.

©Ivezić S.: 26, 29, 37, 60, 154, 178.

Dedicated to

I dedicate these books and express my gratitude to the memory of my parents: my mother Kata, for her tenderness, love and care, for her conscious desire in higher goals, her exceptional common sense, and her sense of order and discipline.

To my father Jovan, for his boundless human goodness, his lessons of tolerance and high moral principles.

I also dedicate these books to the memory of my sisters Marija, Milka and brother Ilija.

I thank my sisters Zorka and Jovanka and brothers Nikola and Milan for their unselfish love and support, especially during the years when I was growing up and being educated.

I am grateful to all my patients, on two continents, from whom I learned a great deal and who gave me inspiration and motivation.

Acknowledgement and gratitude

The publication of these two books about health would not be possible without the help and persistent, continuous work and assistance of a sizeable number of diligent persons and institutions over a period of twelve years. This is an occasion to mention their names and to thank them.

Before everything, I am grateful to the editorial staff of the monthly magazine "Kisobran". While in competition with other magazines, Kisobran has maintained an authentic style and non-biased approach toward the dignity of man and, in such a way, has discovered the true path and found a way into the hearts of thousands of readers on all continents of the world.

Special thanks goes to Katarina Kljajic and her company K–Art for their big effort on the design of the books on which they worked for over six months and to Pavle Kljajic and his company Come2Fix, that made a significant electronic contribution toward the technical make up of the books and for their optimal solutions toward the following text.

I am warmly grateful to Dragana Lalic for her dedicated help and preparation of the text for publication.

My wife Dragica deserves the warmest thanks for her enthusiasm, support and creative ideas about the illustrations and management of these books.

I express my special thanks to my readers who wrote to me or spoke to encourage me or to criticize my articles. All my work and effort has been inspired and performed for their good.

To all my readers, I express my warmest thanks.

Vancouver, 2011

TABLE OF CONTENTS:

CHAPTER I–AN APROACH TO HEALTH

- 14 MEDICINE, HEALTH, AND LIFESTYLE
- 18 LISTEN TO YOUR BODY AND SOUL
- 23 THE PHILOSOPHICAL APPROACH TO BEHAVIOR
- 26 OPTIMISM AND HEALTH IN TIMES OF CRISIS
- 30 IN TIMES OF DARKNESS, THERE IS ALWAYS HOPE
- 34 HEALTHY LIFE AND HAPPY HORMONES

CHAPTER II–A HEALTHY LIFESTYLE

- 40 EXERCISE, BEAUTY AND MOVEMENT
- 44 ALCOHOL–THE TRUTH
- 47 THE ROAD TO HEALTH IS HARD AND LONG
- 50 SMOKING AND CIGARETTES: SAVE YOUR BREATH
- 53 CHRONIC TIREDNESS SYNDROME: CAUSES AND SOLUTIONS
- 57 HUMOR HEALS, SO GO AHEAD AND LAUGH!
- 60 GET YOUR ANNUAL PHYSICAL CHECK-UP

CHAPTER III–FOOD AND NUTRITION

- 66 FOOD: PSYCHOLOGY OF NUTRITION
- 70 REDUCING OUR APPETITE AND PORTION SIZES
- 74 HABITS: HOW DO WE EAT?
- 77 SANDWICHES AND SODA, SAUSAGES AND BEER
- 81 HEALTHY NUTRITION AND CHOOSING FOOD
- 84 PROTEIN: MEAT AND MORE SOLUTIONS
- 87 THE MAGIC FORMULA: THE MEDITERRANEAN DIET

CHAPTER IV–FREQUENTLY OCCURING DISEASES

- 94 LIFESTYLE, HEALTH AND BLOOD PRESSURE
- 99 REDUCE OUR THUMPING HEART RATES
- 103 HEART ATTACK OR MYOCARDICAL INFARCT
- 106 HOW TO AVOID SUDDEN DEATH?
- 109 ASTHMA AND ALLERGIES: OUR PETS OR OUR SPOUSE?
- 112 HEADACHES AND SOLUTIONS
- 115 OBESITY IS AN EPIDEMIC!
- 118 DIABETES: ARE WE TOO SWEET?
- 122 HIGH CHOLESTEROL: AN INSIDIOUS ENEMY
- 125 SMILE, YOUR TEETH ARE SHOWING!
- 128 WHAT'S BUGGING OUR LIVER?
- 132 WARNING: KIDNEY STONES
- 135 CANCER IS PREVENTABLE
- 139 HARD BONES FOR A LONG LIFE

142 JOINTS AND ARTHRITIS, ACHES AND PAINS
145 SAVE YOUR EYES!

CHAPTER V–MENTAL HEALTH
150 PSYCHOLOGICAL ASPECTS ABOUT MENTAL HEALTH
153 HOW TO DEVELOP AND APPLY YOUR OWN MIND?
157 DEPRESSION–RESULT AND PRICE OF TECHNOLOGY
160 MIDDLE AGE CRISIS
164 INSOMNIA: GOOD MORNING, HOW DID YOU SLEEP?
168 QUALITY OF LIFE, HEALTHY MIND AND MUSCLES
171 THE HEALING POWER OF FORGIVENESS

CHAPTER VI–STRESS AND HEALTH
176 STRESS AND CHRONIC STRESS–THE MODERN AGE DISEASE
180 HOW TO SURVIVE PSYCHOLOGICAL STRESS AFTER TRAUMA?
184 STRESS AND TIREDNESS: PATIENT'S AND PHYSICIAN'S RIGHTS

188 BIBLIOGRAPHY

Laurel Phelan–Editor

As an author and editor, I was honored to be asked by Dr. Kljajic to assist in the editing process of his articles and books.

As I read through the articles, I found myself excited and curious to finally read a book on health and healing that was clear, to the point, fluent and truly educational. Over the years I have read numerous books on healing and I find Dr. Kljajic's encouraging articles to be insightful and necessary in our modern world. He not only gives us the benefit of updated medical knowledge and his vast experience as a physician, but helps us realize that "we" are our own healers and the gift of healing is within our grasp.

After reading and working on these books, I have learned that it is indeed possible to take responsibility for our health through well informed approach, common sense and wisdom.

Thank you Dr. Kljajic for writing this necessary body of work.

Laurel Phelan,
Author of Guinevere and Healing Through Time

The Appraisals

This is a wonderful series of articles about healthy living, healthy nutrition, healthy body, mind and spirit, healthy relationships with others and with oneself. Only the wealth of experience and careful observation through many years of practicing medicine can bring such a masterful guide together. While the world has never seen a time in history where so much information has been available to all, true knowledge is difficult to find and wisdom is rather rare. Yet, Dr. Kljajic provides a practical and well written guide to healthy living, so much needed in this world lost in "health information" and society of a consumerism. His thoughts and advice inspires us to remember the beauty of simplicity and the right action. He reminds us how to be true to oneself and to our nature. He provides a much needed disease prevention paradigm, a paradigm that medicine today is being called upon to provide.

Mira Keyes MD FRCPC
Radiation Oncologist
Clinical Associate Professor, Department of Surgery UBC

The Art and Science of Healthy Living–
Thoughts and Recommendations

Among the many books which give recommendations and advice on how to lead a healthy life, there has appeared one, or actually two books, which can be singled out for their uniqueness. Written in an easy style of an author who knows and understands health problems and how they can be overcome and solved if they are recognized and understood. Dr. Kljajic has tapped into his rich life experience and professional experience and his honest desire to help people.

The author describes serious medical and life problems and makes these problems approachable, acceptable and solvable for every reader, whether he is talking about steps toward health and a healthy lifestyle, or discussing the function of food as medicine, or medicine as food, or even about frequently occurring diseases of modern man

Specially worthy is Dr. Kljajic's warm and wise advice about problems raising children and young people. He is critical, but understanding, about why many parents don't spend enough time with their children. He also shows us how institutions, designed to take care and educate children, have often failed them and how modern electronic media negatively affects the psyche and behavior of children, leading them toward destructive actions.

Dr. Kljajic's books are full of practical observations, advice and recommendations which apply for all periods of one's life.

The honesty, simplicity, humanity and wisdom of the author forcefully lead the reader toward the author's goal, which is to help the average man or woman to save the integrity of their personality, their health and their family, in the embrace of the wider social and ecological community. I warmly recommend Dr. Kljajic's books to everyone.

Dr. Sci. Med. Nada Bokan–Erdeljan,
Pediatrician and Professor of Pediatric Medicine at the University of Belgrade

Introduction

My main source of inspiration for these articles were the meetings I had in my office with men, women and children of all nationalities, who came to visit me because of a wide variety of health problems. Many of my articles were also inspired by meetings I had with people outside of my office while attending public meetings, and after giving lectures at various speaker's platforms.

People confronted me with their concerns about their health, psychological problems, worries about their economic survival, maintenance of their families, as well as expressing their concerns about their endless race against time and effort to meet their obligations. All of these problems had a significant impact on their health, feelings and moods. In order to gain knowledge about these problems of health, as well as finding a solution to them, I sought the best available current information to be found in medical journals and I also took advantage of the knowledge and experience I had gained working as a physician for many years.

These books represent a selection of articles which have permanent value and which I believe have general application and significance for a majority of people living in our contemporary society. The articles are not arranged chronologically but according to various themes about health.

Today, modern medicine has attained a high level of development and plays a very important role in the lives of every individual and our whole community. It's evident that a majority of the most important problems in health are covered here and that the reader of these books can find useful and practical suggestions about how to preserve one's health. I have especially covered proactive themes on how to raise our awareness about health, how to learn more about a healthy lifestyle, how to strengthen health and avoid serious diseases of modern time such as: blood vessel disease and arteriosclerosis (clogging-up of the arteries), heart attacks, strokes, malignant diseases and various types of cancers, car accident injuries, degenerative diseases and psychological dysfunctions.

Some of the themes, such as nutrition, diseases of the heart and blood vessels, and upbringing of children, are covered more than once from different perspectives. The attentive reader will spot many themes and topics that tend to be repeated in order to stress the optimistic themes, which I believe are not only useful but are also indispensable.

Dr. George Kljajic

Vancouver–2011

Biography

Dr. Kljajic has been deeply influenced by the rich and multi layered contents of European history and culture. His personality and professional integrity have also been shaped by less harmonious history and the rich culture of South Slavic people, among which he grew up.

Dr. Kljajic completed his medical studies at the Medical Faculty in Belgrade. This faculty was constantly enriched by close contact with medical faculties in Paris, London, Vienna and Heidelberg. After his first few years of medical practice, Dr. Kljajic specialized in transfusion medicine in 1976, and in internal medicine in 1980 in Belgrade.

Dr. Kljajic has worked at medical clinics in Belgrade and at the General Hospital in Zrenjanin. After that, he worked in the Clinic for Internal Diseases of the Medical Faculty of Novi Sad. He continued his medical studies by specializing in haematology in 1986, and obtained his Master's Degree in Medicine in 1988 at the Haematology Clinic of the Faculty of Medicine of Novi Sad. There he worked as an internist and haematologist and an assistant professor from 1986 until 1992.

When he came to Canada, Dr. Kljajic experienced some culture shock and had to adapt to his new social and cultural surroundings. Immigration greatly inspired him to obtain new experiences and knowledge of his new surroundings. Dr. Kljajic was re-certified as a medical doctor at the University of British Columbia (UBC), Vancouver, B.C. Canada.

He received a special award from the obstetric clinic at British Columbia Women's Hospital, for his high level of professional work and his praiseworthy approach in communicating with patients, nurses and other doctors. He lives In Vancouver, works in his private medical office and cooperates with the Royal Columbian Hospital in New Westminster, B.C.

To contact the author: georgejk98@hotmail.com

Book I

A positive approach to health and life in general is, in essence, an awareness of health. The consciousness of health in modern society is often neglected. Many aspects of existence, such as work, career or entertainment, are placed ahead of health. A lot of facts about the value of positive, optimistic and a proactive approach to health show that a positive approach deserves a lot more attention.

There exists strong evidence that a great number of health problems can be prevented through wise planning of one's life, choice of career, as well as type of people and the community one chooses to surround oneself with. Prudent planning is the best path toward realization of health. Such wise planning also enhances the personal, biological and sociological role of a person.

Nutrition is the essential element of a healthy life. There is a lot written and said about nutrition but, despite this, a large number of people, and especially children, continue to have unhealthy nutrition. The main reasons for this are being uninformed, in a hurry, or because of negligence. Every article contains new information, often from a different angle or perspective.

The most frequently occurring diseases of modern time are: diseases of blood vessels and clogging up of the arteries, heart attack or infarct, brain strokes, malignant diseases and various types of cancer, car accident injuries, degenerative diseases, and psychological disorders. The majority of these diseases can be prevented, and many of them may be reduced in severity by planning ahead, and with a conscious choice of a healthy way of life and everyday activities.

The dynamic of modern life is very stratified and often controversial. Many more people today experience psychological problems than in the past. An essential part of this book reports on the psychology of health, and man's desire, not only to survive, but also to make progress and to realize one's potential.

Stress is an essential trait of modern time and I discuss stress in several articles. My goal is to familiarize the reader about how to recognize the nature of stress as a problem, and to learn how to lower stress and how to avoid stressful situations.

I

A POSITIVE HEALTH ATTITUDE

Optimism is a noble plant grown under home conditions

MEDICINE, HEALTH, AND LIFESTYLE

- Introduction to medicine and the definition of health
- Medicine as science, art, and philosophy
- The focus of modern medicine
- Diseases of the poor and diseases of the rich are not the same

"Good day", "How are you?", "How is your health?", "How is your family?" These are traditionally greetings and questions that are asked when friends and acquaintances meet. For centuries this has reflected a list of priorities among the majority of people, not only in our culture but also among many other cultures. The importance of health is stressed as a basic condition of our biological and social existence. Health is the elementary criterion in the evaluation of the quality of our life. Good health is a basic condition needed for our well-being and is seen as life in its most beautiful condition. Good health is also a basic precondition necessary for all other achievements.

- **Introduction to medicine and the definition of health**

The scientific definition of health according to World Health Organization of the United Nations (WHO) is: "Health is not only the absence of disease and disability, but complete psychological, physical and social well-being."

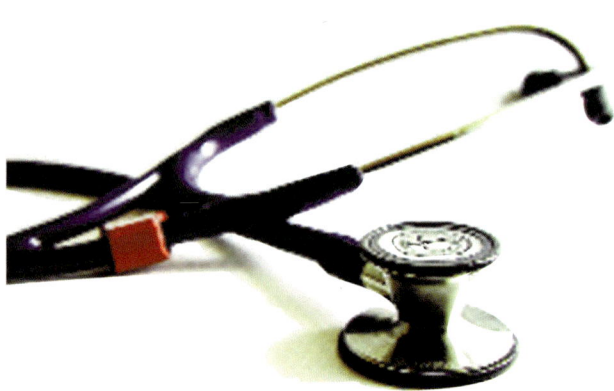

Many people live for years in a state of psychological stress, anxiety, and depression. Many of these people are unemployed, lonely, have high blood pressure, are overweight, suffer from headaches, have pains in their bones and joints, and are overcome with mental problems. All the above named conditions are roadblocks toward leading a healthy life. Are these people healthy? Has medicine advanced to such a level that it can discover in every person a small or a larger health problem, or is everyone unhealthy? When conducting a well researched history of disease and by using a basic medical check-up, a majority of people can be diagnosed with many weak spots in their health. In many of these people, signs of various diseases can be detected, including serious diseases. The above named definition of health by WHO should be accepted as a model and an example to strive for. Common sense tells us that good health is the best gift that a man can possess. Good health is a basic precondition for striving to reach our goals in our personal life, family life, social life, work and career, spiritual and mental life. Do we give enough attention toward our health? Do we do everything in our power to safeguard our health and to improve it?

Leonardo Da Vinci said, "Man spends the first half of his life losing his health, and then spends the rest of his life, after learning what he has done, attempting to regain what he has lost."

An old proverb states, "A healthy man has hundreds of wishes, but a sick man has only one wish, to get well."

According to one study (1), the majority of people who experience some physical difficulty don't go to see a doctor, and only about ten percent actually seek professional help. The rest attempt to get well on their own, seek advice from their friends and relatives, visit naturopathic healers, and take herbal products.

■ **Medicine as science, art, and philosophy**

Medicine as Science

As a scientific discipline, medicine is based on scientific knowledge and scientific studies. Modern medicine is based on evidence which can be measured scientifically, which is tangible and which is based on human experience.

Medicine was founded on Hippocratic ethical principles and humble, basic postulates of natural sciences in Ancient Greece (at that time it was believed that there were only four basic elements in nature: earth, water, air and fire). Medicine as a scientific study was enriched and built up due to great progress in the natural sciences of chemistry, physics, and biology, especially in the nineteenth century and particularly in the twentieth century. The progress in these sciences has been compressed into concepts of biotechnology (genetics, genetic engineering, immunology, organ transplant and pharmacology), which has experienced a great flowering and revolutionary progress in diagnosis and treatment of various diseases in the last few decades. The development of new knowledge in medicine has contributed significantly toward new fields in sociology, philosophy and social sciences during the last 100 years and particularly in the last few decades of the twentieth century.

There is a strong impression that technology is surpassing the development in social sciences, which may have negative consequences in areas of psychological effects, moral norms and legal implications.

Medicine as an Art

The art of medicine consists of the subtle combining of medical knowledge, human compassion and empathy, and choice of the right approach and establishment of good psychological contact with those who need help. Every doctor, health worker, or healer has an opportunity to show their creativity and appropriateness of their behavior, choice of methods of examination and healing, motivation of patients, educating them about nature and duration of the disease, and opening the doors of hope toward recovery and healing. Very often, the first and only effect of healing is understanding, trust, encouragement and a empathetic human word. Support from the doctors and elimination of fear often helps a patient to find a way to recovery on their own.

Medicine as a philosophy

The basic philosophical principle of medicine is to reduce human suffering, to remove pain and to enable healthy functioning of the body and soul. The basic principle of philosophy is the consciousness of morality and sympathy or empathy, which is based on true humanity and ethics of healing. They contain:

Autonomy; the right to self-determination and voluntary agreement, and willingness to cooperate in treatment and examination of disease;

Good intentions; whose goal is a person's well-being, promotion of health, prevention and cure of disease;

Fairness; as a principle of equality of access to medical help which is free from discrimination based on social, racial, gender, nationality or faith orientation; and

Confidentiality and privacy of information; privacy is the highest foundational principle in relations between a doctor and his/her patients and from which one may diverge lawfully only in exceptional circumstances.

■ **The focus of modern medicine**

The main problems that face a medical practice change with time, conditions of life and improvement in diagnostic and treatment possibilities for various diseases. For many centuries people have become ill from many diseases, which at that time were of an unknown cause and origin. In the past, treatment of disease was based on limited knowledge and the eventual outcome of the disease was often negative.

At the end of the nineteenth and the beginning of the twentieth century there was a substantial development of all basic branches of medicine, which helped to establish better diagnosis of disease and to ensure more success in the cure of disease.

For centuries in the past, until the middle of the twentieth century, the main medical problems encountered in most countries were infectious diseases and infections, diseases of improper and insufficient nutrition, most encompassing malignant diseases, heart and blood vessel disease, as well as alcoholism and diseases due to social deprivation.

Because of the strong growth of pharmacology, immunology, programs of vaccination, and better hygiene, the problem of infection has been reduced substantially. On the other hand, intensive industrialization enabled the rise in the standard of living and the lowering of prices for commodities, which largely solved the problem of lack of food, and improved the social status of most people living in developed industrialized countries.

Unfortunately, in many undeveloped countries, especially in Africa and South America, people still experience problems of basic survival such as; unavailability of water, food, housing or access to adequate medical help. In these countries, many people die of starvation, thirst and because there are no medicines to treat diseases such as malaria, tuberculosis or AIDS.

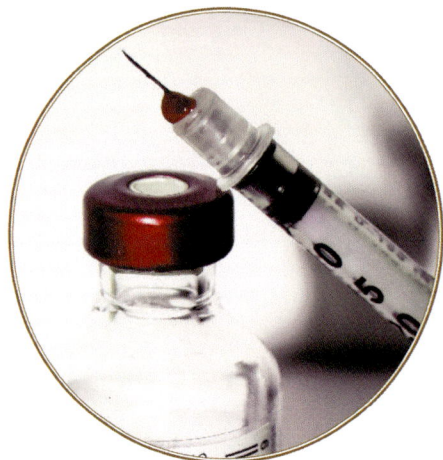

Today, there has been a growth in knowledge about malignant diseases that previously usually ended in death, so that many people who suffer from them, if they are diagnosed early, can be cured.

Current medical problems in developed countries are often due to an overabundance of unhealthy food and improper nutrition. Lack of adequate exercise and a sedentary lifestyle also contribute to many medical problems such as obesity, heart and blood vessel diseases, a rise in blood pressure, heart attacks (myocardial infarction), strokes, an increase in malignant diseases, especially lung cancer (due to cigarette smoking), colon and prostate cancer in men, and lung, breast and uterine cancer in women.

Next in frequency are viral diseases, such as AIDS, and diseases which are due to obesity, such as digestive organ diseases, and joint and bone diseases. Many psychological illnesses are caused by isolation, depression, anxiety and stress.

The focus of current medical efforts is directed toward prevention and treatment of mass occurring diseases of heart and blood vessels, prevention of unhealthy habits (addiction to alcohol, tobacco and recreational drugs), education about healthy nutrition (especially the reduction of trans-fats in our diet, and a reduction in our caloric intake of unhealthy foods), education about safe sexual practices, prevention of AIDS and other sexually transmitted diseases. Significant efforts are being made, and positive results are being achieved, in the fields of genetic diagnosis and treatment, as well as in organ transplant of livers, hearts, lungs, kidneys, retinas and other important organs.

■ **Diseases of the poor and diseases of the rich are not the same**

Unequal distribution of wealth among developed and undeveloped countries that are still growing also contributes to different types of diseases that prevail in these nations. The biggest medical problem of poor countries, such as Africa for example, is lack of clean water, adequate food, and lack of medicines to treat diseases such as malaria, tuberculosis and AIDS. People in more developed and richer nations in western Europe and North America more often suffer from diseases caused by an intake of too much food (often of the wrong type of processed food) which causes obesity, diabetes, heart and blood vessel disease and an increase of malignant diseases.

My advice is that there needs to be a greater level of awareness about general health and a greater knowledge base among our population about the most important aspects of health. What can people do for themselves in this important area? People can do a lot! The first step is to choose to live a healthy lifestyle; avoid excessive alcohol consumption, stop smoking cigarettes, reduce your intake of too many calories, eat more frequent smaller meals, which contain plenty of fresh fruits and vegetables, and start a regular program of exercise and recreation. Reducing stress and nervous energy, relaxing in the circle of our friends and relatives, as well as harmony in our workplace, are all contributing factors in establishing a healthy lifestyle.

LISTEN TO YOUR BODY AND SOUL

- How healthy are we and do we listen to our body and soul?
- The most frequent complaints are emotional
- Don't wait for disease to manifest–prevent it at the start
- A proactive rather than reactive stance toward health and life

Most people experience some kind of health problem from time to time or all of the time. If we strictly follow the definition of health, it would be difficult to find someone who is completely healthy. People often have physical complaints which they suffer for weeks, months and sometimes for years before undertaking something to resolve these problems and often, by that time, it's too late to achieve significant change. Why do these messages from our body remain ignored?

The Canadian magazine Maclean's and Public Health published a study, June 2008, conducted with 5,000 Canadian citizens where it was discovered that a majority of people suffer from complaints related to health, and many of these people had two or more complaints at one time. According to this study, males more often, and in greater numbers, ignore their physical complaints and symptoms and do not pay extra attention to these problems.

- **The most frequent complaints are emotional**

Many people live with stress and psychological pressure, especially those who are employed at regular jobs and don't have enough free time for regularly scheduled meals. They sleep fitfully at irregular hours, have nightmares while sleeping, don't take time to plan ahead and deal with life's challenges. Also, they don't have time to see their own children and to spend quality time with them. It's no wonder then that such irregular life patterns manifest themselves in various complaints and symptoms that signify the beginning of disease or the actual presence and development of disease. Here are the most frequent complaints and health problems found among 5,000 Canadians.

Emotional and psychological problems are first on the list of health complaints

Tension, irritability, feelings of psychological pressure and depression are leading symptoms among the majority of participants in this study, for both males and females. The demands which occupy our time often place much heavier burdens on people. The dissatisfaction with oneself, one's career, co-workers, spouse and children make for an even more complex picture. Along with sadness, hopelessness, feelings of meaninglessness, problems with money and work. This all sounds like a familiar story to many people.

Our soul, mind and body are all connected, and sooner or later, because of too much tension and stress in our life, our body is overwhelmed and begins to be "flooded" with tension. This undesirable state of being produces irritability, headaches, back pain, high blood pressure, exhaustion, tiredness and insomnia.

■ **Don't wait for disease to manifest–prevent it at the start**

Stomach complaints, heartburn and digestion

Problems of the stomach like pinching, bloating, trouble with digestion, heartburn, and burping are second on the list of complaints of people who participated in this study. Causes of these problems are multifaceted; eating unhealthy foods, irregular meals, eating too much food and eating too fast. Beside these causes, as one grows older, the ability of the stomach and the pancreas to digest food weakens, thus one needs to eat smaller meals, more frequently and to consume food that is more easily digested.

The consequences of this type of bad nutrition are not only stomach problems but also the rise of obesity in western countries. This is becoming a social and political problem that is also leading to a rise in rates of diabetes, high blood pressure, a reduction in one's capacity for work, depression, as well as conflict among the general population.

A special danger of our modern lifestyle is a fat stomach or accumulation of fat around the waist. This type of obesity is called, by some doctors, the cholesterol of the twenty-first century; because it represents a big risk for developing blood vessel diseases like heart attacks and strokes.

Solution to problems due to bad nutrition

Proper nutrition is so important that the whole family should participate in the selection of food and its preparation. Eating food at regular family meals, which then become a communal, celebratory time for the whole family, where family members have a chance to talk, exchange information about daily life, and offer help and cooperation to each other, which all represents a form of family psychotherapy.

Headaches, general pains and a stiff neck

Headaches, migraines, problems with vision, hearing, and breathing through the nose, sinuses, and stiff neck muscles are a group of physical complaints which are third in occurrence on the list of complaints mentioned by study participants, both male and female. Possible causes of these problems are nervous tension, being overburdened, depression, loneliness, allergies, bad nutrition, and lack of sufficient sleep. Other causes are a lack of regular exercise and physical activity as well as financial difficulties.

Psycho-social problems

The group of complaints which are closely associated with one's family, career or community in which one lives, takes the fourth place on the list of complaints among participants in the above named study. People are often unsatisfied with one's spouse, with family relationships, their place of work and with people they work with, and they often postpone dealing with these problems and tolerate them without looking for a way out, until the situation boils over in ways that are undesirable.

All small or major misunderstandings among people can be resolved through dialogue, agreement, and through a healthy assertive approach. That means clearly and loudly express in words: I know who I am, what I can do, what I need and what I am prepared to do to learn to obtain new skills and new knowledge.

However, every person has their limitations and can be overburdened only to a certain level. This type of agreement can lead to long term understanding but it demands respect, patience, tolerance and persistent effort of both sides in the family or in the workplace.

Chronic tiredness, slow down and lack of energy

Chronic tiredness is a common symptom and is caused by a variety of causes, including tenseness, worry and stress all definitely contribute to tiredness and often use up energy needlessly. It's comparable to a car engine idling in one place and wasting gasoline. Tenseness and anxiousness are forms of nervous tension. People in such a nervous state experience a high level of negative emotions. It's the same car idling in one place while the driver presses the gas pedal and the break pedal down at the same time. This will cause damage not only to one's nerves but will also damage one's heart and blood vessels.

Of course, it's indispensable to consult with a doctor at this time. A good doctor will take a detailed historical examination of the underlying problem. He or she can undertake a scrupulous examination and order lab tests in order to eliminate the presence of serious diseases such as diabetes, thyroid disease, anemia, diseases of the heart, lungs, liver, kidneys and many other causes which can lead to tiredness and weakness.

Fat stomach–the main health problem of modern time

A fat stomach or the increase of one's stomach around the waist and over the edge of one's pelvis is a serious sign and represents one of the main signs of the presence of metabolic syndrome. Metabolic syndrome consists of stomach obesity, an increased level of cholesterol, inclination toward diabetes and resistance toward insulin. This metabolic syndrome is a very serious factor in the risk of developing heart and blood vessel disease, myocardial infarction and strokes.

Find out the circumference of your stomach! (2) If you are a male and your stomach circumference is over 102 cm (50 inches), or if you are female and your stomach circumference is over 88 cm (42 inches), this is not a good sign. Immediately consult with a doctor, and undertake efforts to lower your caloric intake and begin a regular exercise program.

Besides the above mentioned physical and health complaints, there are numerous other common ones, including, pain in the joints and muscles, back pain, foot pain, inability to sleep, even when tired, disruption of the menstrual cycle in women, and impotence in younger males. Under each of the above named health difficulties one can find many psychological, health and social causes and problems. Such negative health signs are not wise be ignored and serious attention should be given to them while undertaking healthy steps in order to resolve these issues.

■ **A proactive rather than reactive stance toward health and life**

A proactive and optimistic stance toward health means developing a culture of health, informing ourselves, and learning which are the most frequent health problems which await us in the future and how to avoid them.

A reactive stance toward our health is passive, when we don't pay enough attention to our lifestyle and when we wait for symptoms and disease to manifest before we react.

How to achieve a proactive stance?

The real solution is to build a healthy lifestyle and to pay close attention to our psychological and physical health. Pay attention to warnings and signs from our body and our soul and consult with your doctor, psychologist or your well-informed friend.

Making a list of health priorities is important

What is important to me? Is the type of life I am leading taking me toward health? How to better organize and prepare for health? As our health is of first priority, it's important to pay close attention to it! If we lose our health, all else is of lesser importance. What are our other priorities? For the majority of people, besides their health, they worry about their family, work and career, and finances. How to prepare for changing dynamics of our health during our life? What is most important in our life and at what stage of our life, and what can be postponed? How to increase the quality of our work and increase our income, without expending more effort, energy and time?

Continuous learning

The modern world is always changing so that continuous learning and acquisition of new knowledge is a necessity of our time. Our children deserve a lot of love, care and support in order to mature, learn, and accept responsibility for themselves. We need to talk to our children every day, help them with their chores, play with them, and spend quality time with them. Children grow up and learn by playing. Also, pay attention to your spouse. Care for them and talk to them. Establish and define your priorities and look over your problems together with your spouse.

Avoid unhealthy ways to solve your health problems

Denying, ignoring, and postponing dealing with one's health problems doesn't solve them. Also, don't compound stress you experience by further ruining your health with alcoholism, cigarette smoking, and by needless sleep. Our needs for attention, understanding and love can not be met by overeating and consuming junk food. Express your thoughts and feelings in a correct manner and things will go easier for you, and for those with whom you live. Stress is not something that happens to us but is defined by how we react to it.

Create healthy life choices and habits for yourself and for others

One old Chinese proverb says, "If you don't create healthy habits early on in your life, you will have to bear the consequences of bad habits later on in life." Health is the most important thing in life but also there are many other beautiful things in our life which give it meaning and content.

Without good health all our other wishes and needs only remain an unrealized dream.

Quality of life is defined by the care of one's health, says an old proverb.

Key Advice:

- *sharpen your senses and learn to listen to your body and soul. Recognize when you are tense, dissatisfied with little things, when you worry and experience headaches, or have neck and back pain. Feelings of unease and pain are a warning that something is not right;*

- *make a list of the most important priorities in your life. Not all things are of equal importance. What is important to you today may not be so important tomorrow;*

- *put good health at the top of your list of priorities, based on things we do every day;*

- *give awareness of our health constant attention, and learn how to avoid disease;*

- *feelings of happiness, optimism, being energetic, are all a keys to good health; and*

- *being able to recognize, ahead of time, when one is dissatisfied, apathetic, and about to experience a headache or chronic tiredness, and removing the causes of these conditions on one's own or in consultation with your physician.*

THE PSYCHOLOGICAL APPROACH TO BEHAVIOR

- **Our approach to philosophy, values and health are vital**
- **Our conduct has deep repercussions on our health**
- **Preparing and making a decision**
- **Preserving changes and successes**

Medicine has made great strides in technological progress in the span of last few decades. The problem of most infectious diseases has been solved, organ transplant of many vital organs has been achieved (heart, liver, kidney, lungs), the pharmaceutical industry has developed hundreds of new drugs and the food industry, at least in developed countries, has solved the problem of nutrition. The average life span has been extended from just over 70 years to 80 years in many countries.

Despite all of this, the number of patients still continues to grow. People's suffering, unhappiness and affliction, even in developed nations, is greater than ever before. Even those who regularly visit their doctors and take their medications, as well as those who stay silent, all carry their suffering hidden deep within their souls.

For a good diagnosis it's not always necessary to visit a doctor, it's enough to ask ourselves: How are we? How do we feel? Do we feel well and happy? Are we satisfied with what we have done today and what we plan to do tomorrow? An internal examination of our well-being, a feel for happiness of life, and a conviction that there is a meaning and a goal in what we are doing, is a good confirmation of our health. This is a reward that is more important than any material reward or compensation.

A person's right to choose begins with what to think and feel, with how and what to do, and where and with whom, to live. This problem becomes more complicated with the knowledge that many forms of human conduct are subconscious and that they appear when a person is not able to postpone their immediate wants. I want it now! Immediately! This first of all applies to our food, drink, alcohol, physical inactivity, and sometimes drugs. Basic or primitive impulses originate in the middle brain or the so called limbic system, whereas control and postponement of pleasure originate in the brain cortex. Insufficient development of the brain cortex, especially the frontal lobes, during upbringing and education, leaves subconscious impulses which seek direct, immediate satisfaction. There are a number of stages that a person goes through in the process of psychological and mental change. (3)

- **Our conduct has deep repercussions on our health**

Pre-contemplation

The stage at which a problem exists, but a person is not conscious about it, or if he/she is aware of the problem but denies it, or lowers its significance.

A doctor in his/her office is often confronted with people who refuse to acknowledge their obvious behavior problems such as obesity, smoking cigarettes and abuse of alcohol, and who refuse to admit that these habits are affecting their health in a negative manner.

The main task of the doctor is to raise awareness of the patient about his/her existing problems and to educate the patient of the need to change this form of conduct.

J.L., a 63 year old man with well developed signs of diabetes who admitted that he drank three to four beers every day and mainly spent his time at home watching television. He also admitted that he loved to eat sweet things.

When asked if his unhealthy diet, alcohol intake and sedentary lifestyle were affecting his health in a negative manner he answered: "It's not because of that, my father also had diabetes and couldn't be cured." In talking to his spouse, I learned that he was always complaining about being thirsty, being tired and that his eyesight had deteriorated. Even though I respected this man's autonomy, I discreetly showed him a disconnection between the state of his health and his thinking about his health. After several visits, J.L. stopped drinking alcohol, started a healthier diet and began to get regular physical activity. His blood sugar level has become acceptable.

Contemplation

In this stage, people are usually aware of their problem. They think about it, are prepared to talk about it, but are still seeking a way to solve it. At this stage people are less touchy about being confronted with their problem but they often lack enough will and motivation to do anything significant about it.

B.K., a 42 year old woman and mother of two children, smoked a pack of cigarettes per day for over 20 years and was overweight. She was well aware about the harm of her bad habit, and she admitted that it was expensive and dangerous. Besides that, her two children also warned her that they were worried about her and that they didn't want to breathe in cigarette smoke. After repeated consultations and talks with her, I helped her to quit smoking cigarettes, to start eating healthier food and to lower her body weight.

The role of the doctor is to stimulate the patient to seek their own solution to their problem, to consider all pros and cons of the situation, and to choose the best solution to their problem.

■ **Preparing and making a decision**

At this stage, the patient and the doctor form a plan of action and begin to analyze how to overcome some of the barriers to this plan and how to remove them. A patient will often offer a specific date when to begin, such as: I will begin to exercise every day on the first day of this month, or on my birthday. Besides that, "I am preparing a plan for choosing nutritious food or regular attendance of classes at school or at college." This change of lifestyle should be announced in the family and to friends and support should be sought and expected.

Action and its realization

The patient seriously begins measures to change their lifestyle. They begin to exercise with a group of peers, reduce the number of cigarettes or completely stop smoking, taking advantage of "nicotine patches" if necessary. Then they begin to participate with others they live with in choosing and preparing healthy food. The patient suddenly begins to feel better, is psychologically more motivated, has more energy and sees the first improvement as a result of positive changes. Recognizing the price of abstaining from bad habits, the patient is proud to see the positive psychological effects of these changes.

At this stage people are extremely vulnerable, and even a small discomfort or lack of success or suspicion of their friends can make them doubt themselves and return to previous bad habits. It's necessary to offer full support and encouragement to these people. This especially applies to people who have smoked cigarettes or abused alcohol for years. People who are obese are very touchy and vulnerable because the results of a healthy diet and regular exercise program are not immediately obvious, as positive results are only evident after one or two months.

■ **Preserving changes and successes**

This is a period in which corrections to one's lifestyle, changes in one's thinking and concrete actions produce evident results: a much better mental outlook, more energy, more time to spend on beneficial activities, including work, study, planning the future, and establishing contacts with other people who are also successful. This reinforces the knowledge about the importance of good psychological and physical health, which becomes a firm foundation for all other plans and achievements, beginning with basic material survival and extending to education, career and the realization of many of our dreams.

Changes in our attitude and behavior, and the adoption of a healthier lifestyle, gives the patient happiness, self-confidence and opens the doors to many possibilities that, until recently, looked unapproachable. Raising one's awareness about the importance of health, promotion of a healthy lifestyle, and well-being of all the people, gives the doctor a particular satisfaction and intellectual compensation. The role of the doctor is not only to reduce pain and suffering, but even more so, to raise people's awareness about the importance of health, to prevent the manifestation of disease and to alleviate consequences of disease, and then to help in the development of the greatest physical and intellectual potential of every person.

Discussion and agreement lead to solutions

What can you do?

- Before you go to see a doctor, make a list of the most important questions that you wish to discuss with your doctor.
- Seek advice about the most important aspects of a healthy lifestyle and how to adjust it to your own personal needs.
- Make a list of all drugs you are taking including herbal and other preparations.
- If you have any problems understanding the language or terminology, call someone who can help you, such as a nurse or librarian. Even the computer can help.
- Be determined and seek the best solutions for yourself and for your needs, but always control your behavior. It's the best guarantee for a good and productive relationship between you and your doctor.

OPTIMISM AND HEALTH IN TIMES OF CRISIS

- We live in a time of social tension and economic crisis
- The main risk to health in times of crisis is fear and hopelessness
- Going beyond fear and hopelessness to optimism and determination
- Positive emotions come from higher brain centers
- Optimism is a plant that grows in good home conditions

Only a few years ago no one could even dream that the most developed nations in the west would undergo a deep economic crisis that was not seen since the early 1930's. The reasons for this crisis, and seeking blame, is not the most important thing, but the fact is that this crisis has a huge impact on the psychological and physical health of the whole world community.

Thousands of people have lost their jobs and have been left without basic means of survival. Paying rent or credit for one's accommodation, buying food, clothing and other necessities is brought into question not only because our future is uncertain, creates fear and tension, but also because it brings into question our basic elementary survival.

A strong family is made by care, love and togetherness

The modern, well-informed and educated man or woman desires more than just mere survival. They wish not only to overcome the poverty of an elementary existence but also to achieve a higher level of psychological satisfaction, and to offer to themselves and to those closest to them, true happiness of being (4). People want to realize their human potential, fulfill their talents, realize their personality and find meaning in their life.

- **The main risk to health in times of crisis is fear and hopelessness**

In times of crisis it is indispensable to re-examine one's priorities and to find the best way to survive until the crisis is over.

If a person is to make wise decisions, it's necessary for them to consider thoughtfully their situation and to talk it over with members of their family. A person must have "a warm heart and a cool head" as the old saying goes.

It's important to bring tension and fear under control since it's well know that negative emotions like these reduce our ability to reason correctly.

Besides that, tension and fear lead to stress, stress leads to being more tired, increases our blood pressure and reduces our work productivity. Prolonged stress reduces our immunity and weakened immunity makes us more prone to catch infections, more vulnerable to carcinogens, and leads to premature aging and other harmful consequences for our health.

Our decisions about what we buy and our finances can be moderated or postponed until calmer times. Decisions can be made calmly and not in a hurry or under the influence of fear. We can reduce our unnecessary expenses and bring our spending to a tolerable level. Buying fever that possesses all strata in our society during big holidays is a trick played on us by those who want to sell things to us that we don't need.

■ **Going beyond fear and hopelessness to optimism and determination**

Where does pessimism come from? Fear, insecurity, anger and sadness are defensive reactions of a reflexive nature when one is confronted with danger or uncertainty. These reactions are subconscious; they come from the lower centers of the structures of the brain, from the so-called brain stem. These reactions are our evolutionary heritage from lower living beings, from reptiles.

■ **Positive emotions come from higher brain centers**

Today it's known that positive emotions and positive thoughts originate in our higher brain centers. Of course, only if we develop and activate them.

Humans have evolved significantly farther and their brains have a middle brain with a limbic system, from where emotions originate, enriched by thoughts from cortical brain centers.

Why are we given positive emotions like happiness, enthusiasm, inspiration, curiosity, love and kindness? Positive emotions are indispensable for the establishment of healthy relationships between people, for harmony within the family, on the job, on the street and at school.

One brilliant scientist, Dr. Barbara Fredrickson, professor of psychology at the University of North Carolina in the United States, received a high scientific award when she proved the meaning of positive emotions: they enlarge our intellectual perspective, they make creativity possible, they stimulate easier establishment of relationships with other people and with the whole community (5). People who exude positive emotions are welcomed in society, find friends, lovers and work, easier. A positive person sees negative phenomena as accidental, short-term and temporary, but considers positive phenomena as permanent and to be expected.

Whoever has good thoughts, expects good things to happen to them.

In time of crisis we can reduce our spending and buy only what is necessary

Preservation of our basic existence is our primary goal in times of economic crisis.

Our basic existence depends on our lodging, clothing, shoes, food and hygienic needs and everything else can be postponed and reduced to its minimum level.

How do we obtain money and where does it go?

Many people who live together don't share information about their salaries, don't participate in common payments for an apartment or home mortgage, bills for electricity, telephone, heating and other expenses. Mutual agreement and planning about these things is unavoidable in order to avoid disagreements and reduce one's expenses.

We forget that the best things in life are free

Where does the money go, who spends it and why?

Unnecessary cell and mobile phones, unnecessary and expensive coffees, juices, cigarettes and alcoholic beverages appear at first sight to be small expenses, but when they are all added up, it turns out that the total amount spent on these items is significant. There is an old saying, "It's hard to earn money, but it's harder to save it."

Avoid getting into new debt

Specifically, buying with credit cards for which you pay big service charges. Do you know why banks are offering these credit cards? Because they earn a lot of money out of your carelessness. Our modern economy is based on a well researched psychological study of the average, often uninformed consumer.

Are you living beyond your means?

The best financial experts say that even when you have some money, you should live below your financial means! Millionaires don't always live like millionaires. They don't drive the most expensive cars, don't have the most expensive clothing and often don't even pay for expensive meals. They only plan to spend money when they are certain that their salary is secure.

Optimism is a plant that grows in good home conditions

Many of us have forgotten that the best things in life can't be bought with money. What people do for each other and what makes them happy is having good relationships with those they live with, sharing mutual understanding, respect, love and enjoying harmony at home, on the job and in the community. From history and psychology, it's well known that people tend to get closer to each other in times of trouble, crisis and war, than during times of economic prosperity and peace.

Joyful and happy kids radiate positivity and optimism

Coming together and our spiritual development begin at home. Pay attention to your children. Ask their opinion for a change before you command them to do things. Observe what they are doing and with whom, and how they spend their time. Every day I see alienated young people and children who are strangers to their own parents, who have a hard time in resisting momentary pleasures, are poor students, drink alcohol, take drugs and get pregnant at 13 or 14 years of age. The main reason for this is that these children are not receiving serious care and love from their own busy parents, and in an effort to obtain this love somewhere else, these children are getting into even more serious trouble.

Children need to be lead on their way to maturity so that they become responsible for themselves and for their behavior. This is only possible if they receive mature love and a good upbringing. Mature love and a good upbringing are products of noble feelings, good common sense, positive psychology and a long term process of emotional and intellectual maturing of both parents and their children.

IN TIMES OF DARKNESS, THERE IS ALWAYS HOPE

- **The cruel reality of the contemporary world is discouraging and depressing**
- **Enlightenment, optimism and personal commitment offer hope**
- **From material poverty to spiritual growth**
- **Why our brain loves optimism, happiness and enthusiasm?**
- **Spiritual or religious people are happier**

The cruel reality of the modern world, constant wars, economic crises, environmental problems and many other problems, are the reason why people are discouraged and depressed. Since ancient times humanity has tolerated earthquakes, floods, droughts, storms and other natural disasters. On the other hand, human history is full of social disturbances; wars, rebellions, revolutions, persecutions, hunger and disease. Just look at the current news; Iraq, Afghanistan, Rwanda, Sri Lanka, and Pakistan.

Empires were created and overthrown and often, millions of innocent men, women and children have suffered. All these changes have a decisive influence on the lives and health of these people.

If someone is looking from above at our planet from some other world, it would be hard for them to observe anything beautiful about our mental development.

■ Enlightenment, optimism and personal commitment offer hope

The best and most beautiful characteristics of humanity are our education, learning and refinement, which are evident in the fields of science, art and religion. Medicine and psychology have been dealing with problems of the human body and soul: infectious diseases; insufficient nutrition and water; the fight against cancer and dangerous infections; and especially diseases of the mind; including depression, neuroses, obsessions; and paranoia. Many answers have been found to many important questions but progress in science is often hard to observe. Tens of thousands of children die every day in Africa because they lack food, water and medicines, while billions of dollars are wasted on wars.

Higher ethical norms are needed for those who make important decisions. However, these people often place their own personal interests above the interests of the people.

■ From material poverty to spiritual growth

The whole material world can be described with only one concept: money. In the materially developed and rich world many people believe that money is the most important condition of prosperity and happiness. The best examples of this are countries in the developed world, with the top ones being in Western Europe and including the United States. All statistical parameters show an incredible growth of material wealth since the end of World War II. Bigger salaries, bigger and better homes, equipped with the latest technology, more cars, more highways, schools and hospitals. Everything that is material has grown, grown and still grows.

But what about our spiritual condition that's created in a time of peace, prosperity and happiness? It hasn't even advanced a step!! The statistical line of measurement of human happiness is flat and can't be flatter. The same percentage of people that considered themselves to be happy in 1950, about 17 percent (5), is the same number of happy people today, about 17 percent. More money and buying more things doesn't mean a happier life. Money has helped us to escape from poverty but it has also led us to a curse of abundance.

Professor David Myers, who teaches at one of the leading American universities, writes in a very detailed and persuasive manner in his book, American Paradox: Spiritual hunger in time of abundance, about our poor spiritual condition (6). He considers the main reason for this to be our particularly developed moral crisis of society, unhealthy individualism and especially unrestrained sexual freedom, and the break up of the traditional family. This has caused a lot of social disturbances, the rise in psychological problems, the rise in use of antidepressants, abuse of alcohol and drugs, and the rise of criminal activity. Behind all this stands unequal distribution of wealth in our society with a small number of extremely wealthy people at the top of the pyramid and a large number of poor people at the bottom. In this manner, our outstanding material abundance has failed to lead to widespread human prosperity and only demands new questions that await to be answered.

With love and care, all challenges are easier

■ **Why our brain loves optimism, happiness and enthusiasm?**

A joyful and a happy brain significantly better coordinates the functions of the body, increases our immunity, lowers our risk of heart disease and blood vessel disease, lowers incidences of cancer and arthritic diseases, and increases our levels of energy and the ability to work. The center for happiness and joy appears to be located on the left side of the prefrontal lobe of the brain. The essence of the whole story is an optimistic approach to life and problems that are unavoidable. As one psychologist said, "A pessimist sees in every life's challenge a problem, but an optimist sees in every problem a new challenge". Despite there being an inherited predisposition to reacting in a certain way, learning and experience obtained in early childhood shows that happiness in life, and a positive approach to things, can be developed with the influence of a healthy upbringing by parents and teachers who love their children, and know how to make them happy and motivated. People who are taught to be happy in life, and to be grateful to God for their life and their good health, have an easier time overcoming life's barriers, and live a longer and happier life. People who claim that they are always happy, probably aren't. Happiness is a state of complete harmony of our thoughts, feelings, beliefs and actions and only happens periodically. How do we know that we are happy if we are never unhappy?

■ Spiritual or religious people are happier

Many indications exist to show that religious people are happier (4). They are less burdened with problems of earthly life, less worried, and have peace and calmness in their soul, which they find in prayer and in dedication to their Deity. A religious person copes more successfully with stress, pain, suffering, disease and death. This person always believes in the possibility of being saved, of overcoming problems, and finds hope in his/her faith. People who believe have a more compact harmony between their body and soul, are more filled with positive emotions, and have more optimism and hope for a better tomorrow. Religious communities are more ready to help their members. They more openly show their solidarity and support. Belonging to a particular religious community gives these people a strong feeling of security. Their ethical norms are at a higher level. They more readily admit their sins and are more ready to repent. Finally, they believe that their reward for good deeds only awaits them in their next life. The father of western medicine, Greek philosopher Hippocrates, proclaimed that a doctor who believes in God is fulfilling his high calling through the highest moral principles because he/she knows that he/she is being watched from above.

How to rediscover the beauty of existence?

Psychologists have developed several practical approaches that can overcome feelings of hopelessness and can offer new ways of hope for a better tomorrow.

- **Being grateful for one's life, health and intellect.** Life and health, physical and psychological, are the best gifts and the biggest values one can possess. Distinguish and develop your positive characteristics: diligence, honesty, sincerity, altruism and optimism. Every person experiences positive and negative tendencies trying to gain an upper hand. Those things that we focus on will be stronger in us. Maintain optimism, belief, love and hope in us and in those around us. What we give, we will receive.

- **Forgiveness of others and repentance for oneself.** Forgiving those who have insulted us frees us from anger and from negative energy. It gives us a feeling of rising above the fray and gives us power to be optimistic. Repentance is not only a religious but also a psychological category. Repentance is being conscious of sin, admitting that one is a sinner, freedom from blame and a way toward tranquility and mental well-being.

- **Learn and apply kindness.** Kindness and courtesy to other people, having a smile and being ready to help children, the elderly, ill people and unhappy people, creates in a person, feelings of bliss, thankfulness and positive energy. This type of energy can't be lost but only increases!

- **Being thankful to one's teachers.** In the life of every person there exists someone who has taught us something beautiful, good and wise. That person can be our father or mother, a good teacher or professor, priest, doctor or an old friend of the family. We should write a letter to that person, giving them credit for their wisdom and their message which has enriched our lives. That person will appreciate this and we will be left with a feeling of thankfulness as a reward.

- **Recognize and care about happiness that gives our life meaning.** Being happy with a child playing in a field, appreciating bird songs, or watching a beautiful sunset at the end of the day. Remembering moments of happiness during the most difficult times. Singing a song we learned in our childhood which reminds us of our happy and safe days.

- **Care for our family and friends.** Psychologists have proven that all careers, titles and material goods that a person obtains don't even approach the worth of happiness and love experienced inside a healthy family, among our friends and memories that live inside us till the end of our days.

- **To care for our body and soul.** Concern about one's own health, peace of soul, healthy nutrition, physical activity, socializing and smiling, all have their purpose and their mission. The feeling of a healthy body and a healthy soul gives a person initiative and energy to try new undertakings and new ways of doing things.

- **Learning the wisdom of overcoming stress and life's hardships.** "All our failures are only stepping stones toward our future victories", said a famous poet. The struggle with sudden loss of a dear friend, from disease or other difficulties, are part of the reality of life. People who have faith and hope are able to come out of all misfortune, stronger and wiser.

- **Avoiding idleness.** The philosopher Voltaire said, "Work deprives us of poverty, boredom and vice". There is a big difference between unemployment and not working: the unemployed are those who don't work for an employer and don't receive a salary. People who don't work are those who sit idly by with folded arms and wait for other people to help them. Psychologists believe that it's better to work for free than to be idle.

- **Never give up!** A person need never be discouraged by lack of success. Failure is part of our lack of perfection. Failure makes sense if we learn something from it. If a person is to survive, he/she needs a feeling of dignity, a little wisdom, a little hope and a sense of meaning. And meaning of existence is a happy and creative life and empathy of those around us.

HEALTHY LIFE AND HAPPY HORMONES

- **A life full of health and happiness. Reality or dream?**
- **The magic formula is abbreviated as ENHO: exercise; nutrition; and a healthy outlook**
- **Is there a hormone of happiness and joy?**
- **A healthy disposition and psychological health**

Leading a healthy lifestyle is a basic precondition of health, happiness and a long life. A healthy lifestyle is based on our proper approach to life; this approach is based on our convictions which, in turn, are based on our beliefs. We believe what we were taught, which begins with our parents, school and community in which a person is raised and where they grow up.

Probably all of the people in the world desire to be healthy, happy and to lead a long life. However a lot of people don't do a lot in order to realize these desires. What are our missed chances? Incorrect nutrition is one of the manifestations of an unhealthy lifestyle with excessive intake of food, especially food that contains fats and sugar, irregular activity and exercise, weak willpower, life spent under stress with feelings of dissatisfaction, worry and depression.

We can do for ourselves more than anyone can do anything for us. But this can be achieved only with the proper approach to life, health and our basic emotional, cultural and spiritual needs.

In ancient times, the old Greeks and Romans lived an average life span of about 35 to 40 years. In the last century the average lifespan was between 60 to 65 years of age.

Today, in the so-called western civilization, people tend to live about 75 to 80 years and this trend is improving, and many people live beyond 80 years of age. This longer lifespan was made possible with better conditions of life, better nutrition and a great progress in medical science.

The contemporary approach of top health experts is not only to prolong life at any cost, but in helping people to lead a long life with all their powers and capabilities intact, where they can experience the full joy of life.

Prolonging the life of ill and helpless people that are bedridden is not only ineffective but is also very costly and only serves to prolong human suffering.

- **The magic formula is abbreviated as ENHO: exercise; nutrition; and a healthy outlook**

Ancient Greeks spoke about this and later it was adopted by the Romans, "Mens sano in corpore sano" which means "A healthy soul in a healthy body", which also means mutual interdependence between human body and soul.

The fact is that this philosophy originated in Ancient Greece, whose philosophers Aristotle, Socrates and Hippocrates developed solid foundations of our civilization, whereas Romans are more recognized for enjoying pleasures of the body (hedonism) in one of whose branches we are currently leading our lives.

Physical exercise, movement and physical labor

Most jobs in the contemporary world are accomplished without a lot physical labor and sometimes without any physical effort. This is why there is so much talk about the need for regular physical exercise instead of work and physical labor, since between these two things, there is a significant difference.

■ **Is there a hormone of happiness and joy?**

The long-term benefit of physical exercise

Physical labor or sport related play are healthier manifestations of physical activity because they incorporate spontaneity, play, and the spirit of competition, while planned individual exercise lacks some of these characteristics. The most important benefits of physical exercise are (7, 8):

- An increase of secretion in our brain of hormones which promote good moods, happiness and joy. These hormones are called encephalins and endorphins and they have an extremely beneficial effect on human health. The more we exercise, the more we secrete these hormones.

- An increase in circulation of blood in all vital organs: heart; brain; liver and kidneys. Also, the prevention of high blood pressure, heart attacks and strokes, as well as reduction of diseases of all other organs.

- An increase in the elimination of all toxic and poisonous substances through our lungs, skin, stool and kidneys.

- The burning of calories and fatty tissues as well as maintenance of normal body weight, which is one of the main characteristics of good health.

- Physical exercise reduces dangerous levels of LDL cholesterol while increasing levels of good HDL cholesterol, and helps to establish good balance of these two substances in the human body.

- Our bones are made stronger which prevents bone injuries (broken bones); this is a well proven benefit of physical exercise, especially in our later years.

- An improvement in our immunity, which leads to a greater ability to fight against infections (flu, inflammation of the lungs, tuberculosis), and physical activity, and increases our ability to fight against malignant tumors and cancers.

Besides that, physical exercise doesn't only consist of planned physical activity related to sports: we obtain physical exercise when we use the stairs instead of the elevator, and take short walks to a grocery store or shopping centre instead of using our car to get there.

Diet and nutrition

We eat food in order to satisfy our basic needs, in order to maintain normal temperature, create enough energy to be able to move and perform our work, and in order to grow and regenerate (renew) our cells, tissues and organs.

Good nutrition is the intake of nutritious food in a quantity that is necessary to maintain our healthy life and is coordinated with our human needs: a growing child; pregnant woman or a mother that's breastfeeding her child; an active athlete; grown-up young person that spends a lot of time in front of the computer; or an older person–all have completely different needs in relation to their choice and type of foods, and their caloric intake of these foods.

The Main problems of contemporary nutrition are:

- Excessive intake of too many calories that our body doesn't burn up but converts into fatty tissue, which leads to obesity;

- Excessive intake of fats, especially saturated fats that can be found in animal based fats and oils and to a lesser extent, in vegetable oil;

- Unneeded consumption of concentrated sugar and fats, including sweets, cakes, candy, ketchup, potato chips, and processed and instant foods;

- The intake in small quantities of toxic substances, such as herbicides, insecticides, detergents, oil derivatives, preservatives, hormones and food additives, which often reach the food chain through water and through the soil, where our vegetables are grown, or in later added food additives. By careful selection and choice of our food, and careful study of various food labels, it's possible to reduce the above named risks to a minimum.

■ **A healthy disposition and psychological health**

The concept of our psychological health is based on our comfort, well-being and satisfaction of our basic human needs. During the course of the last millennium, humanity has been searching for our origins, our proper path, and the meaning and goal of life.

However, regardless of all our learning and beliefs, every individual has their own philosophy of life, their own motives, sources of happiness or problems, and a particular way to solve these problems.

Our spirituality is based on our need for identity, to belong to a group and is based on our feelings, beliefs and thoughts. In ideal conditions, these three categories are coordinated into one complete whole, which is psychological health. However, there also exist fears, insecurity, crises of identity, and feelings of emptiness, non-existence, and hopelessness, feelings of being overburdened and chronic stress.

How to escape from a circle of problems and begin living on healthy foundations?

How to escape from a vicious circle and see the light of day? There are several very useful and scientifically proven recommendations.

- *Define your value system: What is important to you, what do you believe in, what are your ethical principles and what minimal norms do you wish to fulfill?*

- *Define your goal or goals: What do you wish to achieve and why? What are your short-term and your long-term visions to achieve these goals?*

- *Make a list of priorities! What needs to be done? Start with your most important priorities but make adjustments daily, monthly and yearly. Short-term goals can be coordinated with your long-term goals. Evaluate your ability to do everything that you can on your own, without waiting for others to do things for you.*

- *Organize yourself and how you spend your time. Define your role in your work, education, family, and community, and fit these into your daily activities.*

- *Increase your effectiveness. Do the right things at the right time with well-thought out priority. Determine your weaknesses and work at their removal. Get rid of barriers which are impeding the realization of your goals.*

- *Find time to spend with your family. Music, recreation, sport, art and friends are all important aspects of activity. Be happy, play with your children, but also learn from other people.*

- *Establish a balance in your life: The ideal is to establish a balance between your work, education, family, friends and social activities. This is not simple to accomplish but is of essential importance.*

- *Find a source of accurate information: good advice from a good book, from a wise friend, doctor, psychologist, your advisor, or another person that you trust and that is willing and capable to help you.*

French philosopher Voltaire said, "If a person is to be happy, he/she needs a spirit of a wise person and a body of an athlete."

Children are a source of joy and a great investment

II

A HEALTHY LIFE STYLE

We can do more good things for our self than anyone else

EXERCISE, BEAUTY AND MOVEMENT

- Physical exercise is necessary–It's important to play and be active
- The consequences of physical passivity and lack of exercise
- The benefits of regular physical exercise
- The health risks of physical inactivity

"Good day, how are you?" "Are you tired, or exhausted?" Many people will answer that they are indeed "tired" and "not well" when asked these questions. However, feelings of tiredness come from frustration, stress, unhappiness, anxiety, and insufficient or inadequate level of physical activity and movement, rather than because of too much physical work or movement.

Play, physical exercise and movement are basic biological needs of the human body as well as being a basic manifestation of life. A person will live as long as he/she continues to play and move.

Our modern lifestyle in modern civilization can be characterized as making great technological progress and creating a very comfortable way of life. Many of our needs can be satisfied just by pressing a button, without any physical effort. This includes such activities as turning on various electronic equipment around the house, stoves, washing machines, telephones, computers, cars and other creations of modern technology. There are many jobs where we sit behind a desk and move very little. There are also many jobs that require a lot of physical effort and work. Physical activity and exercise are important because they ameliorate negative effects of our sedentary lifestyle.

Our need for physical movement and play are basic components and needs of our body and soul during our whole life. Because we need to be on the move, and we need to play and be active we have created various physical and intellectual activities which are not characteristics of other living beings: sport, poetry and music. These three activities show in a splendid and creative manner, our integration of human feelings, thoughts, words and movement of our body. As well, they offer a feeling of pleasure, inspiration, ease and vitality. They give our life richness, contentment, quality and meaning.

What is a sedentary lifestyle? It is the type of life where the majority of our time at work and at home is spent in minimal or completely absent movement of the body. If we add to this our prolonged time of "rest" at home, sitting in front of a television set or a computer, time we spend driving our car or at a desk, then this becomes our lifestyle.

■ **The consequences of physical passivity and lack of exercise**

A sedentary lifestyle has been known for decades to be a major risk factor or cause of many diseases such as: obesity; high blood pressure; diabetes; osteoporosis; diseases of bones and muscles; arthritic diseases; cancer of the colon; depression and many others. Physical inactivity, in combination with other risk factors, such as cigarette smoking, abuse of alcohol, drugs, high blood pressure or diabetes, worsen our state of health, reduce our ability for productive work, raise our risk of developing other diseases, lower our quality of life and shorten our lifespan.

The goal of physical exercise

Modern science advises us to be physically active for a total of 60 minutes every day in order to remain healthy, young, and in order to improve our health. Time you spend exercising depends on the amount of effort you have expended during exercise, on your height, age, and your health condition. You must spend a minimum of 45 minutes of exercise four times per week to achieve good physical condition, and to maintain your health and to prevent a variety of different illnesses. After three months of participation in a regular program of physical exercise you will be aware of the difference this will make: you will feel better and you will look better.

The duration of your exercise depends on the effort you expend during exercise

A light effort for a total of 60 minutes per day, including slow walks, light work in the garden or your backyard and stretching of the muscles and joints.

A moderate effort for a total of 30 to 60 minutes per day, including slightly faster walks, bike rides, swimming, dance or aerobic exercise in water.

A high level of effort for a total of 20 to 30 minutes per day, including running, aerobic exercise, basketball, tennis, hockey, swimming fast and fast dance.

Maximum effort: running fast, running a marathon, competitive sports and hard physical labor.

How to evaluate the intensity of your exercise?

This is very simple. On the basis of how you feel, how warmed up you are and how your breathing is.

With light exercise you begin to feel slightly warm and breathe a bit faster.

With moderate exercise you feel a bit warmer and your breathing is significantly faster.

With a high level of exercise effort you feel overheated, and your heart is beating fast and you are breathing rapidly.

With maximum physical effort you feel very hot, you are sweating a lot and you are almost out of breath. You must be careful at this stage, especially if you are experiencing some pain.

■ **The benefits of regular physical exercise**

There are a lot of benefits (7, 8). Here are some of the most important:

- **Better health.** There is no doubt that physical exercise is the elixir of our health, which means: feeling physically and psychologically better, better blood circulation, prevention of high blood pressure, prevention of arteriosclerosis, better digestion, regular waste elimination, prevention of cancers, prevention of osteoporosis (softening of our bones), muscle strengthening, reduction and prevention of obesity, increase of our immunity and ability to resist infections and other diseases.

Different life stages imply different interests and activities

Modern medicine spends billions of dollars on drugs; heart and heart vessel (bypass) surgeries in order to coordinate the quality of our blood vessels and to increase blood circulation to our vital organs like our heart, brain, kidneys and liver.

Stimulation of growth of new blood vessels

However, physical exercise has a fascinating, magical ability, not only to prevent deterioration of existing blood vessels, but to stimulate development of new blood vessels. This is a fact that is well know but is rarely mentioned and is of great significance.

Not only that, in the last few years a new benefit was discovered (2). With regular exercise and proper nutrition, well developed negative changes of arteriosclerosis (clogging up of arteries) can be reversed or at least normalized, which is of great medical significance and offers great unexploited potential.

- **Better posture and balance.** Muscle mass and muscle tone is increased with regular exercise which enables us to maintain a better posture, particularly of our shoulders, back and hips. In this way, we expend less physical effort in maintaining a proper posture, and what's especially important, this prevents the development of degenerative bone disease and joints such as rheumatism, diseases of the spinal cord and spinal disks. This also prevents other damage from occurring to our locomotor body system (system used in movement). At the same time, the center for balance and coordination of movement is strengthened, which allows us to move safely and prevents dizziness and unsteady walk.

- **Better fitness and performance.** This allows us a greater capacity for productive work, better results at work and in sport, and lowers the possibility of experiencing trauma during these activities.

- **A higher level of self-esteem and self-respect.** This is based on our awareness of feeling better and having more energy, greater physical capacity for work and our better overall appearance.

- **Control of our body weight.** Obesity is the most widespread disease of modern time: over 30% of the population or over 100 million people in the United States are obese, and carry all the burdens and risks of this inherent obesity.

- **Relaxation and reduction of stress.** Reduction of tension and stress are very beneficial effects of regular exercise. Stress, anxiety and depression are common complaints of modern time which are caused by being overloaded with responsibilities and feeling helpless to meet all of our expected and required duties. After physical exercise, a person will feel more relaxed and calm.

- **Better mood and less pain (3)!** Science has proven that during intensive physical activity there are substances that are created in the brain called endorphins and encephalins that are similar in their structure to morphine and heroin; these substances make us feel pleasant and they increase our ability to tolerate high levels of pain. But unlike other toxic substances these substances are naturally produced, they are never secreted in great quantities and have no toxic effect like morphine, heroin and other externally taken substances. Besides, these substances are free, which we can obtain through physical exercise!

- **A higher quality of life.** The postponement of old age and continuation of our physical independence in our later years. Better possibilities, results and a greater choice of physical exercise, accomplishments and satisfaction are a priceless gift of continuous physical activity. Regular exercise, along with healthy nutrition, are the best insurance for the maintenance of our youth, vigor and our overall quality of life.

■ The health risks of physical inactivity

People who lead inactive and sedentary lives are unnecessarily sacrificing the best gift that nature gives us; our body, our soul, in other words, our health. These are the beginning stages of our complaints about little things that bother us; weakness, headaches, not feeling well, being apathetic, constipation, obesity, erectile dysfunction and sexual problems, social isolation and reduction of our ability for productive work. Sooner or later these minor complaints lead into more serious health problems and signs of developing diseases like; high blood pressure, arteriosclerosis, diabetes, heart attacks, strokes, osteoporosis, depression, cancer of the colon, disability, need for greater medical care, reduction of our lifespan and premature death.Regular physical activity and play is first of all one of the most beautiful sources of childhood and adult happiness, inspiration, rest and relaxation. Physical exercise is the cheapest source for improvement of our health, prevention of disease, as well as being the way to treat and rehabilitate a great number of diseases. There was a study done recently where patients with terminal heart insufficiency (heart strength is less than 20% of normal heart function and where patients are practically bedridden) were encouraged to participate in regular physical exercise (which was considered at the time to be medically absurd) (4) . More than half of these seriously ill patients were able to improve their health condition, lower their physical complaints, increase their mobility and decrease their need for medications.

ALCOHOL–THE TRUTH

- The truth about recommendations on alcohol
- Is a glass or two of alcohol daily a benefit for health?
- Why alcohol is a toxic substance for our body?
- Recognizing an alcoholic
- Weekend drinking or "binge drinking"

In the public media and especially on TV and newspapers, despite bans on alcohol ads, there often appear ads for beer and wine. What is even more surprising, famous producers of alcoholic drinks become sponsors of famous sports and cultural events. An intelligent person would be hard pressed to find any connection between sport and the use of alcohol. Real sportsmen and sportswomen don't drink alcohol. Alcoholics never really care about sport.

Unfortunately, sports also includes sports spectators who sit and watch sports on TV or in person while eating huge amounts of unhealthy food and "drowning" themselves with copious amounts of "good" beer. Advertising has become an integral part of any business: which means that the most important thing for businesses is to sell their products regardless of the consequences.

In the last few years, the consumption of alcohol has risen and it's estimated that about 30% of people who work regularly also drink alcohol. There are about 7% of alcoholics in the adult male population. (5)

- Is a glass or two of alcohol daily a benefit for health?

According to a significant number of studies conducted with a large number of participants, it was discovered that one or two glasses of alcohol for an adult lowers the risk of heart disease and disease of the blood vessels. From this comes the suggestion that adult males can drink one to two drinks three to four times per week, while for women this quantity is one or two drinks two or three times per week. This of course applies if a person is not suffering from any serious disease, especially diseases of the liver, is not on any medication that does not combine well with alcohol, is getting proper nutrition on a regular basis, and what's most important, they exercise self-control and that one drink is one drink and that's all!

In order to find a proper balance about alcohol consumption, it's necessary to warn about several facts:

Most people can control the amount of alcohol they drink, they can abstain from alcohol before driving a car and they don't drink alcohol at work.

- Why alcohol is a toxic substance for our body?

Concentrated alcohol is easily dissolved in the food and water and is even more absorbed in our mouth through small capillaries and through tissues inside the mouth. Alcohol can be absorbed very easily in fats, and fats and cholesterol are the main ingredients of our brains. That's why alcohol is easily absorbed by the brain. The most sensitive structures in our brain are the brain cortex, where our thoughts, control of our behavior, memory and planning functions occur. That's why alcohol serves to reduce inhibitions of these functions, and that's why people are less inhibited and feel more free when they drink alcohol.

A larger quantity of alcohol serves to free our lower motor and emotional centers and leads to freer expression of our thoughts and emotions, and in some people, this produces hyperactivity, aggression and anti-social behavior that can harm the person who drinks, and those people who are around him/her (6).

A very large quantity of alcohol depresses proper functioning of the brain. Breathing and heart rate slows down, acute toxicity occurs and if it's not treated, one can lose consciousness, go into a coma and death can result.

Long term or chronic abuse of alcohol leads to serious damage to a large number of organs, including stomach ulcers and chronic gastritis, heavy damage to the pancreas, which produces pain and impairs digestion, liver damage in the form of cirrhosis of the liver, or long term destruction of liver cells.

Alcohol causes extremely heavy damage to the brain and leads to brain atrophy, destruction of brain tissue, alcohol psychosis, as well as damage to peripheral nerves, which manifests itself as neuritis or inflammation of nerve lining, producing paralysis of arms or legs and loss of sexual potency in males.

■ **Recognizing an alcoholic**

The inability to control your alcohol intake is the main sign that you have a serious alcohol problem. An alcoholic is someone who can't abstain from drinking alcohol every day and who is not able to stop. With such loss of control, all other functions are brought into question, including personal behavior, care about one's health, nutrition and putting on clothing. To this can be added problems with one's spouse, children and the whole family is negatively affected by the presence of the alcoholic. Problems arise at work, one doesn't complete one's work related duties and there is conflict with co-workers which may get one fired. This creates new problems: lack of money, inability to pay one's expenses and endangers one's basic survival. Driving while under the influence of alcohol is one of the most frequent causes of car accidents with serious injuries and huge material damage.

Alcoholism results in damage to one's health, family function and disability

■ **Weekend drinking or "binge drinking"**

Binge drinking is defined as taking five drinks during the day in the course of several hours. A large number of people, especially young people, consume large quantities of alcohol at the end of the work week: Friday evening or Saturday evening are our "days of rest and relaxation" where many take 6-12 drinks, often beer, wine or various forms of hard liquor and cause acute toxicity or complete intoxication to themselves. Being drunk, these people cause public disturbances such as aggression, rapes and car accidents, which all may have irreparable consequences (7).

Being drunk over the weekend causes serious consequences for one's health and relationships and should be avoided.

Alcohol reduces our reasoning powers and makes us uninhibited, causing all other forms of behavior which are likely to damage our health, including aggressive conduct, being sexually uninhibited with consequences of contracting sexually transmitted diseases, driving while drunk with a high possibility of being involved in a car accident, use of other drugs and many other negative consequences.

When I ask a patient in my office, "Why do you drink so much alcohol?", I often receive this answer, "To feel high or to be in a good mood." Alcohol doesn't make us happy but instead it frees lower brain centers from control of higher brain centers. That's why many people experience a feeling of acute depression, feelings of guilt and dissatisfaction when they get sober.

A proper choice in order to achieve a better mood is to participate in creative play, sport, or good conversation with one's friends; those activities that mobilize us to engage in our best qualities.

A worrying trend in our society is the use of alcohol by children and young people (8). In the United States over 4,500 boys and girls lose their lives annually because of abuse of alcohol in car accidents or murders, which are alcohol related. This also leads to a significant rise in teen pregnancy.

Take care of your children; be sure that you know where they go, what they are doing and who their friends are. Teach them to take care of themselves!

A mature, responsible person plans all one's activities and makes an effort not to damage one's health, one's life and the lives of people close to them, because only one additional glass of alcohol can turn one's life upside down with disastrous consequences.

Many young people resolve their stress by using alcohol–especially on weekends

Curing alcoholism is a serious business and a long term process. It requires co-operation between teams of doctors, psychologists and sociologists with the patient, his/her family, and community in which the patient works and lives. This problem is even more pronounced for those who live on their own and the number of such people is on the rise. In our rushed and hurried lives, where families are damaged or dysfunctional, it's difficult to establish this co-operation, which is indispensable for the successful cure of alcoholism.

THE ROAD TO HEALTH IS HARD AND LONG

- Effort–not wishing, improves our health
- The heart–my broken heart
- Blocked arteries
- How to lower our risks and improve our health
- AIDS–It's still here

It's nice to hear people's wishes to be healthy but wishing is not enough. It's necessary to make an evident effort to improve our lifestyle, the manner of our nutrition, reduce the burden of stress, and to increase our physical activity and regular exercise.

Most people living in developed and undeveloped countries continue to have problems with unhealthy, hyper caloric nutrition and obesity. The consequences are diabetes, strokes, diseases of the aorta and arteries in the lower extremities.

- The heart–my broken heart

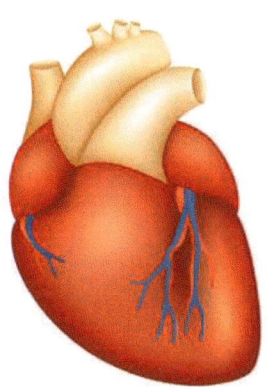

It's well known that the heart is damaged because of high blood pressure, high cholesterol, diabetes and clogged arteries. Recently, it was proven at an American hospital, John Hopkins, that even the so-called "broken heart", because of strong emotions at the loss of a loved one, can lead to serious heart damage.

It's assumed that by experiencing strong emotions there is a secretion of large quantities of adrenaline, hormones which increase blood pressure, speed up heart rate and literally "freeze" the heart, lowering its contractibility and its ability to relax, and reducing its capacity to pump and to receive new blood.

For most study participants, mostly women, these changes were temporary. It's believed that a long term increase of adrenalin can permanently damage the heart muscle.

- Blocked arteries

Diseases of the aorta are being discovered more frequently. The aorta is the main artery that distributes blood from the heart to the whole body and aorta's branches, especially to arteries for the left and right legs.

I was recently called to the hospital to visit one of my patients: a man of about 50 years old, who had led a life filled with stress and suffering, who was a smoker for many years, with high blood pressure. He was admitted to the hospital because of pain in his stomach and in his legs, especially when he took long walks. The pain would subside when he stopped but would shortly resume. He also experienced dizziness and weakness. Urgent tests found out that he had a sclerotic and an enlarged lower aorta with its main branches, pelvic and leg arteries also being affected. Today, vascular surgery is achieving miracles. The heavily damaged part is cut out, a graft inserted in the form of a "sling" and the person is allowed to go home.

Justified anxiety and worry develop into basic lifestyle changes; healthy nutrition, rest, quitting smoking, taking easy walks and later maybe even light work.

The purpose of education about health is not to instill fear but to inform people to take care of themselves and those close to them, and to prevent what is possible to prevent. Why is it necessary to wait for worsening of our health and our life before we do something and learn something?

■ **How to lower our risks and improve our health**

Cute and chubby

Our normal body weight can vary by about 10% from our ideal body weight. People who are 20% over their normal body weight are termed as being "overweight" or obese and those who are significantly over 20% of their normal weight are called pathologically obese. Obesity by itself carries many serious health risks, including diabetes, high blood pressure, high cholesterol, breast cancer, cancer of the uterus and large intestine, arthritis and rheumatic diseases, depression and many other others. The epidemic of obesity is growing all around the world. The World Health Organization estimates that in the year 2005, the number of obese people reached over one billion, which is about 20% of the total world's population.

The greatest increase of obese people has occurred in the United States, England, and Eastern Europe and in the Middle East. The reason for this is the same; reduced activity, unhealthy nutrition, which contains lots of animal fats from hamburgers and fried meats, lots of sugar and lots of pop drinks like Coca Cola. In some countries, the number of obese people has tripled and is approaching one half of their total population. An especially worrying trend is the rise of obesity among young children.

Is it going to be "normal" to be obese when the majority of people are obese?

Too sweet

Diabetes is a serious disease where there is an increase of sugar in the blood. Most frequent is Type II diabetes where insulin (hormone that lowers blood sugar levels) continues to be produced but is inactive. Just in the United States, about 7% of the population is diabetic (over 21 million people) while almost double or 41 million people are in the early phase for developing diabetes. This means if nothing is significantly changed in our nutrition and physical activity in a year or two, these people will develop full diabetic disease. It's well known that diabetes Type II in about 80% of cases can be successfully controlled and managed through healthy nutrition and regular physical activity.

Drugs used to treat diabetes exist but are very expensive and have negative side effects. Complication of diabetes like heart attacks or strokes, blindness, loss of male potency, deterioration of the kidneys and heavy nerve damage are all main components of this serious disease. However, these symptoms can be prevented through the use of a healthy diet, physical exercise, drugs and self-control.

Tumors and cancers can be prevented

By far the most frequent cause of tumors in males is lung cancer, prostate cancer and cancer of the colon. Among women lung cancer is also in first place because of female "emancipation" which has led more women to smoke cigarettes, and many women also develop breast cancer and colon cancer.

The risk of these above named cancers can be significantly reduced: lung cancer by quitting smoking and by not breathing in polluted air. A recently published study shows that second hand smoke, or sharing accommodation with a smoker, damages the health of non-smokers, mothers and their children. About 30% of these people will develop lung cancer, breast cancer or cancer of the uterus.

That is not all; children who live with smokers, develop asthma more frequently.

Cancer of the prostate can be prevented by taking licopene which is contained in tomatoes and Vitamin D, which can be obtained by sun tanning. Cancer of the cervix in women can be successfully prevented with the use of condoms which stops transmission of various sexually transmitted diseases like papilloma virus, and can be discovered with regular pap tests.

The American government is going to approve the use of a vaccine against the most frequent type of virus which contributes to cancer of the cervix.

Over emphasized problems of bird flu

Avian flu or bird flu is dominating our news recently with warnings that it may be transmitted to humans. Is this risk of transmission so great? Until now, about 132 people have died because of this disease. We are talking about a virus that mainly attacks birds, often wild birds but even domestic birds. The virus of bird flu is not very infectious for humans because it's not easily transmitted from birds to humans. There is intensive work being done to come up with a vaccine against bird flu and there also exists an antiviral drug which is believed to reduce the risk of developing this disease.

■ **AIDS–It's still here**

AIDS is a chronic, difficult, infectious disease which is most frequently transmitted through sexual contact and from which is causing the suffering of a great number of people in the world. The World Health Organization estimates that there are 40 million AIDS patients in the world: men, women and children (children are infected by this virus while in the womb of infected mothers). The question to ask here is, why is Avian flu which has killed 132 people is more interesting to our news-media than AIDS which daily kills tens of thousands of people? Just in the United States alone, there are over one million infected AIDS people. Doctors have recently warned against the appearance of a special type of AIDS virus, which is resistant to all drugs used to treat this disease. This dangerous new type of AIDS virus has been observed in New York City in their homosexual male population.

The risk of being infected with this disease can definitely be reduced by reducing one's promiscuous sexual activity, through the use of condoms and by complete sexual abstinence.

CIGARETTES AND SMOKING–SAVE YOUR BREATH

- Tobacco smoking is one of the leading causes of disease
- Is smoking a disease?
- In what psychological phase of smoking are you?
- How to develop and maintain your motivation to stop smoking?

Greater awareness about the harm of smoking cigarettes has been proven by many studies which have examined a large number of healthy and ill people during the last few decades. There is no doubt that smoking cigarettes leads to damage of our circulatory system, impotence in men, clogging up of blood vessels, heart attacks and strokes, and a whole series of cancers with cancer of the lungs at the top of the list, cancer of the throat and cancer of the colon. In women smoking contributes toward development of breast cancer and cancer of the uterus.

The problem is much deeper because it involves large industrial corporations and companies that earn multimillion dollar profits by the manufacture and sale of cigarettes. Of course, this also includes government administrative departments that gain a great deal of money through taxes on cigarettes.

The only losers in these processes are consumers of cigarettes who pay a steep price for their temporary pleasure and all they get in return is a great deal of harmful consequences. In the last few years, there is talk not only about diseases which result from smoking cigarettes, but also about huge material loses sustained by our medical services and by our whole society.

- Is smoking a disease?

According to the 1999 definition of Canadian Medical Association among diseases of dependence is also included nicotine dependence with the following justification:

Dependence is the primary disturbance among people who show reduced control in their use of psychoactive substances.

Changes among smokers manifest themselves in changes of moods, unburdening oneself from negative emotions, feelings of a certain level of satisfaction, compulsive behavior and persisting in certain types of conduct despite unfavorable physical, psychological and social consequences (coughing, struggling for breath, headaches, predisposition to catch colds and resistance of one's family and work place colleagues).

- In what psychological phase of smoking are you?

The pre-contemplation phase (9, 10) is one during which you don't think about quitting smoking because you are not prepared to think about this. You need to talk to someone about this or you need more information about this.

Consider the consequences of smoking on your health and the health of people who live with you, including your family, work colleagues and friends.

Smoking is linked to cancer of the lung, oesophagus, stomach, breast and faster aging

The contemplation phase occurs when you become interested in the problem, you think about the problem and consider its pros and cons; why do you enjoy smoking cigarettes, what kind of pleasure do you derive and can you substitute something else for cigarettes, which is a healthier, less harmful pleasure? What do you gain and what do you lose if you stop smoking cigarettes? If, in this evaluation of pros and cons of smoking, you have a clear balance on the side that you should stop smoking cigarettes, then it's time to put this plan into practice.

The decision phase. I am definitely quitting smoking! Determine the day: an important date, a holiday or birthday. Prepare yourself mentally and physically, make an appointment to see your doctor, ask your doctor to hear you out, to give you support and together make a detailed plan and choose the best method for helping you to stop being dependent on cigarettes. Openly talk to your doctor about your previous unsuccessful attempts to quit and reasons that you failed. Ask your doctor for a detailed examination of your health. Most changes that you make can be reversed (can be normalized) after a short or long period of time.

Maintaining your decision phase. It's done, I don't smoke any more! You deserve honest congratulations and you have a reason to be proud of yourself for your decision. Ask support and encouragement from your family and your friends. Talk freely about signs of abstinence syndrome, like irritability, being upset, going without sleep, increase of appetite and your desire for a cigarette and other things.

How to develop and maintain your motivation to stop smoking?

- *Your strength and decision to persist in it is confirmation of your self-confidence. It's now clear to you that you've gained a great deal. You feel better, your strength has returned, your thoughts are clearer, you have fresher breath, you don't cough, your conscience is not bothering you about hurting your children, friends and co-workers.*

- *There are a lot better and healthier ways to relax and to resolve stress, including deep breathing with the use of your stomach muscles, regular exercise, walks in clean air, meditation, good music and a good book!*

- *Talk to other smokers and tell them about your own example. It will not only help to strengthen your position as a non-smoker but you will also help other people by being a good role model, especially to your children and to those people that trust you.*

- *Are there pros and cons of smoking? Of course there are! Just like in every human imperfection a person sometimes gives in to things that are against us and which we are aware are harmful. Let's be realistic, human beings are imperfect. The most often mentioned reasons for smoking are; mental relaxation, control of our appetite and our body weight, improvement of our concentration, feeling of satisfaction and a way to socially interact with other people ("I don't know what to do with my hands"). Among young people smoking may be a way to get noticed: "Oh you are a smoker, man!" or a way to establish contact: "Do you have a match?"*

- *Of course, there is no doubt that there are other ways to show your maturity and to interact with people.*

- *Reasons against smoking are by far more numerous and can be applied immediately; cough, struggle for breath, asthma attacks, headaches, being a nuisance to other people, especially to children with a sore throat, eye irritations and a predisposition toward infections.*

- *Consequences of smoking which manifest themselves later are; diseases of the heart and of blood vessels, strokes, problems of blood circulation in our arms and legs, male impotence, lack of fertility of both sexes, lung cancer, emphysema of the lungs and many other diseases.*

- *Consequences for other people who live with or near a smoker are; higher risk of developing lung cancer for family members, higher risk that children of a smoker will also smoke, greater predisposition of children to get infected, lung infection, asthma, infection of the middle ear and many others.*

- *How to definitely determine that one has a bad habit? It's necessary to distinguish people who have a true nicotine dependence from people who smoke because of psychological or social dependence.*

- *If you smoke more than 10 cigarettes daily, if the first thing you want in the morning is a cigarette, if you begin to sweat and are upset when you go without a cigarette for a prolonged period of time, then you probably have a chemical dependence. In order to quit, you need to make a detailed plan in co-operation with your doctor, who has enough time and understanding to hear you out and to help you.*

- *To be a long-term smoker is a state of mind, lifestyle and takes into consideration the whole organization of your conduct and work, which is dominated by your constant need to smoke cigarettes. It takes about 5 to 15 minutes to smoke one cigarette. If we multiply this time by about 20 cigarettes per day we can see that a significant amount of time is wasted here which we can spend in doing something more beneficial.*

- *Treatment of nicotine dependence is composed of three basic approaches: pharmacological, psychological and social.*

- ***The pharmacological approach*** *consists of the application of drugs in the form of tablets that don't contain nicotine but reduce our need for tobacco (Bupropion) or skin patches, which contain various amounts of nicotine, depending on the number of cigarettes smoked daily. There are also chewing gums which contain different concentrations of nicotine.*

- ***The psychological approach*** *consists of educating the smoker and changing their behavior, especially avoiding a situation which leads us to smoke a cigarette and developing new interests and activities. Instead of smoking that first cigarette in the morning, go for a jog or a walk outside, then take a shower and the whole world will be in front of you! After dinner, instead of a cigarette, get up immediately from the table, wash the dishes and brush your teeth. If later you feel a need for a cigarette, eat some finely chopped up fruits that you prepared previously. Instead of coffee you should have fresh fruit or vegetable juice.*

- ***The social approach*** *consists of family support and support of your friends who are aware that you have made a decision to stop smoking, will respect your decision, and will help you to remain consistent.*

- *What are the benefits for health and the community of someone who stops smoking? By quitting smoking you not only benefit your own health and the health of your family, but you also improve your appearance, slow down skin aging, slow down development of wrinkles and aging of your blood vessels, increase your self-confidence, and of course, you improve the state of your wallet.*

- *It's been calculated that a person who smokes a pack of cigarettes daily for 40 years spends so much money that he/she could afford to buy a fine house worth about $300,000. During that same time period from a lung capacity of about 5 liters there is a loss of half that capacity, every third smoker has developed lung cancer and every fourth smoker has had a stroke (11).*

- *Just two hours after stopping smoking the amount of nicotine in the blood is lowered by half.*

- *Eight hours after stopping smoking oxygen levels begin to rise, lowering carbon monoxide in the blood and our blood pressure begins to be normalized.*

- *The smell of your body, breath, hair, clothing and your whole house will be much better.*

- *If a woman doesn't smoke during her pregnancy she will reduce her chance of having a miscarriage, premature birth and newborns will have a normal body weight.*

- *Your teeth will be less yellow and will last longer. You will feel stronger and will have more energy. Your life insurance will be more expensive if you are a smoker! Many companies and businesses don't hire smokers! You will have more money left over to spend on better things.*

- *No one can teach us and do well for us that we can teach ourselves and do for ourselves. By helping ourselves we also help other people as well!*

CHRONIC TIREDNESS SYNDROME: CAUSES AND SOLUTIONS

- Tiredness is an alarm signal
- The most common reasons for chronic tiredness
- The primary syndrome of chronic tiredness
- Lessons for removal of chronic tiredness

Modern society of western civilization at the end of the 20th and the beginning of the 21st centuries can be described as a time of very rapid technological progress and development. Computers, biotechnology with genetic engineering, highly productive industries, high level of consumerism and consumer power with many dynamic social changes occurring. These changes refer not only to our economy and agriculture but have a deep impact on society, the family and on an individual. Before us are heavy duties and responsibilities, not only at a professional level but also at a private level, including work, career, family, personal needs and desires.

Continually present duties raise our feeling of responsibility, psychological tension and often increase our feelings of dissatisfaction, lack of accomplishment and loneliness.

These rapid changes increase psychological tension and produce muscle pain. Feelings of tiredness reduce our good mood, mental concentration and work efficiency. So the vicious circle closes and things get worse until there is a "car wreck" and we start to seek the causes of our complaints. Tiredness is an alarm signal, it's a warning that something is not right and we need to seek out and remove its cause (12).

Fatigue and exhaustion are frequently caused by neglected health care

- The most common reasons for chronic tiredness

Improper nutrition which is rich in fats, large meals, insufficient levels of vitamins and minerals in our body, irregular meals and food which contains unhealthy preservatives (monosodium glutamate) can create a feeling of being tired and weak.

An insufficient amount of healthy sleep, irregular sleep, disturbance of day-night rhythm, and insomnia, all prevent the body from recovering and to refresh from daily efforts and duties.

A lack of regular exercise lowers our sense of well-being, reduces our ability for productive work, has a negative influence on healthy sleep and prevents the accumulation of sufficient energy necessary for daily activities.

A state of long-term stress, tension, anxiety, increased level of adrenaline, high blood pressure, raised pulse and burning up of oxygen and energy, all lead toward tiredness and weakness. Unburdening through rational planning and use of our time, techniques of deep breathing, recreational activities, socializing and relaxation all reduce tenseness and stress.

Nicotine and smoking of cigarettes produces chronic poisoning of the body from substances which result when tobacco is burned, increase the concentration of carbon monoxide, which is a poisonous gas that blocks hemoglobin and so lowers the amount of oxygen in the blood, resulting in headaches and muscle pains. These are only the most frequent acute consequences of smoking cigarettes.

Abuse of alcohol and consuming large amounts of alcohol leads to speeding up of the pulse, an increase in oxygen absorption, with additional overloading of the liver (the main organ used in detoxification of poisonous materials).

Misuse of caffeine contained in coffee and sweetened juices leads to an increase in irritability, sleeplessness and a higher need for oxygen.

Pregnancy, breast feeding and menstruation are all normal physiological states that demand a higher level of energy and special attention to our nutrition, rest and moments of relaxation.

Tiredness as a consequence of psychological disturbance

Depression, which is manifested through apathy, disturbance of our sleep patterns, disturbance of our appetite, bad mood, and lack of interest in our basic joys of life, which is sometimes accompanied with suicidal thoughts, are all states that are occurring more frequently in our alienated and technologically advanced society. Everyone now has a computer, telephone and email, but our overall communication with other people is poorer and doesn't make us happier.

Depression can occur at every stage of our life but manifests itself more frequently among males over 40 years of age, who are lonely, isolated, who drink more alcohol or have other health problems, such as high blood pressure, diabetes or chronic bronchitis.

People who manifest signs of depression should visit their doctor or their psychiatrist in order to take measures to investigate their situation and to begin treatment.

A state of anxiety is manifested as chronic nervous tension, panic attacks, fear of being in public, fear of being in the presence of other people, various obsessive/compulsive states (which are always in our thoughts), and a state of urgency to do something about this, are some of the most frequent forms of this type of psychological disturbance.

Hormone induced neurotic states which occur during early puberty can lead to a revolutionary state in the body, especially among young girls, and among post-menstrual, mature women in their 50's, can cause psychological changes, changes in behavior with a feeling of tiredness, and can lower our ability to do productive work. Consulting with your doctor in order to eliminate the presence of more serious diseases is invaluable at this stage.

Physical disease as a cause of tiredness

Diabetes patients as well as those with high blood pressure and heart weakness or patients who have survived a heart infarction, all can have a more or less expressed feeling of tiredness.

Lung diseases especially among long-term smokers with emphysema or chronic bronchitis are often causes of permanent weakness. Diabetes, disease of the thyroid gland, liver diseases, disease of the kidneys, rheumatic diseases of the bones and joints are all frequent diseases that can be recognized only in its later stages.

Thyroid gland. According to one big American study, about 20% of so-called healthy women have a mild form of lowered functioning of the thyroid gland whose main sign is experiencing chronic tiredness. This disease can be easily diagnosed and treated.

Anemia. A large number of young women and girls have an increased blood flow during menstruation, which can lead to long-term anemia on one side and lack of iron in the blood which is necessary in the production of red blood cells. Anemia leads to weakness because of reduced production of one of the main proteins of the blood, hemoglobin, which works to supply the body with oxygen. Not only lowered oxygen levels but also lowered reserves of iron in the blood produces chronic tiredness, as iron is a key component of developing immunity and defense against various infections.

Infectious diseases like tuberculosis, jaundice, AIDS, infections that are sexually transmitted and other viral infections can all cause significant tiredness.

Diseases of the liver and the kidneys are often the cause of long-term tiredness and have complex, multifaceted causes. That why it's necessary to devote special care to early signs of these diseases and to begin treatment.

Many drugs, especially if they are taken in excess and without control such as pain killers (analgesic drugs), anxiety reducing drugs (benzodiazepine), allergy drugs, heart and blood pressure drugs can all cause a feeling of tiredness and weakness. Every one of the above mentioned diseases requires extra attention, investigation and treatment.

Psychosomatic diseases are a group of disturbances with a psychological basis which manifest themselves through physical symptoms. These types of diseases manifest themselves through permanent or frequent headaches, chronic back pain, muscle and bone pain but, in reality, they project a long-term accumulated level of psychological unease, loneliness, apathy, dissatisfaction with oneself or with other people, and unrealized wants, needs and dreams.

■ The primary syndrome of chronic tiredness

The basic criteria used for diagnosis of chronic weakness according to The American Center for Disease Control are: new manifestation of persistent, sometimes oscillating weakness which can not be recovered with normal sleep and which reduces our level of activity over 50% over a period of six months. As well as these main complaints, there exist a large number of other complaints that can be observed; unexplained muscle pain, rise in temperature, sore throat, bone and joint pain, headache, changes in our sense of taste and smell, irritability, lowered level of concentration, memory lapses and other complaints. Diagnosis of primary weakness is only established when the presence of other physical or psychological diseases (that have a different nature, course and treatment) are ruled out (13).

■ Lessons for removal of chronic tiredness

By studying a detailed history of disease and examination of the patient, many of the previously mentioned diseases can either be ruled out or confirmed. If it is proven that there is no presence of other serious diseases, then people who are suffering from a primary weakness can be helped in the following manner:

- regular, moderate and healthy nutrition;
- well organized day-night rhythm with a sufficient level of healthy sleep;
- regular physical exercise, participation in sports or other recreational activities;
- avoidance of tobacco and moderation in use of alcohol and caffeine;
- lowered level use of drugs or complete avoidance of unnecessary drugs;
- fulfillment of one's spiritual, emotional and mental needs; and
- the establishment of a dynamic balance between one's professional, family and personal needs.

In the case that none of the above ways to treat tiredness helps, there exist a wide spectrum of drugs that can significantly reduce complaints and can help the patient. This syndrome is not fatal but can last anywhere from 3 to 4 years and can significantly lower the quality of life.

HUMOR HEALS, SO GO AHEAD AND LAUGH

- Humor and personality
- Humor in a relationship between doctor and patient
- Humor at school and within the educational system

We live in a world where intense changes occur daily. A world in which deep social trends are boiling over, as well as continual economic and political crises. The modern world is full of problems, such as in Africa and parts of Asia, where people are dying because of hunger and because they lack basic necessities for survival like bread, clean water and medicine. While in the rich, developed world people are dying because of an overabundance of food and alcohol, and because they are unsatisfied with their lives, and are beset with depression and worry. In these rich western countries, because of this overabundance of food and excessive food intake, people are fighting various diseases such as high blood pressure, high cholesterol, diabetes, obesity and other diseases caused by unhealthy habits and an unhealthy lifestyle.

Humor can reduce pain, stimulate our immunity, help with digestion and improve our general feelings of well-being as well as psychological health. Even the greatest problems in life, such as serious diseases and death, look less frightful if we approach them with a sense of humor.

Humor and laughter are very powerful communication tools which help to establish good relations between people and help make them relaxed and comfortable. Victor Borge, one of the most recognized comedians and virtuoso piano musicians said, "Humor is the shortest distance between two human beings."

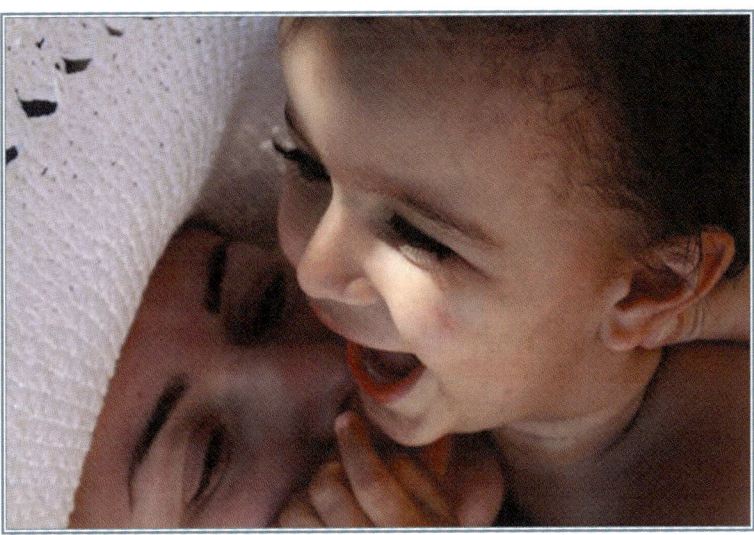

Laughter and joy are signs of optimism and health

Humor has a therapeutic effect on our health and that's why it's recommended in medical practice, between the doctor and his/her patients, because good humor has multifaceted beneficial effects for us. Nothing relaxes us more and lightens our burdens due to stress and tension like good humor (14). Humor that is tasteful and humane is not made at the expense of someone's racial, national, or religious characteristics, nor is it based on someone's physical and mental weakness or disability.

The basic principle, of course, is very simple; we need to laugh with people and not at them. People often laugh at their own minor flaws, overlooking a detail, making mistakes of memory or remembering something or at their own small or great foolish acts. A mature adult often laughs at their own foolishness in their youth and that's why they are more understanding or tolerant toward their children and the younger generation.

A doctor said to a patient "You should quit smoking and drinking alcohol." "But doctor, I neither smoke nor drink." "Okay, Okay," said the doctor, "Then I'll have to ban you from something else."

■ Humor and personality

Through a sense of humor can be discerned many positive characteristics of human personality. A person with a well developed sense of humor possesses a high level of intelligence and quick wit, and can come up on the spur of the moment with an apt and funny answer, which is gladly accepted in any social setting. Recognizing someone's humorous side of their personality means that very often we discover a new dimension to them and sometimes a whole new world. In a healthy and mature person, a sense of humor exists alongside their intelligence, dignity and responsibility toward oneself, and to other people.

■ Humor in a relationship between physician doctor and patient

In his office, the doctor turns to a middle-aged woman and says, "You said that you drink two glasses of wine every day?" "Yes, doctor, you told me that one drink every day is good for my heart." "But you are taking two glasses, every day." "One glass is for my heart, and the other glass is for my head. My headache goes away after I have the second glass."

Laughter in the doctor's office is not only permitted, it is also recommended. A tasteful joke reduces patient's worry, pains and traumatic experience. However, during this whole process the doctor must remain calm and not even for one moment should his/her serious professional stance and treatment of the patient come into question. At the same time, it's necessary to maintain the patient's self-confidence and dignity. Demeaning laughter or sarcasm should never be present because such an approach can significantly damage the relationship between the doctor and the patient. Humor needs to be good natured, inspirational and relaxing.

■ Humor at school and within the educational system

Researchers who study the effect that humor has on education have discovered that good and healthy humor attracts the students' attention, improves their concentration, and reduces stress and tension (15). Humor can improve our approach toward learning, our literacy, and can lead to a better understanding of education. When you learn something with the help of humor and laughter, you remember it better and retain it longer. Cruel reality looked at with a sense of humor can look less terrifying and less drastic. One man who managed to survive all the horrors of the Nazi concentration camp during World War II claims that humor helped him to survive all the torture and persecution to which he was exposed. He says that laughter and humor put all this suffering in a different light and more tolerable. Laughter is a special form of human freedom and helps people to rise above all sorts of meaningless situations. Humor is way to "rub it in" even to the highest authorities, all without actually insulting them.

Whenever we are too serious, our excessive seriousness narrows our objectivity and creates tunnel vision, limits our perception and serves to deform reality.

Isn't laughter with children at the start of the day often the best way to establish good contact with them and also with the parents? Jokes, laughter and play are the basic manner of child behavior. Children communicate the best and easiest among themselves and with adults through play. Humor is one of our most humane characteristics. An adult who retains the nature of a small mischievous child remains young, humane and creative much longer.

Many waiting rooms of doctors' offices are stocked with children's toys, funny picture books, humorous magazines and cartoon films. The idea is clear; for doctors and for medicine, just as for children and for adults, humor is always welcome. In many waiting rooms there are caricatures and funny anecdotes placed in a prominent place at the expense of other health personnel.

Humor doesn't only mean making jokes and telling good jokes, humor means happiness and joy at life, even when things are not going as they should. The basic characteristic of human psychology is the human longing for joy and happiness. This is the most significant motivation of our being and all our activity. Humor is the best way out of depression, boredom, sadness and hopelessness.

Together with love, toward everything that's good and humane, human happiness and humor deserve a special place in the life of every person.

GET YOUR ANNUAL PHYSICAL CHECK-UP

- Stages of growth and maturity
- Promotion of health and risk factors at different periods of life

During life, a person goes through different periods of growth, maturity and functioning with many changes occurring at a psychological and physical level of our health, so that every distinct phase of life has its own specific characteristics.

The earliest growth of a child from birth to two years of age can be characterized by great physical and mental development. The transition from breast feeding to regular food, beginning to walk, learning our first words and speech, as well as the development of the senses, and fitting into a family.

The most important parameters of healthy development of a child in this stage are proper and healthy nutrition, growth in height and weight, and proper mental development which includes movement, speech, and safety of hearing and sight. At this stage children need a lot of love and care, with a good relationship with their parents and the surrounding in which they live.

The most common causes of disease at this stage of life are infection of the breathing passages, manifestations of inherited diseases and general injuries. The duty of the parents is to ensure a safe and comfortable environment for the development of their children and to provide them with healthy food, warmth and love. A regular consultation with a doctor should ensure proper growth of the child, along with regular vaccinations and prevention of injuries at home, in the car and outside the home. A simple cold with an infection of the middle ear can slow down speech and mental functions of the child because of damage to his/her hearing.

- Promotion of health and risk factors at different periods of life

Children from two to six years of age

At this stage of growth it's necessary to monitor a child's height and weight (there is more childhood obesity), perform eye examinations to determine nearsightedness or farsightedness and to control development of speech.

Changes in behavior can be observed at this stage in children, and learning and psychological problems can manifest themselves, especially in children from dysfunctional families. The first signs of bad teeth or losing teeth because of improper nutrition or bad hygiene need to be noticed in time and removed. Children's injuries at this stage include those they sustain when playing, riding a bike and accidental swallowing of foreign objects or poisons, or chemicals that need to be placed out of their reach. Consultations with a doctor or a psychologist, and education of children and their parents can help to prevent and remove many of the problems which can occur at this sensitive period.

Children from 7 to 12 years of age

During this period children fit into life beyond the home, their education begins and they start to perform regular chores at home and at school. The most frequent injuries at this stage include physical injuries during play, such as riding a bike, or injuries they sustain as pedestrians or as passengers of vehicles.

Regular monitoring means closely following children's height and weight, having their eyesight and hearing checked, as well as blood pressure. Advising children at this stage about healthy nutrition and the need to develop a healthy culture of regular physical exercise and participation in sports are of essential significance, and are a long term value and investment.

Period of puberty from 13 to 18 years of age

During the time of puberty or adolescence, many big psychological and physical changes occur in children, which can lead to rapid growth in height and rapid emotional, mental and sexual development which also leads to an inner search for their identity.

Besides regular check-ups about height, weight and the evaluation of mental development during this stage, it's indispensable to monitor any manifestation of symptoms of depression, abuse of alcohol, tobacco or toxic substances, such as recreational drugs. The most common injuries sustained at this stage are tied to the use of motor vehicles, suicide and poisoning. More that half of young people begin sexual experimentation at this stage, so advising them and educating them in order to prevent early pregnancy and transmission of sexually transmitted diseases is of great significance.

Puberty is the age of great mental and biological changes

Period from 19 to 39 years of age

In this period of adulthood, a manifestation of other serious diseases can begin, such as problems of the breathing passages like chronic bronchitis and emphysema, diseases of the heart and blood vessels, diseases of organs used in digestion and diseases of sexual organs (16).

Healthy nutrition, participation in sport and regular exercise needs to be an essential part of the everyday lifestyle. Regular annual check-ups of the heart, blood pressure and a blood test to determine sugar level, as well as a urine test, should all be performed each year. Women need to have a regular annual gynecological test called the pap-test and a breast examination for early detection of breast cancer which are essential in the examination of their health status (17).

An examination of the mouth and teeth should be performed every six to twelve months by your dentist. Immunization and vaccination against tetanus and diphtheria should be renewed every 10 years and special risk groups should be vaccinated against Hepatitis B, pneumococcal virus and influenza virus.

Period from 40 to 64 years of age

The main causes of disease during this period are diseases of the heart, most of all, high blood pressure, heart attack, lung cancer, and cancer of the large intestine. A regular annual examination of the prostate among males and the uterus among females should be performed to discover early stages of disease of these organs. Breast examination known as a mammography during this period has the goal of early detection of breast cancer.

A consultation with your doctor needs to cover very important aspects of your health such as healthy nutrition, regular exercise, avoidance of tobacco and moderate use of alcohol. Examination of eyesight and hearing and appropriate correction can significantly improve functioning at a professional and personal level of activity among people in this age category.

During this stage of life there is a reduction in the secretion of sexual hormones among both males and females, which on one side facilitates large emotional, psychological and physical changes and on the other side, leads to stoppage of the menstrual cycle among women around the age of 50 and weakening of male potency. Many of these disturbances are correctable and we need to devote care and time for them.

Period of life after 65 years of age

The number and frequency of illnesses during this period occur more often and require regular annual checkups, even among people who don't have any health complaints. A comprehensive physical examination can include, regular monitoring of blood pressure, the heart, lungs, stomach organs, digestion organs, especially the liver, colon and after that, an examination of the uterus and the prostate gland at least once a year (18). An evaluation of one's mental state, family relationships and community relations are of vital significance. During this stage of life we begin our retirement, and it's important to find other avenues and interests for our activities and recreation as well as to find new meaning and purpose in our everyday activities. Healthy, moderate nutrition with small intake of calories, avoidance of fats of animal origin, plenty of fresh fruits and vegetables along with taking regular walks and work in the garden can improve not only our overall physical condition, but can also help our psychological state during this period in life. A regular checkup of eyesight and hearing can not only serve to improve the functioning of these organs, it can also raise the quality of our life.

The most frequent causes of disease and mortality during this period are diseases of the heart, strokes, obstruction of breathing passages as a consequence of smoking cigarettes and air pollution, lung cancer, cancer of the colon, prostate gland cancer and breast and uterine cancer. Through regular care and doctor examinations many of these diseases can be prevented and if they appear, they can be detected at an early stage of development.

Good care about our health, regular consultations with our doctor and healthy lifestyle are all basic preconditions for the realization of our desires, goals and plans.

An old, wise proverb defines this for us in the following manner: "A healthy person has a thousand wishes, but an unhealthy person has only one wish: to get well!"

III

HEALTH AND NUTRITION

*"Our food should be a medicine–
and our medicine should be our food"*

FOOD: PSYCHOLOGY OF NUTRITION

- The physiological basis of nutrition
- The psychological motives of ingesting food
- Food and feasts as a social act
- The spiritual or religious approach to food and the meaning of a fast
- The most frequent problems of improper nutrition

The leading Canadian professional medical journal *Canadian Medical Association Journal (CMAJ) in its February 1999* issue dedicates three main article to obesity among Canadians: "Over 30% of Canadians are obese (women–27%; men—35%). Obesity is defined in Body Mass Index over 27. The Index is a relationship between body weight and body area. The most frequent medical complications of obesity are high blood pressure with its negative consequences on vital organs, diseases of heart arteries and brain arteries along with infarction of the heart and strokes, increased level of fats in the blood (cholesterol and triglycerides) and diabetes, with its harmful effects on blood vessels, kidneys, nerves, eyesight etc. It has been estimated that the cost of treating obesity and its negative consequences in Canada in 1997 was over 2 billion dollars. There are over 100 million people in the United States that are obese and their costs of treating obesity are much higher (this is more than one third of the total U.S. population and this number has increased significantly in the last 10 to 15 years). Obesity carries not only medical but also social and psychological implications; lowered capacity for productive work, increase of disability, lack of self-esteem, insecurity and depression which all leads to a lower quality of life (1).

Where do these problems come from and is it possible to prevent them?

- The physiological basis of nutrition

Do we eat to live or do we live to eat? Even if the answer appears to be self evident and simple this is not the case (2, 3).

Human beings ingest food in order to satisfy their hunger and for pleasure. This is a basic biological and also deeply human motive. Hunger is the basic physiological signal, over which we have no choice, and can be satisfied with all sorts of food. This is the first step toward variety in choice and structure of food, its availability, quantity, different methods of its preparation and serving; this great variety of food further establishes big personal, cultural, geographical, ethnic and other variations in food.

Why is food necessary?

Our body requires materials to produce energy for; the maintenance of normal body temperature, energy for our heart to work, for blood circulation, muscles to work, for movement, secretion, etc. In addition, we need building block materials for everyday growth and regeneration of our body tissues (bone marrow, epithelium cells for all mucous membrane tissues, liver, bones, skin, etc.) to be used during the growth of the individual and also to be used in the reproduction and division of cells.

These essentially very complex functions can only be performed if the body possesses these materials that are indispensable, including proteins, starch and sugar, fats (glycerol, fatty acids, and cholesterol), vitamins (A, B, C, D, K, and E), minerals (nutrients, calcium, potassium, magnesium, bicarbonate), and water as the main dissolvent.

■ The psychological motives of ingesting food

Besides the basic physiological motive of satisfying our hunger, a person often ingests food for a completely different psychological reason, such as anxiety, nervous tension, depression, dissatisfaction, anger, boredom, along with the frequent absence of hunger as a basic motive (3). Ingesting food creates a feeling of pleasure, which can subconsciously serve to satisfy other pleasures that are unattainable or are hard to obtain, which leads to the concept of substitution. Regression is a concept where we return to our lower biological instincts in the absence of moral, pedagogical, or social limitations or norms.

■ Food and feasts as a social act

In many cases, our social gatherings, beginning with simple friendly, family and work related meetings, including birth of child, birthdays, weddings, funerals and other jubilees, are all marked with good food. Good dining and appropriate food has for centuries been considered a sign of success, achievement, prestige and good hospitality. Today, during official dinners, it's socially accepted to prepare 5 or 6 types of food or courses during only one meal, which is totally unnecessary! In developed nations of the west food is relatively cheap, easily accessible and of great variety. This has led to a virtual cult of food and excessive intake of food. However, are we really aware of our real needs of food and calories? Are we also aware of large social changes that have occurred in the last few decades; our reduced need for heavy physical labor, our lack of ambulatory movement, rise in many sedentary professions, long rides in our cars and sitting for a long time in front of TV sets and computers? Are we making a proper selection when we buy food?

Do we know how to prepare food so that it keeps its nutritious qualities (vitamins A and C) and so that it doesnt lose its organic characteristics; smell, color, taste? Do we have food when we really need it or when it's socially acceptable?

According to the state of nutrition of the general population in developed countries, it's obvious that everyone needs to exercise more self-discipline in this area and also people need to be more informed about food (4, 5).

■ The spiritual or religious approach to food and the meaning of a fast

Even ancient wise men, philosophers, and authors of the Bible recognized the significance of proper nutrition and the periodic need for abstinence from bodily pleasures, which includes food, especially food of animal origin.

Fasting, as recommended in the Bible, more than once during the course of the year, suggests that we avoid all sorts of fats, milk products and all animal products and carries a deep medical justification: after a long winter with many feasts, celebrations and holidays with huge quantities of food and drink (coffee, tea, alcohol) we need a period of "cleansing" of the body just to burn up all the surplus calories but also to take a break from all the pleasures of the body. The goal of this abstinence from food is to move our desires from pleasures of the body to the strengthening of our spiritual powers, our self-confidence as well as moral re-examination. The ability to abstain from bodily pleasures is, according to many psychologists, the basic condition of mental maturity of an individual.

Abstinence from bodily pleasures can become a new source of spiritual satisfaction and thus become a new motive. This act serves to regenerate our body and our soul; healthy functioning of our soul and body requires a dynamic and continuous balance. Through disciplined nutrition and by regular exercise, our body can maintain its youthfulness and significantly postpone the aging process. By clinical examination in the last few years it has been proven that even damage by arteriosclerosis of our blood vessels can be reversed (it can be reduced or completely eliminated) if the principle of healthy nutrition is consistently and extensively applied.

■ The most frequent problems of improper nutrition

Modern medicine considers that the main problems with today's nutrition are (6, 7, 8):

- ingesting too many calories that don't get burned up but accumulate in the form of fatty tissue;
- excessive intake of fats, particularly trans fats of animal origin;
- excessive intake of proteins (eating more than one 3 ounce steak between 90 to 100 grams is unnecessary and can have negative consequences);
- excessive intake of concentrated sugars, including ice-cream, cakes, candy and chocolate;
- intake of food additives: herbicides, antibiotics, and food preservatives;
- ingestion of genetically modified food, including practically all sorts of vegetables and fruits are already genetically modified and consequences of ingesting such foods are yet to be determined; and
- irregular scheduling of meals, often our main meal is taken in late afternoon or in the evening. Our food is often consumed in a hurry and when we are on the move.

Aloe vera is believed to have many healing properties

What we can do for ourselves?

- We need to adjust our caloric intake according to the needs of our body, the type of work we perform and the time of day.
- We should reduce our intake of fats to a level below 30% of our total calories, we should use exclusively vegetable oils (canola, olive oil, sunflower oil) not more than 50 ml/24h (two tablespoons per person).
- Fish is healthy and should be consumed at least twice a week because it contains Omega 3 fatty acids.
- Our main meal should be consumed in the morning and our afternoon dinner should be light.
- We should consume leafy and root based vegetables that are fresh.
- We should walk daily for about 4 to 5 km, or exercise for about 45 minutes 4 to 5 times a week.
- We need to check our body weight, blood pressure and fats in our blood, they can be high for a long time before we feel any complaints.

What we need to avoid?

- We need to avoid fats and fat of animal origin: chicken, beef, and pork.
- We shouldn't consume excessive meals.
- We should not consume our meals late at night or before we go to bed, this is the fastest way to gain weight!
- Don't skip breakfast, if you do, you will be more tired and less productive at work.
- If you have to sit while you work, get up and take a short walk every one hour and thirty minutes for at least 10 to 15 minutes.
- Don't eat in a hurry, you need to devote enough time for each meal. Your health depends on it. What you fail to do now is hard to make up in the future.
- The Canadian Medical Association as a leading professional medical organization which is responsible for creating medical policy in Canada, recommends use of the cookbook, New Light Cooking by author Anne Lindsay.

REDUCING OUR APPETITE AND PORTION SIZES

- Is our food intake greater because of better appetite?
- Is food cheaper and more accessible than ever before?
- Is food a substitute for our dissatisfaction, depression or loneliness?
- Which diet is best?
- Don't give your children Coca Cola and Pepsi!

The problem of healthy nutrition and obesity has gone beyond personal care and the doctor's office, and has become a widespread social, and even, political problem. The number of obese people has doubled in the last 15 years and the problems that result from this have quadrupled. The number of obese people, according to various statistics and criteria in developed countries of the west, which includes Canada and the United States, has reached 40% of the population.

Obesity significantly damages health, reduces the ability to move and create productive work, creates depression, high blood pressure, diabetes, rheumatism and inflammation of the joints, colon cancer, breast cancer and uterine cancer (high estrogen level).

The costs of treatment from the consequences of obesity are reaching astronomical sums, which is beginning to seriously worry even the most optimistic economists, sociologists, doctors and politicians.

A 27 year old single mother with a 7 year old daughter entered my office recently. There are over 3 million single mothers today in the United States. She was very pleasant but had a worried look on her face. She was evidently very, very obese, was sloppily dressed, and smelled of tobacco smoke from a recently smoked cigarette. She complained of pains in the soles of her feet and she wanted me to prescribe her some pain killers immediately and asked me to refer her to a foot specialist. She did not, at least not out loud, ask to know the cause of her foot pain. To my persistent question if she had any other problems or if she any other questions for me, she said: "Yes, I need a prescription for birth control pills."

I kindly asked her several more questions about her life. She told me that she lived alone with her daughter, was on welfare, her parents were divorced, she did not graduate from high-school, was abandoned by her boyfriend, was very disappointed, unhappy and unable to change anything in her life. She admitted that she didn't prepare her food or cook; bur rather ate out with her daughter at fast food restaurants like McDonald's or bought processed food. She smoked one pack of cigarettes every day and took birth control pills. She denied using alcohol and drugs. She was extremely pessimistic about her future.

It was difficult to conduct a physical examination. With reluctance she agreed to be weighed. The scale showed 270 pounds or about 123 kilograms. This was more than double her normal body weight for her height.

After a lengthy talk we made a program of action which sparked some hope in her. We agreed on a change of lifestyle, including a gradual change in diet to healthy food, mostly of plant origin, vegetables, whole wheat grains, fish, salads and fruits. She would start a regular program of exercise or at least take daily walks, reduce the number of cigarettes every day and eventually stop smoking altogether. She needed to attend psychotherapy sessions with a psychologist. She would also continue her education as a long-term goal. She also needed to get help with the upbringing of her daughter. Her progress needed to be monitored periodically by coming to see me in order to evaluate her participation in the program, and to ensure that her daughter was receiving a good upbringing. Her path toward recovery and health would prove to be long and strenuous!

■ **Is food is cheaper and more accessible than ever before?**

Our food intake hasn't increased only because people have a better appetite. This problem is much more complex. Here are a few main causes.

All studies show that people today eat significantly more food, their caloric intake is much greater, especially of animal based foods, including meat and fat and large quantities of unnecessary sugar, particularly white sugar contained in cakes, chocolate, candy and pop drinks. Cheap "junk food" that is widely available is rich in fats and the most popular drink is Coca Cola. Therefore, the quality and composition of food not only doesnt meet our human needs (not enough minerals and vitamins) but also leads to harmful consequences for our health, including a rise in obesity and all the negative consequences for health that obesity brings.

Excessively large portions of food (9, 10, 11, 12, 13)

Many women have forgotten how to cook; they are more used to going out to eat. Restaurants compete with each other for who will offer you a greater portion of food with more calories, and with many free additions that you can choose.

Overabundant choice of food

During private celebrations, not only during weddings, holiday celebrations and feasts, but even during a friendly meeting of a few friends, it has become accepted to prepare 5 or 6 types of food. And of course, nothing less than a full stomach, with heartburn and bloating, accompanied by a difficult sleep and a hangover morning, are just short term consequences of this overeating. Some long-term unwanted consequences are obesity, arthritis, high blood pressure, high cholesterol and heart attack, among many others.

■ **Is food a substitute for our dissatisfaction, depression or loneliness?**

These are diseases of modern time and of an alienated man or woman, who often doesn't have the courage or ability to face reality and, as such, turns to food, and frequently to alcohol, tobacco or drugs. They find comfort in the form of this temporary pleasure; however, the heavy price they pay are many negative consequences and even worse dissatisfaction.

What is the lesson? You should buy fresh and healthy food, according to availability, without chemicals and you should prepare a variety of healthy meals at home in moderate amounts. You should serve your guests with a smaller number and smaller quantity of foods. Hospitality can be expressed through nice conduct, creating a pleasant atmosphere and with more meaningful friendships. The lesson of the previous example is quite simple but it demands persistence, discipline and consistency.

■ **Which diet is best?**

Is a diet with a lot of protein (Atkins diet) the best or are low carbohydrate diets (Low carb diets) better. Or is there something else?

There is much talk about the diet designed by Dr. Atkins, which recommends an intake of a lot of protein as a way to lose weight (18). An average adult requires one gram of protein for one kilogram of body weight. Only children going through their growth spurt and pregnant women require more protein, about 1.5 to 2 gram/kg. A larger quantity of protein represents an additional burden for the stomach, liver and the kidneys. Proteins have to be absorbed, which requires more energy, and degrading products of proteins have to be secreted, which overloads the liver and kidneys with too much ammonia and other toxic substances.

Information about diets with low carbohydrates is everywhere. There are many versions of this type of diet and all have been commercialized. The issue of Journal Match from July 2004 contains information about these diets. All of these companies print information about themselves in brochures. Many of these brochures give the wrong picture about the value of various food products. The leading organization for control of drugs and food in the United States is the Food and Drug Administration (FDA), which is responsible for labeling food, has been unable to come up with a clear definition of what constitutes diets with low carbohydrates, their quantity and content. The recommendation for those who are interested is clear. Ignore all brochures which describe "low carb diets" and stick to information from the FDA given in their "Nutrition Facts". If you decide to go on a low carb diet you should choose the one with servings of less than 150 calories, where you obtain less than 50 calories of carbohydrates per serving.

The problem with the above mentioned diets, as well as with many others is that these diets often don't contain what we need (minerals, vitamins and high fiber). They offer what can be harmful instead, such as too many calories, fats, sugar and, frequently, unlabeled chemicals in the form of preservatives.

■ **Don't give your children Coca Cola and Pepsi!**

One of the things we often forget is the overuse of sugar laced carbonated drinks such as Coca Cola, Pepsi, Canada Dry, ginger ale and others (19). These drinks drastically increase our unneeded sugar intake, and lead to obesity and diabetes among children and teenagers. In order to reduce the level of obesity among children in England, a group of doctors there conducted a study. This study included 644 children from 7 to 11 years of age from six different schools. Half of these children were regularly informed during the year about the harmful effects on health from carbonated sugar drinks while the rest of the children in this study were not informed about this. After one year, the number of carbonated drinks consumed and levels of obesity among the informed group of children was significantly reduced, while in the group that wasn't informed these numbers were significantly increased.

Their conclusion was very simple: children can be positively influenced through proper upbringing and proper education. The best way to teach children about this is by setting an example and being a good role model. It's not appropriate to tell children and young people not to drink Coca Cola or beer because it's not good for them if we ourselves consume these drinks. This is not healthy for anybody!

HABITS: HOW DO WE EAT?

- Many of our convictions and habits have been confirmed by modern medicine
- Drinking too much alcohol increases the risk of developing colon cancer
- Vitamin D strengthens the muscles and bones
- Song birds live longer!

In the last few decades modern medicine has intensively been dealing with questions of healthy lifestyle and our habits which relate to nutrition, choice and selection of types of food, drinking of alcohol, and our use of supplements such as vitamins, hormones and minerals.

There have been many studies done in these fields of knowledge. Results of these studies show the significance and consequences of habits which have been adopted by many people. Grains of knowledge in these fields are invaluable to all people whose priority is to keep their good health and to live a long life.

- Drinking too much alcohol increases the risk of developing colon cancer

Colon cancer is one of the top three types of cancers (together with lung cancer of both sexes and breast cancer in females and prostate cancer in males) on a list of cancers in the general population.

Colon cancer is the disease of modern civilization among people who eat too much food of animal origin, especially red meat and large quantities of animal fats (14). These foods have a carcinogenic effect, especially if they are prepared by frying which produces carcinogens (chemicals that cause cancers). If we add to this an increased intake of white sugar then the risk for developing colon cancer is even greater. Besides the creation of poisonous materials, this type of nutrition leads to chronic constipation, which complicates things even further. Namely, constipation or irregular bowel movement leads to intoxication, either because of poisoning of the body from slowed down or irregular elimination of toxic materials, or because of prolonged contact of this type of material with the lining of the colon, which is a precondition for developing colon cancer. The signs of this chronic intoxication are being tired, being in a bad mood, and experiencing weakness and stomach pains.

Research studies show that even a small increase in alcohol intake can raise the risk of getting cancer of the colon. It was specified, namely, that even an intake of 30 gm of alcohol daily raised this risk factor in an unspecified manner and an intake of 40 grams or more of alcohol (which is over two glasses of wine or two small glasses of hard liquor) per day significantly raises this risk (15, 16).

Researchers have concluded that the lowering of alcohol intake to just two drinks per day serves to lower the percentage of cancer patients by a very significant 5 percent. Maybe this is not a big number, but even if you are one of these cancer patients than it's 100 percent for you!

Alcohol raises the risk of developing gout

Gout is an extremely painful illness. It's an acute inflammation of joints (most frequently the inflammation of the first joint of the big toe). This disease manifests itself with a great increase of pain in this joint, followed by evident swelling and redness, which poses a great difficulty when walking. The attack of gout usually occurs after a big meal which contains lots of meat, such as liver and kidneys with wine. This description is a classic case of this disease which can be determined during an examination.

Recent studies with over 50,000 participants who were followed for over 12 years through an officially sanctioned scientific argument, prove what medical experience has known for over 100 years. It was discovered in these studies that even a small amount of alcohol increased the chances for an attack of gout and that this risk increases linearly with an increase of alcohol. People who take up to 30 grams of alcohol per day have a one and a half greater chance of developing gout, people who take from 40 to 50 grams of alcohol double their chance of getting gout and people who take more than 50 grams of alcohol per day, two and half to three times greater chance of an attack of gout. These studies once again demonstrate that classic wisdom which recommends moderation is the "mother" of all proverbs!

Small advantages –and huge draw backs

- **Vitamin D strengthens the muscles and bones**

As we age, our body uses up tissues and organs, there is a decrease of our mental and physical power, and physical deterioration after 65 years of age and especially after 70 years of age. One of the most significant problems of old age is weakening of the muscles (loss of muscle strength and muscle thickness) and loss of bone mass (people become lighter and are smaller because of this). People also grow more helpless because of this loss of muscle mass and because they gain fat tissue instead of muscles. These phenomena can significantly be slowed down by leading a healthy lifestyle: regular mental and physical activity and healthy nutrition. In a recently conducted study (*Journal Watch, June 2004, New England Journal of Medicine*) it was discovered that a regular intake of 800 units of Vitamin D or 1,200 mg of calcium increased muscle and bone strength significantly, and served to prevent falls and injuries among the elderly, which is one of the most important problems in this population bracket. In other words, healthy nutrition, regular physical movement and supplementing of Vitamin D and calcium can postpone problems of aging and can improve the lives of the elderly.

- **Song birds live longer!**

It's well known that when we exercise our muscles we increase muscle mass and muscle strength. The exercise of our brain has recently been proven to lead to an increase in brain mass but also to an increase in brain cells. Researchers studied brains of song birds that only sang in the first half of the year. By measuring bird brain mass and brain activity, it was discovered that certain parts of the brain responsible for the production of bird songs were more developed during the time that these birds sang. Birds that sing live longer and are happier.

In order to confirm this discovery, a team of German scientists conducted a study with volunteers who were taught intensively to play a musical instrument or to perform various manual skills and tricks with their hands.

The result of these experiments confirmed that through these intensive exercises, participants developed the parts of their brain responsible for learning and storage of special information in the frontal lobes of the brain, and that these changes did not occur in people who did not perform these exercises. This investigation did not end with this study, only after three months, after discontinuing these exercises, did brain mass return to its previous states before exercise.

The moral of this is more than clear: we need to sing like the birds, learn and develop new skills, activate our brain and our soul, and our life will be better and happier.

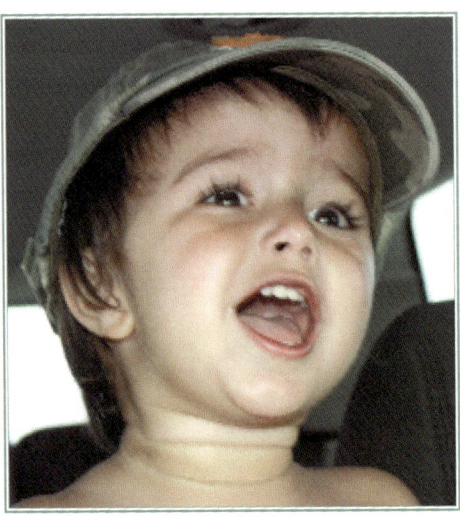

A peace of grain from the physician's brain

Mental dementia or loss of memory and intellectual functions can be prevented or postponed through healthy lifestyle, recommends the magazine Healthy Aging.

There are many things which we can do in this area:

- *staying mentally active, learning new skills and knowledge, taking music lessons, dance lessons, learning new unknown games and doing math and geometry problems; and*

- *ingesting foods that have antioxidant properties such as strawberries, raspberries, raisins, vegetables of different colors, spinach, beets, cauliflower, radishes, cabbage with a different color, always makes sense! Tomatoes, besides containing large amounts of Vitamin A and C also contain a special substance called licopene, which prevents prostate cancer and is highly resistant, even to high temperature, and is not diluted–even in cooking!*

A healthy lifestyle, good nutrition, and maintenance of our mental acuity not only serve to make us live longer, but also raises the quality of our life!

SANDWICHES AND SODA, SAUSAGES AND BEER

- **Unhealthy nutrition is in full bloom in developed countries**
- **In Europe, Germany, the Czech Republic and England have the most obese people**
- **Modern industry produces huge quantities of cheap, unhealthy food**
- **Obesity has become a virtual epidemic and a world-wide problem**
- **Personal initiative and education are the way toward health**

Modern life imposes on us a fast tempo as we seek a better job, bigger salary, higher standard of life and greater material goods. A better job usually entails greater responsibility, longer hours, higher levels of stress as well as a higher salary. A growing number of women are employed and spend a lot of time at work, where their nutrition is taken in a hurry, in a peripheral manner, and is often not very healthy. Having our meals at fast food restaurants and going out to restaurants for dinner, lunch and even breakfast, have become a common occurrence.

However, this type of nutrition is often unhealthy because we eat too much food containing too much fat, without enough vegetables, minerals, vitamins and fiber without which our health will suffer. As a consequence of this improper type of nutrition, we now have an epidemic of obesity taking place in all developed countries of the world.

In North America, at many leading restaurants, sandwiches are full of fats and sugar, mainly of animal based fats, and juices are full of artificial color, sugar and additives. Sandwiches and Coca Cola have become prominent but an unhealthy symbol of our time.

■ In Europe, Germany, the Czech Republic and England have the most obese people

Germany is leading Western Europe in the number of obese people (20). Their affinity for beer and sausages has led to an explosion of overweight and obese people. Between 60 to 75 % of Germans are either overweight or obese. That means that between 36 to 53 percent of Germans are obese with a body mass index over 27. Between 22 and 23.5 percent of Germans are pathologically obese with a body mass index of over 30. Body mass index is the best measurement of body weight and takes into account the relationships between body weight and body height. This standard has been established by experts in the World Health Organization and has been adopted by all countries in the world.

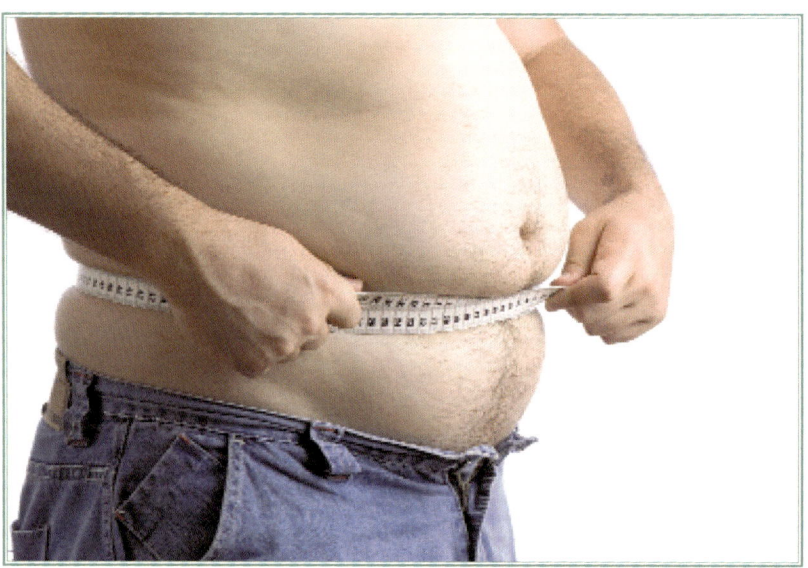

■ Modern industry produces huge quantities of cheap, unhealthy food

The origin of obesity is very simple: men and women eat too much food and ingest more calories than they need to maintain their everyday level of activity. The lesson is clear: don't eat more than you need! The explosive development of technology has made possible fast production of cheap food that's affordable even to those who have little money. Unfortunately, this type of food that's produced in huge quantities is often unhealthy. It contains growth hormones that animals are exposed to in order to make them grow faster. It contains antibiotics given to these animals to prevent the spread of infections and diseases, which still periodically break out nevertheless, and this food contains preservatives, which are supposed to keep the food from spoiling and also give it better color (21, 22).

However, all these chemicals and substances have a detrimental effect on our health.

The problem of nutrition is not only in the quantity of our food but also its quality. The average meal on this continent contains more fats than we actually need. Many daily meals also contain more than 30 percent of calories from animal sources and fats which often contain trans fats, which are the unhealthiest types of fats.

An optimal level of nutrition should contain about 25 percent of calories originating from animal fats, and the rest should be obtained from vegetable based oils, olive oil, canola oil and sunflower oil.

Besides that, today's nutrition contains too much concentrated sugar in the form of granulated sugar, sweets, cakes and chocolate. All of these unneeded calories that don't get burned up during the course of our daily activities are converted into fat, which accumulates under the skin or in our organs. Healthy nutrition should predominantly be based on plant based food, proteins obtained from grains, and should contain a large intake of fresh fruits and vegetables.

A sedentary lifestyle means an insufficient level of physical exercise and movement.

There are many jobs today that are done sitting at a desk in an office and that don't require a lot of physical energy or activity. Many people have a hard time reducing their daily meals and their appetite to a level that they actually require. Younger, as well as older people, often spend hours sitting in front of the TV set or the computer, which is another reason for their low level of physical activity.

- **Obesity has become a virtual epidemic and a world-wide problem**

The increase of obesity among our population represents a major health risk and has contributed to the appearance of many diseases, including high blood pressure, diabetic diseases, myocardial infarctions, strokes, diseases of the gallbladder and bile passages with gallstones, as well as diseases of the joints, bones and muscles, in the form of different types of rheumatism. Psychological problems lead to depression, and dissatisfaction with one's appearance lead to social isolation and an unwillingness to appear in public.

Obesity also represents a significant risk for the appearance of cancer in males and females. Breast cancer, uterine cancer, cancer of the colon is seen more frequently in obese people because fatty tissue is an endocrine organ which produces several hormones, one of the most important being estrogen. An increased level of estrogen facilitates the development of the above mentioned cancers.

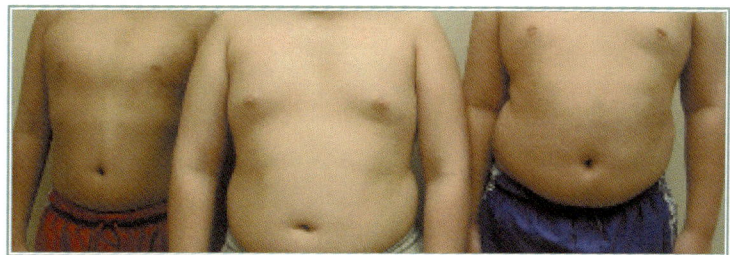

All of the above mentioned facts show that unhealthy nutrition and obesity has for a long time overburdened our health and medical institutions, and has become a social problem that our political institutions are trying to solve because it impacts negatively on our ability for productive work, it damages our economy, and it even endangers our national security.

- **Personal initiative and education are the way toward health**

In order to reduce obesity we need an organized approach and a solid program of education about health. We need to be well motivated and persistent, and we need to continue with proper and healthy nutrition to lead a healthy lifestyle.

A peace of grain from the physician's brain

Here are several recommendations:

- *prepare your own food and reduce the number of times you go to a restaurant;*
- *buy healthy food with plenty of fresh fruits and vegetables;*
- *carefully read directions on how to prepare food and reduce to a minimum level your meat and animal fats consumption;*
- *choose the least amount of saturated fatty acids in your food and eat more unsaturated fatty acids;*
- *eat fish at least twice a week. Cook with canola oil and not with animal oil;*
- *eat whole wheat bread and use only whole wheat flour for all your baking needs instead of white bread, which is not as healthy;*

- *maintain a regular program of physical exercise and activity in order to maintain your muscle tone and to feel better. You will also burn up unnecessary calories;*

- *in new studies conducted with obese people it has been discovered that persons who try to lose weight always underestimate the amount of food they actually eat;*

- *it's necessary to design an individually tailored, detailed plan of action in consultation with your physician or dietician, taking into consideration your age, sex, employment, inherited factors, diseases and lifestyle; and*

- *for all individuals who suffer from a serious disease like diabetes, high blood pressure, liver disease, kidney disease or breast cancer, or cancer of some other organ, it's necessary to follow detailed directions about nutrition. With proper and healthy nutrition your treatment will become easier and your chances for improvement will also increase.*

The road to good health is long and hard but in the end it's worth it. With improvement of your health and normalization of body weight, your mood and psychological state will improve significantly, you will be more physically fit and your quality of life will improve too.

Place a belt not around your waist but around your stomach!!!

Recently, I read one more unbelievably interesting thing about how to control your weight. Until now there have been various methods developed in modern medicine; diet with a reduced level of calories; control and intake of food; avoidance of sweets; increase in physical activity; and exercise, but all of these things did not achieve satisfactory results. Then, surgeons found a new solution: literally cut off one part of the intestine so that only a small quantity of food can be absorbed or; an even more drastic solution; reduce the size of the stomach so that a person can't eat as much food because the stomach is now smaller. Is this modern medicine?

The latest technique for weight reduction is to build in a track or a belt with holes between the connection of the esophagus and the stomach (through the technique of laparoscopy through small openings in the wall of the stomach using a small camera and a television screen). The openings on this track or belt can be adjusted according to width of the patient and according to the recommendations of the doctor. For those who want more information about this, here is a website: realizeband.com

There is a good common expression about this: "If you lack a knot in your own head with which to control yourself, building in this knot on some other spot will not help you very much."

HEALTHY NUTRITION AND CHOOSING FOOD

- Is a glass of alcohol beneficial or harmful?
- Individual types of food
- Should we drink coffee and how much?
- Eggs and cholesterol

Consuming one to two alcohol drinks daily protects our heart and blood vessels. A glass of alcohol before meals or after meals to help with digestion is the part of many cultures and is also included in many cookbooks, as well as being considered a good way to entertain your guests. Is this healthy or not?

According to older beliefs a glass of wine with a meal benefits our health. Modern research confirms that a glass of good wine, beer or a small glass of hard liquor (50 ml) can have a positive effect on our heart, blood vessels, prevent arteriosclerosis (clogging up of the arteries) and lower our risk of sudden heart attack.

Alcohol is not the only substance that has a beneficial effect if taken in moderation. The best approach to alcohol is through moderation. By consuming more alcohol we don't raise its beneficial effects but expose ourselves to becoming alcoholics, which is a serious disease with harmful consequences. Different alcoholic drinks have different properties, such as plant derived substances, and vitamins and minerals that can also have a beneficial effect for our health.

- Individual types of food

Yogurt. It's been believed for a long time that yogurt is healthy for us and that it contributes to a long life. Yogurt is a good source of protein, calcium and other minerals especially low fat yogurt (less that 1% fat content). People who are allergic to milk can still eat yogurt because it doesn't contain milk sugar (lactose). Yogurt contains bacterial substances that establish a normal bacterial balance in our intestines (especially among people taking antibiotics) and can help women in the production of vaginal flora and those suffering from vaginal yeast infections.

Garlic and onions. Research has shown that garlic and onions strengthen our immune system, prevent development of cancer and have a beneficial effect on our blood vessels (23). Garlic contains a chemical substance called alicin which has a multifaceted beneficial effect. It reduces coagulation of the blood, has an anti viral effect and prevents the inflammation of the joints. There is evidence that onions reduce the level of cholesterol and fats in the blood and that they even help in metabolizing sugar. Cooked and fried onions are much less beneficial, so raw is best.

Hazelnuts, almonds and walnuts. Research shows that hazelnuts are rich in unsaturated fatty acids and fibers, Vitamin E and folic acid, that are also an important vitamin. All these substances in moderate amounts are beneficial in case of heart disease, especially if they are taken in salads, rice and other foods (24).

Chocolate is considered today to be better than it was before. New research shows that chocolate is not bad for our health, on the contrary, chocolate contains plant substances that reduce the risk of cancer, and contains antioxidants that prevent heart and blood vessel disease (25). One recent study with people who exercise regularly and eat two to three bars (a small amount) of chocolate a month tend to live longer. It's not known why this is so, but moderation is the mother of wisdom.

Tea is always our good friend. Old beliefs are that tea is a pleasant drink that is accepted in all social settings. It's popular in the palaces of kings, as well as being popular among the poorer classes. New research proves that green, black and brown teas contain a whole group of chemical substances, including antioxidants that can reduce our risk of developing arteriosclerosis, heart disease and make us more resistant to carcinogens. Drinking tea doesn't increase our loss of calcium from bones as it was believed earlier (26).

Tomatoes are a heavenly plant. Tomatoes have an especially beneficial effect in neutralizing acidic products in the body and that is why they make a good combination with foods rich in proteins like various meats, cheeses and legumes. Tomatoes are not only rich in vitamin C and potassium but also in a substance known as licopene. This substance has the ability to stop the development of prostate cancer! There is much more licopene in cooked tomatoes than in raw tomatoes.

Soybeans are a rich source of food. It was believed in the past that soybeans were just another source of calories. New research shows that soybeans are very rich in proteins, plant oils, minerals, and vitamins. They contain substances that reduce cholesterol and have an antioxidant effect. Soybeans can be used in the form of soybean grain, flour, and tofu, or soybean milk. The use of soybean products have a protective effect against heart diseases.

Cherries, Sour Cherries, Strawberries and Blueberries. Colored or pigmented fruits and vegetables contain more vitamins and minerals than originally thought. These special fruit pigments have a protective effect against a variety of chronic diseases and carcinogens (27). They have a powerful antioxidant potential. This doesn't mean that we shouldn't eat less colored fruits and vegetables like cauliflower, green peas or potatoes. It's recommended that we find a place in our daily diet for darker vegetables and fruits like plums, red grapes, cherries and sour cherries, radishes and carrots.

■ **Should we drink coffee and how much?**

Coffee and caffeine. People believed in the past that coffee can be harmful for our health. New research shows that coffee doesn't produce heart disease, cancers or ulcers in the stomach, as it was believed in the past. Coffee helps us to stay awake and gives us more energy, however, it doesn't improve our concentration. For healthy people, coffee is not harmful. However, coffee can be harmful if it is consumed in large quantities (more than 3 cups daily), and it can also be harmful to people with high blood pressure, heart arrhythmia or to people suffering from heartburn. More than 3 cups of coffee daily, among others things, increases the secretion of calcium in the urine, especially in women over 50 years of age and women going through menopause. Sudden stoppage of drinking coffee can lead to abstinence syndrome in the form of headaches and nervous tension, and that's why it's recommended to reduce one's level of coffee consumption gradually.

■ **Eggs and cholesterol**

Eggs and cholesterol. It's been known that an egg contains between 250 and 300 mg of cholesterol, which is almost the total maximum amount of the daily recommended dose. Newer research shows that eating one egg a day doesn't increase the risk of developing heart disease among healthy people. This doesn't apply to people with high levels of cholesterol, diabetes or who have other risk factors such as high blood pressure. There is proof that two egg whites with one egg yolk completely neutralize any harmful effect. If you are sure that you are healthy and that your cholesterol level is not high, then periodically eating eggs is okay (28).

A combination of nutritious food, so that our meals produce acidic substances and also substances that neutralize these acids is a special skill. That's why fresh salads, leafy vegetables and tomatoes are so valuable to us; because they neutralize the surplus of acids that are produced when we digest proteins from various meats and other food products which create substantial amounts of acids.

Healthy nutrition is one of the most important factors of good health. The basic characteristics of good and nutritious food are that it looks good, tastes good and smells good. This nutritious food also includes a wide variety of food choices, all of which are rich in indispensable materials like proteins, minerals, vitamins and unsaturated oils. It's also necessary to plan and to space one's daily and weekly meals so that we consume smaller meal portions of freshly prepared food.

The father of modern medicine Hippocrates once said,
"Our food needs to be our medicine, and our medicines need to be our food."

PROTEIN: MEAT AND MORE SOLUTIONS

- How much meat do we consume daily, monthly and yearly?
- What are the consequences for humans and the health of future generations?
- Why is animal fat unhealthy?
- How to change our habits and open new doors to healthier nutrition?

In a recent, leading medical *Canadian magazine, Canadian Medical Association Journal*, it was reported that the average Canadian consumes 2.8 grams of protein (mostly of animal origin) daily. This is four times more protein than is actually required. Protein is composed of albumin which is indispensable as a building block and regenerative material for all living cells of the human body.

We need about 0.8 grams of protein daily for each kilogram of our body weight. That's about one piece of meat half a palm in size that we need daily. This doesn't include all the other meat products, milk, cheese, eggs or fish, which all individually contain their own proteins.

It has been estimated that the average American during the course of his/her life consumes 15 cows, 25 pigs, 12 sheep and about 900 chickens, and about 1,000 pounds (about 450 kilograms) of other animal proteins: fish, venison etc. This adds up to whole herds of animals for each person!

Big changes have taken place during the course of the 20th century. From the beginning to the end of it there has been a drastic change in the structure of yearly nutrition of the American population:

- consumption of grains has dropped from 300 pounds to 150 pounds
- consumption of potatoes has dropped from 200 to about 100 pounds
- consumption of meat has increased from 50 pounds to 150 pounds
- just the amount of chicken meat consumed has increased by 280%

The industrial revolution and modern technology have made possible a huge development of agriculture and have led to an increase in the production of food. Greater employment in industrial and social institutions has led to a need for nutrition outside the home. A large number of people eat at restaurants, where they often consume too much unhealthy food. Our bad habits in nutrition are also a consequence of large changes that have taken place in the structure of the average family. Family dinners and family celebration meals, including meals consumed during religious holidays, which were once highly respected in many homes, have been eroded or have almost disappeared.

Of the total budget used for nutrition in the United States, over 36% is spent on nutrition outside the home, which mainly includes buying food at fast food restaurants such as McDonald's etc.

- What are the consequences for humans and the health of future generations?

There are three major problems.

First: this type of food contains 60 to 70% of fats and sugar, which is too much.

Second, this type of food lacks important ingredients such as vitamins, minerals, complex carbohydrates, starch and fiber.

Third, this type of food contains too many chemicals used as preservatives to ensure that food lasts longer, and improves its taste and smell. There are about 2,000 such food additive chemicals that are currently on the market and many of these are extremely poisonous. The average American ingests about 3 to 5 pounds of such chemicals every year!

■ **Why is animal fat unhealthy?**

Because it's largely composed of saturated fats, which contains a lot of hydrogen. These fats are solid at room temperature, contain a lot of cholesterol and make blood more viscous, which all contributes to arteriosclerosis. Arteriosclerosis is the clogging up of blood vessels. Many negative consequences originate for human health because of these basic problems. Most frequent of these are: • **Arteriosclerosis** leads to high blood pressure, heart disease and heart attacks, strokes (accompanied with paralysis), male impotence and other diseases;

• **Cancers**. Animal fats and proteins don't contain fiber or roughage which are vital for proper digestion and detoxification (elimination of poisons from the body). Because of this, there is a greater risk of developing colon cancer, breast cancer in women and prostate cancer among men;

• **Osteoporosis** or softening of the bones. Animal fats contain too much protein or albumin. Dissolved proteins contain lots of ammonia, ureic acid, sulfur and other chemicals. These materials are especially harmful to kidneys and the liver. They also facilitate calcium loss through the kidneys and can lead to softening of the bones or osteoporosis which makes bones prone to breakage, especially among elderly people. The Chinese rarely suffer from osteoporosis because their diet contains a lot of grains and foods of plant origin;

• **Cholesterol** is one of the main factors in the risk of developing disease of the blood vessels. Animal fats, milk and meats contain a lot of cholesterol. One egg has 200 mg of cholesterol and this amount raises blood cholesterol immediately by over 30%. Plant based foods don't contain cholesterol!!! Normal amounts of cholesterol should be less than 200 mg in the blood and no one with a cholesterol level of less than 150 mg gets a heart attack;

• **Cows milk** is loaded with fats, cholesterol and salt. All these substances are harmful for human health. One of the leading experts for nutrition in the United States, Dr. Klapper, said that the only thing that cow's milk is good for is to make a 50 kilogram calf into a 300 kilogram young bull in only a year. Milk is not the best source of calcium. A better source is plant based food;

• **Diabetes** is a disease that goes along with unhealthy nutrition and too much fat intake and can today be encountered among adults, especially among obese individuals;

• **Poisonous substances** such as herbicides, pesticides, antibiotics and bacteria that we ingest with our food, stay in the body for a longer period of time because they are not secreted from the fat tissue of obese people. Such substances also more easily dissolve in fat; and

• **Childhood diseases**. Children today eat too much meat and fat of animal origin. Because of this unhealthy nutrition many children develop obesity, diabetes and high blood pressure. In the United States over 1,000 teenagers get strokes every year.

■ **How to change our habits and open new doors to healthier nutrition?**

Family agreement and a plan

The best way to change our bad habits and move toward healthy nutrition is to reach a family agreement about nutrition, to educate all members of the family in good nutrition, and to plan, choose and cook food together as a family. Instead of drastic changes it's easier to gradually reduce the quantity of meat and introduce more plant based foods.

Are humans meat eaters? The biggest animals like horses, cattle, giraffes, antelopes, deer, stags, and elephants, are all vegetarians. Human beings are primarily vegetarians, if we take into account the structure of our body, mouth, digestion organs (especially the length of our intestines) and our muscle and bone composition. All the substances that we need to maintain our life can be found in plant food. Such food is also much cheaper, healthier and is easier to obtain. What do we really need in our nutrition?

- Proteins or albumin, which can be obtained from grains (5-10%) and legumes such as peas, beans, lentils and green vegetables.

- Vitamins, which are most abundant in plant food such as fruits, nuts and fresh vegetables.

- Minerals, especially calcium, potassium, magnesium, zinc, iron and other minerals are important for the normal maintenance of tissues and are all available in abundance in plant food.

- Energy which can be obtained from plant based oils, the best being sunflower oil, canola oil and olive oil. These oils don't contain cholesterol and remain liquids at room temperature. Then we need complex carbohydrates and starch, which are abundant in grains and root based vegetables such as potatoes, radishes and carrots, green vegetables, fruits and sunflower seeds.

- Liquids. Clean drinking water and a good selection of natural fruit juices without additives as well as a good selection of teas.

We need all of the above mentioned things to maintain our health, normal body weight, to prevent disease, to feel better and finally, to extend our biological life.

Is there anything more important than our health? Is there anything more concrete than what we ingest every day? We need to begin healthy nutrition today.

Someone once said, "Show me what you eat, and I will show you who you are!"

THE MAGIC FORMULA: THE MEDITERRANEAN DIET

- It has been proven scientifically that Mediterranean food is the best
- What is the Mediterranean diet composed of?
- Valuable benefits of the Mediterranean diet
- The Mediterranean diet is a fountain of youth and longevity
- Is the Mediterranean diet only for those living around the Mediterranean Sea?

There is much talk in medical literature in the last few years about healthy nutrition. An overabundance of information available in various public media creates confusion among the average member of the general public because there is so much contradictory advice. The reason for this is pretty clear: many companies are pushing their products with the help of often compromised and unreliable research, while authentic and reliable studies done by reputable medical experts often get lost in the sea of unreliable information.

It has recently been revealed that the average Canadian family goes to "fast food" restaurants about 500 times a year!

In order to study this dilemma of best quality food and nutrition, several American and European medical institutions conducted a scientific study in which over 2,000 participants were followed for a period of two years.

The results of this study were published in one of the best medical journals, *The New England Journal of Medicine*, on July 17, 2008.

All participants in this study were overweight and had a body mass index (the relationship between body weight and height) of over 31. The normal body mass index is between 21 to 27. These people had three types of specially defined diet:

1. the Mediterranean diet, with a limited number of calories;
2. a diet that contains a lowered ingestion of fats; and
3. a diet with a limited amount of starches and sugars.

At the end of two years, the patients that followed a Mediterranean diet had the best metabolic balance: they had lost excess body weight, had the lowest concentration of sugar and the lowest concentration of total cholesterol.

- What is the Mediterranean diet composed of?

The Mediterranean diet is the most frequently used diet in countries situated around the Mediterranean Sea. These countries have a suitable climate with easy access to the sea and as a result have a diet that is rich in fish, fruits and vegetables, and lots of olives, from which olive oil is made. Foodstuffs that were used in this study have a limited amount of calories, about 1,500 daily for women and about 1,800 calories daily for men. This diet also includes a lot of vegetables which contain fiber, including beans, onions, garlic, carrots, green lettuce, cabbage, broccoli, cauliflower, beets, whole wheat bread, olive oil, fish, and a small amount of almonds, peanuts or walnuts, not more than 20 grams daily.

During the whole duration of this study all participants were observed by dieticians every day. Their main meal was dinner, and all food was clearly labeled about its contents and was taken in limited amounts. Dinner was taken during the middle of the day and the majority of participants who took part in this study were regularly employed.

The many studies show that the Mediterranean diet is the best composed type of nutrition because it safeguards our best health, has the lowest chance of causing distress, disease and ensures that we will live a long life.

Ancient gods from Mount Olympus in Greece knew about this healthy diet almost three thousand years ago. It's another question altogether if this type of diet was actually accessible to thousands of slaves of that time.

Whole grains, vegetables, fruits, fish and olive oil

The Mediterranean diet is not the case of a planned type of nutrition but consists of the type of lifestyle that is lived in countries around the Mediterranean Sea, including Greece, Italy, Spain and France.

The main ingredients of the Mediterranean diet are grain based foods made from whole grains like wheat, oats, barley, rice and dough made from these ingredients.

What are the good substances that these grains contain? Complex carbohydrates or starch materials that are digested, diluted and absorbed gradually, providing blood sugar, which is necessary in creating energy for our body. They also contain a lot of cellulose and fiber, whose role needs to be emphasized. Fiber materials serve to clean out our body from potential toxins; they reduce the level of cholesterol; assure proper functioning of our intestines and prevent the development of colon cancer, breast cancer and cancer of the uterus! A small amount of proteins and minerals are an important source of these indispensable materials of daily nutrition. An important quality of this type of diet is the lack of cholesterol and low level of saturated fatty acids.

Nuts, legumes, fruits and vegetables represent an especially important group of foods in this diet. Nuts like almonds, hazelnuts, walnuts, peanuts, pistachio nuts and similar nuts are an important source of unsaturated fatty acids, minerals, starch, vitamins and a small amount of protein. Nuts are always best when taken in moderation, usually one handful daily. People who experience problems with cholesterol, diabetes and other diseases need to be more cautious and consult their family physician.

Legumes include all sorts of beans, soybeans, peas and vegetables such as potatoes, tomatoes, cabbage, cauliflower, broccoli, onions, garlic, carrots, radishes and green lettuce, all represent a good framework. Some of these products need to be exposed to a greater degree of heat during cooking. These include: beans, peas and soybeans. Others, which should be exposed to minimal heat during cooking are cabbage, cauliflower and beets. Vegetables like onions, radishes, carrots, tomatoes and green salad can be used in their raw state. Fresh vegetables contain, besides starch, a small amount of fat, protein and minerals that are diluted and lost during cooking. Items from this food group can be used daily and in a variety of ways. Choose a wide variety of different vegetables of different color in order to increase their antioxidant properties.

Olive oil, especially extra virgin olive oil, contains a large concentration of unsaturated fatty acid, will meet all our oil needs and provides a valuable protection against arteriosclerosis (which is the main cause of clogged arteries), heart attacks and strokes. It's best to use olive oil when it's cold, because it's diluted when hot or during cooking. The next healthiest oil to use is canola oil, which is also a good source of unsaturated fatty acid and can be used more frequently.

Fish, especially sardines and salmon, are an excellent source of fish oil. This oil is a source of important Omega 3 unsaturated fatty acids which have been proven to play a role against inflammation and degenerative reactions. Their role is not only important in the protection of blood vessels and prevention of arteriosclerosis but also helps to protect joints and prevent development of rheumatism. It's a good idea to eat fish at least twice a week.

Chicken, beef, pork and other red meats ought to be lowered to a minimum intake because they are rich in saturated fats and contain too much protein. These meat products are, unfortunately, often the main ingredients of nutrition in western, developed countries. The increased use of red meat has been proven to significantly raise the risk of developing heart and blood vessel disease, diabetes, arthritis, gallbladder stones and obesity, which all by itself, contributes to depression and other mental disturbances. Quantities of these types of food are significantly lower in the Mediterranean diet, which has left evident positive consequences for the health of people who use this diet. Red meat is best avoided or limited to only once a week.

The use of alcohol is only recommended in a moderate quantity (a glass of wine during dinner two times a week), for those people who can control their alcohol intake, for those people who are not suffering from serious disease and for people who don't have a history of alcoholism in their family.

■ Valuable benefits of the Mediterranean diet

The benefits of the Mediterranean diet are many and this has been demonstrated in many studies (29, 30).

- Prevention of heart disease. Lowered level of cholesterol, blood pressure, obesity and diabetes. This diet can lower the risk of developing diabetes by 30%.

- Prevention of repeated heart infarction. People that have had a heart attack or infarction can lower their chances of having another heart attack by over 75% in comparison to people that use a "western style of diet".

- Lowered occurrence of rheumatism and inflammation of the joints, with less swelling and pain in the joints. This is probably due to the presence of Omega 3 fatty acids but also due to the intake of lowered levels of other fatty acids because of using less red meat.

- Protection against breast cancer. Oleanic acids in olive oil lowers the activity of one gene which is responsible for breast cancer. It has been proven in scientific studies that oleanic acid has significantly lowered the activity of genes that cause breast cancer.

- Prevention of gallbladder stones. Food that is high in saturated fats, including pork, beef, lamb, chicken meat, etc., significantly contributes to the development of gallbladder stones. By using the Mediterranean diet this risk can be lowered by over 50%.

■ **The Mediterranean diet is a fountain of youth and longevity**

- The Mediterranean diet improves health, prevents continuation of disease, raises the quality of life and contributes to longevity.

- Several studies on this diet have proven that it improves the quality of life and that it contributes to a long life, which is in direct proportion to one's application of this diet (31, 32). In other words, the more you follow this diet, the more your overall health benefits will be.

- Avoid using margarine and butter and limit red meats to only once per week. As well, use other meats in moderate amounts and avoid cigarettes.

- Avoid processed white bread. There was an article written in a medical journal with title, "The whiter the bread, the sooner you're dead." This sounds a little drastic, but there's some truth to it and its certainly wise advice to follow. Reduce "junk food" from fast food restaurants like McDonalds, Burger King and others. Just one meal obtained at these restaurants has too many calories, saturated fats and sugar.

Is the Mediterranean diet only available to people living around the Mediterranean Sea?

Other studies that were done at other institutions, proved the value of this diet, even for people who did not live around the Mediterranean Sea. People who used this diet live a healthy life; they have less heart disease, fewer problems with diabetes and usually live longer.

Similar studies were done with the Japanese who live on the island of Okinawa. They live longer and healthier lives, and that island has a great number of people who live over 100 years.

When nutrition experts, doctors, dieticians and anthropologists finished their study in Japan, it was determined that the Japanese diet is very similar to the Mediterranean diet, with access to a warm sea, a lot of vegetables and fish.

It's clear that you don't have to go to Greece, Italy or Spain–or even Japan–in order to enjoy the Mediterranean diet.

IV

THE MOST FREQUENT AILMENTS

*A healthy person has a thousand wishes
and the sick one only one–to get better*

LIFESTYLE, HEALTH AND BLOOD PRESSURE

- Are we aware of our lifestyle?
- How to test and check one's own lifestyle?
- Recommendations in relation to salt
- Recommendations about stress reduction

Many things in our actual life are of such a nature and scope that we can't influence them or change them. But there are many things in our life that we can significantly improve for the better; this includes ourselves and people around us, our perceptions, acceptance and understanding of reality, of our nearby locality where we live, our work and our creative life. If we help ourselves and other people we will feel better and be healthier.

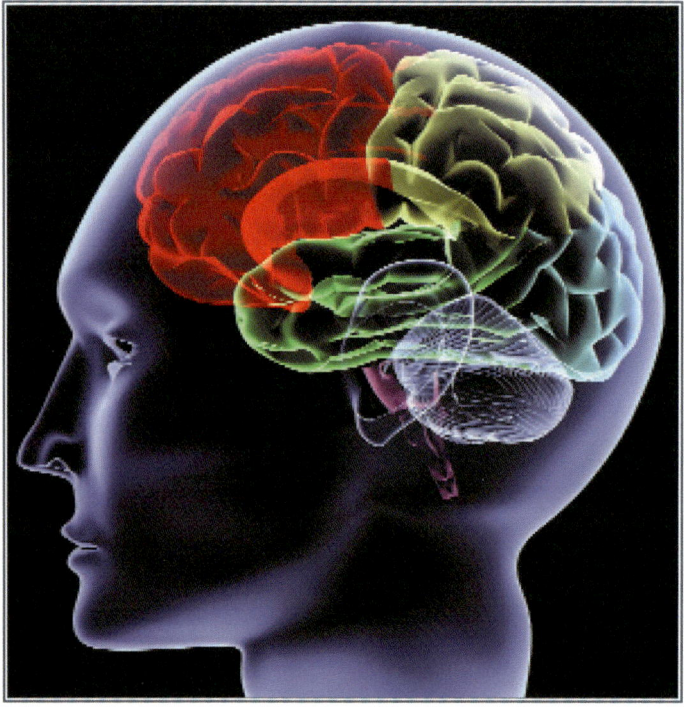

Health awareness and planning–the first step to good health

Lifestyle as a basic philosophy of life encompasses the type of life we lead and is an extremely wide concept which takes into account everything that life means; how we think and feel, what is our main occupation, what we eat, how and if we socialize with other people, what we believe in, as well as many other things. There probably exist as many types of lifestyles as there are people, however, it's possible to make psychological and sociological categorizations of different lifestyles.

From a medical perspective it has been experientially and scientifically proven that there are two basic approaches to type of life and choice of habits. These two approaches are:

A Healthy lifestyle that protects and improves our health prevents the development of disease and increases the quality of our life. This lifestyle means a positive, optimistic and realistic approach to life. It's demonstrated when we show our good and beautiful side rather than our negative side. How we treat people who live with us and who live around us; our willingness to help other people, and our empathy and cooperation with them; our selection of good and regular nutrition; our development of positive and qualitative relations with members of our family and our social community; our participation in regular recreational activity; our willingness to avoid and lower stress; and many other things.

A Less healthy or totally unhealthy lifestyle which is passive, pessimistic, sometimes chaotic, and which carries within itself a high risk of developing various diseases. Typical examples of this type of lifestyle include: being disorganized with one's time and energy, unhealthy habits like eating too much caloric food, being inactive and not exercising, drinking too much alcohol, passivity, being socially isolated, smoking cigarettes and leading a life spent under stress. These people more often have high blood pressure, heart disease and obesity, with all the inherent risks of these conditions such as developing diabetes, cancer, depression and many other dysfunctions.

High blood pressure is undoubtedly the most frequent disease of the last few decades among modern people and carries many harmful health consequences with it. These include: arteriosclerosis (clogging up of the arteries), heart attacks and strokes, which have been the leading cause of death and disease that by far outnumber other serious diseases like cancers of all types, various infectious diseases, traumas sustained in accidents and diabetes.

Over 20% or about 60 million Americans suffer from high blood pressure. Among Caucasians this disease affects 15% of the population, while among African Americans it's over 25% of the population. The reason for this discrepancy is still unknown. High blood pressure develops with age and is more pronounced in older people. In relation to gender, high blood pressure is more pronounced among males than females under 50 years of age, and after 50 years of age women more frequently suffer from high blood pressure, which confirms a theory about hormonal protection from this disease while they are in their reproductive period.

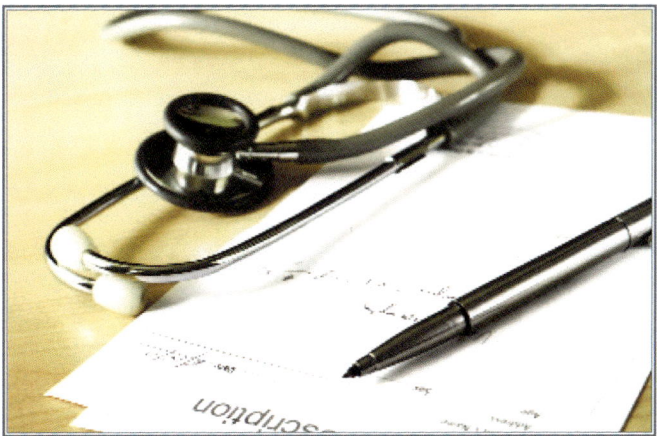

In one of the issues of the leading *Canadian medical journals, Canadian Medical Association Journal, May 4, 1999*, there is a whole special section dedicated to studies about modification of lifestyle and how it affects blood pressure and its negative consequences. These studies included tens of thousands of participants in a large number of medical centers on the North American continent.

- **How to test and check one's own lifestyle?**

Testing one's lifestyle is based on clear cut parameters and is accessible to every individual even without medical education; however it's recommended that one should still consult with their physician.

Recommendations for changing one's lifestyle and dietary habits

- determine the height, weight and body mass index in every individual;
- determine the level and type of physical activity;
- define the amount of daily consumption of salt;
- define the amount of daily consumption of alcohol; and
- examine the presence of stress in everyday life.

To hear and to understand is of mutual benefit

In the above named list are not discussed the use of tobacco, stimulants like coffee, tea, drugs and other things. These substances without a doubt have a big impact on health, disease and mortality of people who use them and will be looked at in more detail in subsequent articles.

Recommendations for people who are overweight

The use of too much food has led to a rise in obesity by 30% in the last several decades on the North American continent. The number of obese people has risen from 20% to over 30% and carries with it not only undesirable medical consequences but also negative social and economic consequences.

It's recommended that a health care worker measure your body weight, height and calculate your body mass index (BMI) among those people who are overweight and especially among people who have high blood pressure.

This is done in order to prevent the development of high blood pressure or to lower high blood pressure among people who already suffer from this dysfunction. The goal is to reduce BMI to a normal level which is 20 to 25.

All people with BMI over 25 need to be advised regularly to lower and to maintain their normal body weight through a regular program of exercise and by lowering their caloric intake of food.

Recommendations for physical activity and exercise

Healthy people or people with slightly higher level of blood pressure need to participate in moderate, rhythmic exercises by walking and riding a bike at least 3 to 4 times a week for about 50 to 60 minutes in duration.

Physical exercises need to be coordinated with the rest of one's dietary and pharmacological therapy and with the approval and care of the family physician.

People who don't have high blood pressure can still continue to exercise regularly because this serves to prevent arteriosclerosis, diseases of the blood vessels, heart disease and strokes first of all and also serves to improve our general physical and psychological health. The type and variety of exercise depends on one's height, health state, gender, availability of exercise and many other factors.

Regular physical activity has multifaceted positive effects on health

- Improves general blood circulation and prevents aging of blood vessels by maintaining their elasticity and by preventing arteriosclerosis.
- Makes possible the development of new blood vessels, which is of vital importance for the heart, brain, kidneys and muscles.
- Improves the tone and quantity of muscle tissue, which increases vitality, physical and psychological endurance, prevents deformation of bones, spinal cord, and bone and joint diseases.
- Improves general and special immunity from infections, prevents the development of cancer and other malignant diseases.
- Physical exercise improves general emotional well-being and intellectual capacity, psychological motivation and a feeling of satisfaction.
- The above listed items are only the most common effects of exercise on health.
- Recommendations in relation to salt

In order to avoid ingesting too much salt, it's recommended that we consume fresh fruits and vegetables as often as possible. Avoid canned food and restrain from adding salt when cooking, and raise our awareness about the amount of salt in food that is prepared in restaurants.

For people with high blood pressure, especially for people over 45 years of age, it's recommended that they ingest moderate amounts of salt which means not more than 2 to 4 grams a day (a tablespoon).

Increased salt intake may lead to increased blood pressure

Recommendations about intake of alcohol

It's recommended that each person's amount of alcohol be determined individually by the family physician based on social and genetic factors, if they can drink any alcohol, and how much they can drink and tolerate.

In order to reduce the risk of high blood pressure it's recommended that the intake of alcohol agree with Canadian recommendations about intake of alcohol, which carries a smaller amount of risk. This means:

- a healthy adult should not drink more than two standard sized drinks a day, with consumption not more than 14 drinks per week for men and nine drinks a week for women; and
- a person with high blood pressure needs to consult their physician who will determine their alcohol intake based on their individual characteristics.

- **Recommendations about stress reduction**

For all people who live under significant levels of chronic stress, it's recommended that they reduce this stress by relaxation, physical exercise, change in behavior and habits through psychotherapy under the supervision of an expert (1).

For persons with high blood pressure, reduction of stress is of even more importance and can represent the main component of a plan for treatment of their high blood pressure. Individually tailored psychotherapy and change of behavior in such a case is most effective.

The following are simple, useful and effective measures in reducing stress: modification of one's lifestyle, which includes control of your intake of food, salt and alcohol, avoidance of tobacco and other toxic substances, and participation in a regular program of physical exercise. Another advantage of these stress reduction activities are that they are inexpensive to apply.

An old proverb says, "Prevention is better than treatment."

"Yes it's better but it's not easier!" some hedonist might say sarcastically. However, self-discipline, maturity and responsibility toward oneself and to those who mean a lot to us, could be our motivation, inspiration and lead us on the right path.

A healthy lifestyle will help to keep young even a person who is older than 60 years, but an unhealthy lifestyle will make even a 40 year old person into someone with characteristics of old age. Every person desires to live a long and a healthy life and no one wants to get old before their time. This is indeed possible! But the only way to achieve this is through a healthy lifestyle. Investment in our own long term mental and physical health should be the most important investment of every person! All our other investments lose value and become meaningless if we get sick and lose our health.

REDUCE OUR THUMPING HEART RATES

- Stress and heart rates
- Warning signs to watch for
- What to do at the beginning?
- Have you slowed down your heart rate?

We live in a time that's full of dynamic change, where people are burdened with many duties and responsibilities. Most of these activities are causes by themselves, but even more so because of the presence of high emotional stress and the speeding up of the heart rate.

Intense feelings and emotional stress cause tension and tension causes anxiety, which is due to fear of failure. Modern psychology believes that anxiety results when we feel loss of control at our job, in our community, where we live, or in our life.

- Warning signs to watch for

Many cardiologists say that human longevity is genetically determined from birth, by the number of heart beats. This means when our heart beats a pre-determined number of total beats, it automatically stops. There are signs in the functioning of the human organism which are warning signs that something is wrong.

Pay careful attention if you have been given a warning sign and the red light is already on.

- Have you become very irritable and nervous?
- Do you experience frequent headaches that last longer?
- Do you have trouble sleeping?
- Do you frequently get colds which last a long time?
- Do you lose or gain weight without any intention to do so?
- Do you feel that you are missing something in your life?

If you even have one of the above symptoms, you should think it over. If you are not suffering from any serious disease, then you are certainly living under stress.

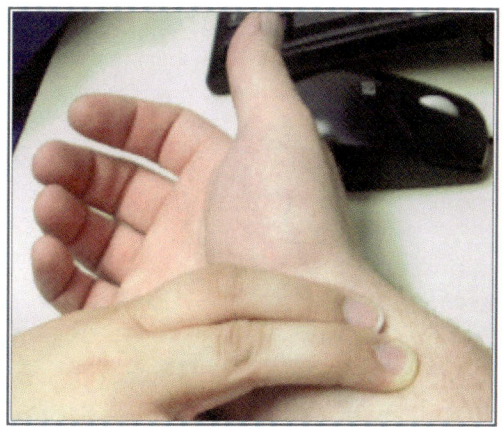

Heart rate and pulse regularity–an important sign of a healthy heart

What you have to do to unburden yourself and to come to your senses? Are you rushed for time? Good time management should be a priority. If you don't take care of yourself, no one will do this for you. Spending between 25 to 30 minutes every day in thinking about your life, in contemplation and meditation and re-examining things in your life is enough to establish a balance and to regenerate yourself (2).

Are you worried because of conflict with your boss? If you do your job responsibly and conscientiously, and if you openly share your personal needs with an understanding person there shouldn't be any problems. A proactive, creative approach to problems will yield good results (3).

Are you worried because of your family? In many families there are common and individual duties and if every member of the family fulfills these duties and accepts what is demanded of them, then it's easy to maintain the internal harmony of the family.

Having too many duties and plans? This is normal because life is complex and everyone has many duties. Not everything is of the same importance. A list of priorities can be made where things should be rated from the most important to least important. This list could contain things we need to do immediately and things that we can afford to postpone.

Do you lack money? Few people are so poor that they can't dedicate a little time to themselves, to take care of themselves and to feed one's body and one's soul. Some of the most beautiful and important things in life such as meditating, listening to good music, a walk in the park and reading a good book don't cost a lot of money.

■ What to do at the beginning?

A talk and a confession. Talk to a good friend that you trust and who can listen to you without criticizing. A short confession, re-examination and a search for ways to solve your problems are the main role of a psychologist, sociologist, physician or a priest.

Make a good plan. Such a plan could contain your short-term and long-term individual and family goals, list of priorities, your debts, plans in relation to your job, profession, education, finances, expenses, cultural needs, participation in sport, recreation, and healthy nutrition. We often make temporary simple mistakes and apply wrong solutions to problems, which then require a lot more time and energy to remedy.

Build up a healthy lifestyle. Lifestyle includes everything that we do beginning with; do we get enough regular sleep, do we eat a proper healthy diet every day, do we know which food is indispensable and which is potentially harmful, do we get enough physical exercise or do we sit for hours on our couch in front of the TV or at our office desk. Do we take long walks every day? Does our job consist of hard physical labor where it's beneficial for us to relax afterward? A healthy lifestyle means adopting habits that are good for our body and our soul, and avoiding those habits that are potentially harmful or toxic such as smoking cigarettes, drinking too much alcohol, drugs and unnecessary prescription medications. This list can be a lot longer and can include bad friends, bad wine and too much caffeine. Research studies prove that more than three cups of coffee daily is harmful. Watching too much television is harmful for the souls of children and adults. Television destroys one's motivation, provides us with the wrong type of information and often teaches us to do bad things. It's rare to see a really good and educational program on TV.

The need to establish and maintain true friendships. A good friend is invaluable to have, particularly if such a friend has a positive approach to life. A good friend can possess good common sense, be open, willing to listen, willing to console and to help. The true measure of a man may not be how much money he makes but how many real friends he has.

Maintain a useful and healthy hobby. Here are a few of such hobbies: going fishing even if you don't catch any fish; picture painting; growing flowers in your garden or on your terrace for your own pleasure. Such hobbies will help you to relax and to unburden yourself. A good hobby will help you to escape from everyday reality, help you to rest and recharge your emotional batteries so that you can tackle new jobs and duties with renewed energy.

Go to church even periodically. Many physicians recommend that we go to church. Not all of our questions can be answered by science, medicine, psychology, philosophy or art. Such disciplines can't give answers to the most important questions in life such as, where do we come from, what are we and where are we going? When in church a person can appreciate our earthly dignity and our cosmic significance. One can also find peace and consolation in church. In church we remember those who passed on. Our faith is not only a matter of personal preference; faith is also the deepest expression of our mental state that we experience from birth. Some people cultivate their faith more and some people less. I remember for a long time the saying of Christ that was written in large letters in church: "Come to Me, all you who are weary and burdened, and I will give you rest."

Forgiveness. Forgiveness is not only a Biblical category. A willingness to forgive is a sign of deep humanity and a confirmation of human qualities. We need to forgive even those who have insulted us. We need not remind people about this, but rather, to remove anger from our soul. Being angry for a long time is toxic for our soul and harms both us and those with whom we are angry. Anger displaces other noble feelings such as understanding, respect, generosity and love. We need to forgive ourselves and to unburden ourselves from a feeling of guilt. We are all imperfect and we learn and grow by making mistakes. The problem is not in making mistakes but in not learning from them. It's human to sin, it's divine to forgive (4, 5).

The need for laughter. It has been proven in medicine that laughter is healthy and beneficial. When we laugh there are beneficial hormones of happiness that are secreted in our brain. These happiness hormones help to decrease the workload of our heart and to lower our blood pressure. Laughter puts us at ease and relaxes us. It makes us happy. A five year old child laughs about 400 times a day, but an adult only laughs about 15 a day. People need to laugh; things are not as bad as they appear. I just happen to know a very grumpy person who hasn't laughed in the last 20 years. You should subscribe to a humorous magazine like Reader's Digest, comics, or watch a funny movie, and you will always have a reason to laugh and to share your source of laughter with those around you.

Get rid of negative thoughts! If you are always preoccupied with negative thoughts like: everything is meaningless, there is no solution to my problems, I am completely alone and lost, no one needs me, or I don't stand a chance. Get rid of all these negative thoughts! Keep in mind that every person is unique, original and is only born once!

Think positive thoughts! Here are just a few of these great positive thoughts: I am an intelligent human being, who occasionally makes a mistake. However, tomorrow is a new day, the sun will rise again, and tomorrow I have a new chance for new success and happiness. This applies especially if we learn something from our mistakes. Nothing brings us more joy and strengthens us than small things we do to help ourselves and other people including, helping around the house and in the yard, helping children to do their homework or learning a new song, giving a bouquet of flowers to a dear friend, particularly if you grew these flowers yourself, passing a hard test, a day filled with good work and meeting our dear friends from whom we have learned a lot of good things. The long journey of life is made up of many little steps!

- Have you slowed down your heart rate?

Physical exercise and movement help to improve our physical condition and fitness, they improve our overall endurance and increase our stores of energy in our muscles, and they prevent high blood pressure and heart disease, and prevent obesity. Regular physical exercise has at least 50 more positive biological benefits and psychological effects. Physical exercise helps to slow down our heart rate! The average heart rate of a healthy adult is about 70 to 80 beats per minute. A person who is in good physical condition has at least 10 beats less per minute or 60 to 70 beats. Measure your heart rate. If it's above 70 beats per minute, go outside for a jog or for a walk. I have already talked about the need for regular physical exercise and healthy nutrition in my previous articles.

Medicine has already proven that human feelings are created and deposited in the brain and not in our heart but there is no doubt that our heart is the best signpost of our feelings of excitement or our feelings of suffering. When such thoughts occur our heart "skips a beat", or our heart rate speeds up.

A calm and unburdened heart works peacefully and carelessly like a wide river that flows slowly down the valley without any sound and carries everything that surrounds it forward. And the slower it flows the longer it will last.

HEART ATTACK OR MYOCARDIAL INFARCT

- A heart attack is the most frequent cause of death in developed countries
- What is a heart attack?
- How does a heart attack manifest itself?
- What is the treatment of the heart attack?

The leading cause of morbidity (illness) and mortality (death) in highly developed nations is a heart attack or myocardial infarct (myocard = heart muscle, infarct = deterioration). A heart attack is the most frequent complication of diseases of the blood vessels, called arteriosclerosis or clogging up of the blood vessels by the development of blood clots or blockage on the walls of blood vessels (6).

A heart attack or infarct occurs four times more frequently among males than females.

- **What is a heart attack?**

A heart attack occurs when one of the arteries of the heart muscle becomes momentarily blocked and prevents the part of the heart muscle from receiving blood and oxygen. Lack of oxygen to the heart muscle produces a

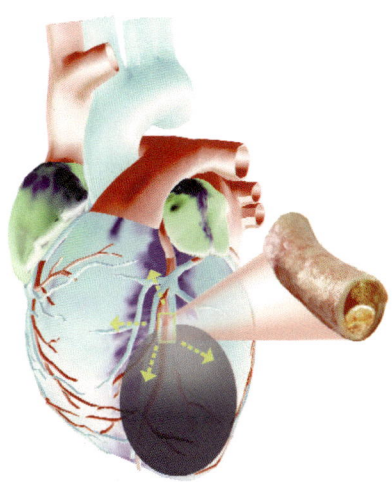

distinct, sharp pain. On the other side, the heart as a pump momentarily weakens, which leads to a lack of sufficient blood supply to the brain, kidneys and muscles, and to difficulty in breathing and a general weakness. If this lack of blood to the heart muscle lasts longer than 15 to 20 minutes, the part of the heart that is affected can die, which can lead to all the negative consequence that result from this.

What are the causes of a heart attack or a myocardial infarct? There are a large number of causes and they can be divided into two groups. The first group of causes are predisposing factors and the second group are provoking, or triggering factors.

The most frequent factors for developing a predisposition for a heart attack or a tendency to develop this serious illness are atherogenic factors (which stimulate arteriosclerosis) are:

- **High blood pressure** stretches the wall of blood vessels and leads to the damage of the inner layer of arteries. This makes the depositing of cholesterol on the inner layers of the arteries possible, which leads to the reduction of the diameter of these arteries and reduced blood flow. A high salt intake also leads to the retention of surplus water in the walls of blood vessels and this further leads to damage to the walls of blood vessels.

- **Diabetes mellitus** or sugar disease, an ever increasing disease which can be seen among adults and children. This disease manifests itself when too high a concentration of sugar occurs in the blood. A long-term increase of sugar in the blood is toxic because sugar by itself damages the endothelium of blood vessels and stimulates the development of arteriosclerosis. People who suffer from sugar disease have other potentially toxic chemicals in larger quantities than normal. These chemicals include; acetone, milk acids, and they often have a high level of cholesterol, which further damages the blood vessels.

- **Obesity** or being overweight, a prominent risk factor because it is well known that heart attacks occur more frequently among obese people. This occurs because they often have high blood pressure and high levels of cholesterol. Obese people are also more predisposed toward developing other diseases.

- **A sedentary lifestyle** is an ever increasing cause of heart attacks in western countries. As a consequence of lack of movement and physical activity there has been an epidemic and an explosion in rates of obesity among the general population.

- **Increase of concentrations of fats in the blood** such as cholesterol and triglycerides are also distinct atherogenic factors. Especially worrying is a total increase of cholesterol over 5,2 of the so-called bad cholesterol or LDL increase of 3,4 and decrease of good cholesterol or HDL below 1,0. Cholesterol all by itself is a normal component of blood but in combination with other factors such as high blood pressure and diabetes, cholesterol more easily sticks to the inside walls of blood vessels and contributes to long-term damage to the endothelium of blood vessels. Triglycerides are prominent types of fat in the blood which occur when a high level of sugar is ingested and also when high level of animal fats are taken in. Triglicerides represent an indirect cause of heart attacks if they reach levels over 2,3 Mmol/L.

- **Stress and chronic stress** have a very negative effect on the function and the structure of blood vessels. People who experience stress for a long time have an increased level of adrenaline and cortisone in the blood. If these hormones remain for a long time in higher concentrations than is normal (in the blood) they can lead to high blood pressure, high levels of sugar in the blood, lowered immunity and can cause other negative consequences for one's health.

- **Smoking of cigarettes** and cigarette smoke releases several hundred toxic chemicals that also damage blood vessels. The most frequent chemicals are carbon dioxide, derivatives of sulphur, cyanide and arsenic, and cyclic benzene. These harmful chemicals not only contribute to the destruction of blood vessels, they speed up aging and damage the heart, brain and whole body.

- **Infectious and inflammatory diseases,** such as chronic infections, can lead to large changes in the composition of blood. Such diseases can lead to an increase of some biological markers in the blood such as C-reactive protein, fibrinogen, can activate components of the complement, complex system of immune defense, damage of endothelium in blood vessels and can all by themselves cause a distinct group of atherogenic factors. Acute infectious diseases such as colds and flu, throat infections, bronchitis, lung infections or urinary passage infections, to mention just a few, can lead to the inflammation of the walls of arteries and so promote arteriosclerosis. Chronic diseases such as chronic bronchitis, emphysema, chronic hepatitis, rheumatoid arthritis, lupus and other infectious or inflammatory diseases, speed up the aging process and contribute to clogging up the blood vessels.

Diseases of teeth, diseases of gums and inside of the mouth also have an undesirable effect on health and speed up arteriosclerosis. It is known today that damage to teeth enamel and tartar build up periodontal (around the teeth) disease with chronic inflammation of the gums. The accumulation of plaque and stains on teeth and gums, can be absorbed by the blood and can seriously damage endothelium of blood vessels, which may lead to clogging up of the arteries.

The most common provoking or triggering factors are: physical effort, heavy work or exercise, cold air, and stress. Sometimes, a combination of more than one of these factors plays a role.

The main event in developing a heart attack is a disproportion between the need and supply of oxygen to the part of the heart muscle.

■ How does a heart attack manifest itself?

A heart attack can take place without the patient showing any previous symptoms and can pass in the form of a cold or flu. It can manifest itself in the form of stable or unstable angina, with signs of heart infarct or as sudden heart death.

The appearance of a heart attack usually goes along with previously experienced angina or pressure in the chest, which can spread up into the neck or left arm and left shoulder. A heart attack can usually result because of physical over-exertion and can pass away spontaneously when we stop walking or working and take several deep breaths. If a heart attack persists and pains in the chest increase (patients often complain that they feel a crushing pain or as if "someone is sitting on top of their chest") and are followed by a feeling of choking for breath, followed by a sudden sweating fit, dizziness and even a loss of consciousness. There is often an occurrence of incorrect heart rhythm, which can create new complaints, with heart palpitations, unrest and further deterioration of the patient's condition. Such a patient should be sent to the hospital immediately. If waiting for an ambulance, the patient needs to lie down, be given oxygen by mask if it is available, nitroglycerin spray applied under the tongue and a physician called immediately.

■ What is the treatment of the heart attack?

The first few steps in treatment of a heart attack are to apply pain killers such as nitroglycerin or morphine and then to increase the patient's oxygen supply with the help of an oxygen mask. Normal blood circulation needs to be restored with the application of intravenous infusions. The next step is to monitor and to control the heart rate of the patient and give drugs to correct the heart rhythm if necessary. It is necessary to ensure that the patient is placed in a quiet and a comfortable room with a half-raised bed. All this can ensure the quick recovery of the patient. The modern approach in larger hospitals provides an even more aggressive treatment where so-called thrombolitic therapy is immediately provided with the application of drugs to thin the blood and to open up blood vessels. Such an approach has contributed to more successful treatment of heart attack victims in the last 25 to 30 years. After that, blood thinners are applied such as Aspirin, Plavix or Warfarin, and drugs used to strengthen the heart muscle (angiotension inhibitors, angiotension receptor blockers), to control heart rhythm (beta blockers) and to reduce any surplus of liquid diuretics.

If the above means don't improve the condition of the patient, then a coronarograthy is performed and a catheter is inserted into the patient's arteries, which supply the patient's heart, to discover which artery is blocked. Then cleaning out the blockage with a tiny balloon at the end of the catheter, angioplasty is performed and a stent left in, which is a small metal spiral loop that holds open the damaged artery. The recovery of a heart attack patient can last several weeks to several months. The length of recovery depends on the damage that was done to the heart muscle and other developed complications and the condition of other tissues and organs.

The majority of heart attack sufferers today, probably over 90 percent, survive their first heart attack and continue to live with greater or with lesser level of disability. A heart attack patient must go through a long period of education during which he or she must learn to change and to put their life in order. The patient is advised to improve their nutrition, lower stress and body weight, control their blood pressure, sugar blood levels, cholesterol, stop smoking cigarettes and begin a regular program of physical exercise (7).

Regular visits and care by their physician is indispensable so that a patient's recovery can be monitored, drug dosages adjusted and new complications are prevented.

The heart is not only the main motor which makes it possible for normal blood circulation to occur but it is also the main means of biological existence and psychological stability.

HOW TO AVOID SUDDEN DEATH?

- Heart stoppage during physical exercise is a well known and dangerous risk
- Physical exercise is necessary but risky if you are not fit
- Existence of undiagnosed illness raises the risk
- How to recognize warning signs of heart disease?

Recently a forty year old man went for a jog in a nearby park. He felt a sharp pain in his chest after 15 minutes, he felt dizzy and he fell down clutching at the left side of his chest. Unfortunately, he died before the ambulance arrived.

On the east coast in Baltimore in one of the leading hospitals in the United States, John Hopkins Hospital, three of their top surgeons at the top of their profession suddenly died. All these physicians were between 40 and 50 years of age and all died during physical exercise because their heart stopped suddenly.

A sedentary lifestyle is one of the leading risks of developing coronary heart disease. In order to prevent this, a regular program of physical exercise is recommended. Physical exercise has numerous positive effects for human health. However, this may sound paradoxical but nothing in our life or health is absolutely certain. Physical exercise, which everyone recommends can, in a small number of cases, have very negative consequences for our health. What is sudden heart stoppage?

Heart stoppage is a sudden end of the work of the heart pump due to sudden weakness of the heart. For example, this can occur because of a heart infarction (blockage of one of the heart arteries and death of the affected heart muscle) or due to a sudden irregular heart rhythm which after a short time leads to fibrillation of the heart chambers and can lead to heart stoppage. Both forms of this disease occur when there is a big disproportion in the amount of oxygen needed by the organism and by the heart and the amount that is actually available. In other words, there is a sudden appearance of oxygen hypoxia (lack of oxygen) which is due to heart stoppage. Any type of physical exercise or activity can lead to these disturbances. Such a dysfunction most often occurs in people who are physically unfit or who already have undiagnosed illnesses such as arteriosclerosis, heart valve disease or excessive hypertrophy or enlargement of the heart muscle.

- **Physical exercise is necessary but there is a risk among people who are not fit**

Persons who perform physical labor or participate in a regular program of physical exercise practically have no risk of sudden heart stoppage.

On the other hand, people who are not fit must be very careful and need to gradually increase the length of exercise and physical effort because this enables the muscles to gather enough energy and for the heart muscle to obtain enough oxygen.

What are the most prominent risks and how to reduce them? The victims of sudden heart stoppage are most often men after 40 years of age. The risks are significantly increased if a person is a smoker, has diabetes or high blood pressure, a high cholesterol level and a person who has a sedentary lifestyle or who sits behind an office desk during the course of the day.

The formula for reducing your risk of sudden heart stoppage, according to recommendations of leading American health experts, consists of Activity, Blood Pressure, Cholesterol, Diabetes, Cigarettes and Diet or Body Weight: ABCDE.

Activity should be present not only during physical exercise but also during the course of the whole day by moving around and walking. Walk to buy groceries rather that ride your car for a short distance, don't use an elevator but take the stairs, walk with your child to school rather than using the car and use every chance to take short walks whenever you can (8).

- **Existence of undiagnosed illness raises the risk**

Taking an Aspirin every day is recommended for people who have changes of their heart arteries and blood vessels because it helps to lower blood viscosity in the arteries.

High blood pressure has been proven to be one of the most serious risk factors. However, with regular control, healthy lifestyle, healthy nutrition, blood pressure can be maintained at a level around 130/80 mm/Hg. A level of blood pressure at 140/90mmHg is considered to be too high.

Cholesterol is a normal component of the blood. It's believed that about one third of people who are middle aged and older have a higher level of cholesterol. Total amount of cholesterol should be between 2 to 5.2. Two types of LDL cholesterol or bad cholesterol should not be higher than 3.5. Good cholesterol or HDL cholesterol should be between 0.9 and 1.1. It's important to understand that a high level of cholesterol may be harmful to human health. It's also important to know that if the ratio between good and bad cholesterol is upset, this can also carry negative consequences for our health.

Diabetes, especially type 2 diabetes, is on the rise because of a simple reason, obesity is also on the rise. Lack of control of sugar levels in the blood leads to many serious long term diseases, including heart damage, blood vessel damage, strokes, kidney disease and eyesight damage. It can also lead to mental disease, depression and male impotence. All these complications of diabetes can be prevented with healthy nutrition, taking appropriate drugs, participation in a regular program of physical exercise and by being under the supervision of a physician. Medical research shows that in a majority of patients who suffer from diabetes, their disease can be controlled with good diet, physical exercise and through a healthy lifestyle.

Cigarettes. Smoking cigarettes has far-reaching negative consequences for health. It can lead to blood vessel disease, disease of the breathing passages, lung cancer, pancreatic cancer and cancer of the bladder. Cigarette smoking is one of the most harmful habits in the general population. If you are a smoker think well about reducing the numbers of cigarettes you smoke or quitting altogether. Your physician can help you to quit by recommending a number of methods like nicotine patches, gums or drugs which reduce your nicotine craving.

Diet and body weight. Under this category it is understood that you are not to starve yourself but to adopt a culture of good and healthy nutrition. Above all else, this means that you eat healthy food, mainly of plant origin, containing lots of grains, use whole wheat flour, food that contains a lot of fiber and eat a lot of fruits and vegetables. You avoid animal fats because they contain unhealthy saturated fatty acids and cholesterol. You also reduce your daily intake of meat to one gram per one kilogram of your body weight, or less. The main trick is to balance the right amount of calories with your actual daily needs (the amount of calories you burn up daily). Your surplus calories accumulate in the form of fat tissue under your skin and this leads to obesity. Obesity is, by itself, a big risk factor in developing diseases of the heart and blood vessels, diabetes, high level of cholesterol, rheumatic diseases and diseases of the joints, depression, cancers especially cancer of the colon, cancer of the uterus, breast cancer and many other diseases. Body weight is best expressed through body mass index (BMI). This measurement is the relationship between weight and height and a normal value for this should be between 19 to 27. Everything above 27 is a sign of being overweight or obese.

- How to recognize warning signs of heart disease?

Diagnostic examination. If you intend to begin a program of physical exercise or if you experience chest pains, shortness of breath when exerting yourself, become dizzy or if your heart rate speeds up significantly, consult your physician. It's also useful to have your blood pressure checked regularly, a blood test should be done to determine your blood sugar level, you can have an EKG (electrocardiogram) test done and you can even have a stress test. Further examination depends on your initial test results, on how you feel and if there are any signs of disease or dysfunction.

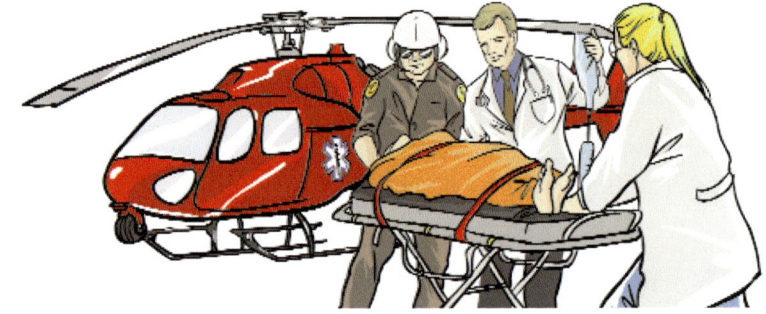

Sudden heart problems–usually the sign of a pre-existing heart condition

Emotional, psychological and social balance. Modern human beings live in times of rapid technological and social change, which place daily demands on them. There are demands of the job, of the family and of our social community. Everyone tries to fulfill their demands, while working under time pressure and other people's demands. In order to meet all these demands, a person can often neglect their own personal emotional, physical and cultural needs while trying to meet demands of other people. It's vital that we continue our education, acquisition of new knowledge and skills, that we organize and manage our time and continue to perform our work in a systematic manner. A well developed system of values and choice of priorities for every moment of our life is not easy to achieve. Wisdom and living our life well is something that we work on all our life. It's only by making dramatic changes in our life that we can continuously maintain our psychological balance.

Raising the level of awareness about the importance of health is perhaps the most important task of our general culture. Good health is the most valuable gift that we receive when we are born. Preserving our good health should be a priority of every moment of our life. Conditions of life are bound to change and a person will go through different phases of development, but one unchangeable principle still remains: we need to continuously maintain our health, to improve it and to control it.

ASTHMA AND ALLERGIES: OUR PETS OR OUR SPOUSE?

- Why are we allergic and what is causing our allergy?
- Allergies can be caused by: pollen, dust, furnace air, animal hair, foods and insect bites
- Are your pets more important than your spouse?
- An environment that's too clean and dust free can be harmful for our health
- Be aware of anaphylactic shock

Allergies in many forms are appearing more frequently, not only among children but also among adults. People suffer from many types of allergies: they complain about itching, skin changes, burning eyes, burning sensation in their pharynx or their nose and catching frequent colds, especially in early spring. Allergies manifest themselves most frequently by itchy red patches on the skin, asthma attacks with pressure in the chest and being short of breath, red itchy skin rashes, cracked and painful skin, frequent colds which make it hard to breathe through the nose and many other complaints.

- Allergies can be caused by: pollen, dust, furnace air, animal hair, foods and insect bites.

Spring fever, which is a common name for one allergy, is appearing more frequently. There has been a triple increase in this type of complaint over several decades. It has been estimated that about one third of the population suffers from pollen allergies and that this number will increase to 50% of the population in the next 10 years.

Pollen and flowers may be the cause of a serious allergy

Allergens can be: flower pollen, household dust, mold, furnace air, animal hair and food (9).

Allergens can be all those substances that can cause an allergic reaction. Such substances can be parts of flowers, pollen, leaves, roots and fibers from the stem, various components of household dust, beginning with textiles, wood particles, paper, clothing particles and bedspreads, and from insects who live in such material. Allergies can also be caused by various substances in our food. Such substances are contained in walnuts, chocolate, peanuts, fish and milk products.

Household pets that live in the home or in the apartment can also cause allergies. Such pets including birds, dogs and cats, with their fur and feathers, can often cause allergies.

■ **Are your pets more important than your spouse?**

Recently, I met a young man in his early 30's who was married several months ago and who entered my office, pale with swollen lips and a frightened look on his face. He complained that he had a hard time breathing. When I obtained information about the conditions of his life, I learned that he had gotten married about 3 months earlier and that his complaints started from that day. I asked him what else had changed in his life and he answered that his wife had a household pet–a dog that lived with them in their apartment. He believed that he was allergic to animal fur, but his wife was not willing to get rid of their pet.

After an examination, I concluded that he was suffering from a serious asthma attack. After inhaling some drugs his condition had significantly improved. However, besides his need to take drugs to control his asthma, he had to come to an agreement with his wife. What was more important, her husband's health or her pet?

■ **An environment that's too clean and dust free can be harmful for our health**

A leading medical journal, *The British Medical Journal, published, as long ago as 1989*, a study which shows that an overly clean environment is not that good for our health, particularly for children. It was discovered that people (especially children) who live on farms have better immunity, are healthier and less frequently suffer from many diseases, even allergic diseases.

The explanation for this is very simple. These children often come into contact with dirt and many substances in animal stalls, on the field, around plants and animals. This serves to familiarize their immune system with many bacteria, viruses and parasites, which creates long term immune resistance to these substances! It turns out that our so called civilized progress which has produced overly clean and kept homes and apartments, is not the best thing for our health!

Overuse of drugs lowers immunity

In the last few decades the use of antibiotics (drugs that kill bacteria) has unnecessarily increased by a substantial amount. Not all bacteria are harmful. The majority of bacteria is not harmful and is needed and only rare bacteria cause disease. Misuse of antibiotics, even for common colds and against viruses, is not only ineffective but is also harmful because it destroys good bacteria in our intestines which are needed there, but are also beneficial. If you want to take antibiotics or to give them to your children, take yogurt at the same time. Yogurt contains healthy milk bacteria which renews normal bacterial flora in the intestines.

Chemical air pollution and new harmful substances

Air pollution has reached critical levels; a person who lives in a city with a well developed industry breathes in over 20 millions harmful particles a day. These particles are in the air and can harm our breathing system, our immunity and can lead to allergic diseases. It's well known that residents of cities have more problems with breathing, skin diseases and allergies. In the last few decades, thousands of molecules of new substances have been produced that our immune system doesn't recognize, and this is also another reason for the appearance of allergic diseases.

Air pollution is bigger in big cities

- **Be aware of anaphylactic shock**

Anaphylactic shock is the most extreme form of an allergic reaction that it can seriously affect health and even lead to sudden death. The most common cause of this syndrome is insect bites: bee or wasp stings, or bites by other insects. It can also be caused by eating certain types of food: walnuts and peanuts among children, or by some drugs, like penicillin, and some other substances. It's useful to check out and perform certain special tests for these diseases by your family physician or an allergy specialist (10).

People who definitely are at risk for allergies need to always carry an anti-allergy kit (which contains an injection of adrenalin–Epi-Pen) in case it's urgently needed and which can be self-administered, or administered by another person, by an injection into the muscle and thus save that person's life. Consulting your family physician about this is very important.

A peace of grain from the physician's brain

Beware of the most common and frequently used drugs such as acetaminophen or Aspirin.

Acetaminophen or Tylenol is used for all sorts of pain and to treat high temperatures of children and adults.

This drug can be very toxic for the liver. More than one third of the population takes this drug daily or in combination with other drugs. More than 50% of cases of poisoning of the liver are due to the use of acetaminophen. This is particularly common among people who drink from one to two alcoholic drinks per day because the liver is responsible for detoxification from alcohol. It's unwise to take more than 8 tablets (4 grams) of acetaminophen per day and for people who have a weakened liver and who drink alcohol, these doses must be even lower.

Aspirin often used as a blood "thinner", for rheumatic complaints, pains and high temperature, can harm the lining of the stomach and intestines, and can cause serious bleeding or development of stomach ulcers. It's always wise to take Aspirin with your meals. For people who are too sensitive to Aspirin there are other alternative drugs and they should consult their family physician about this.

HEADACHES AND SOLUTIONS

- Why do so many people suffer from headaches?
- What are the most common types and signs of headaches?
- What is a migraine headache?
- How can you stop or prevent a migraine headache?

A headache has been traditionally seen as a sign of worry, being overburdened and having too many duties which are hard to fulfill. We live in a time when people have high ambitions, with many duties and real needs just to survive, and to endure and improve their life. In the last few decades the average duties (at work, in the family and in the community) of an individual have gone up. More is expected from people and more is required of them. There has been an explosion of progress in technology and science and every field of knowledge is influenced by these changes. Every area of our life is affected by these changes in communication: in our home, in our cars and in our workplaces. These places now all contain such things as computers, printers, cell phones, email, and many other technological innovations. Television sets with aggressive ads appear everywhere and are no longer just a home appliance!

New information is raining down on us and this information is constantly changing and grows all the time! How to find what we need in the sea of information? What is really important and how to choose proper information? What information is of main priority? Isn't this enough to cause a headache? A chronic headache (11)!

Too much information and many duties lead to an increase of tension, anxiety, to distraction or inability to concentrate, cause sleeplessness and waking up with a headache, as we confront a new day and new duties. Besides all this, problems within the family, with one's spouse, unruly children, financial debts, trouble with one's boss at work and many daily misunderstandings, all this may cause endless headaches.

- What are the most common types and signs of headaches?

A headache can be primary if it's caused by changes in the structures of the brain, in blood vessels of the brain or in the meningeal layer of the brain.

A Migraine is the most common type of headache. Then there is a depressive headache, tension headache, migraine neuralgia or headache experienced after a head injury.

Secondary headache is due to eye diseases, the need for glasses, diseases of the sinus, ear, teeth, or the jaw bone. It can also be caused by general diseases like high blood pressure, diabetes, liver and kidney diseases, and many other diseases. A headache can be a sign of the presence of a tumor in the brain, but can also indicate disease of the neck, spinal disk injury or muscle or joint injury.

Migraines are more frequent in females

The sudden onset of a headache that requires immediate medical attention is acute meningitis or infection of the membrane around the brain and acute hemorrhage in the brain. Besides experiencing a headache, such patients can experience loss of consciousness which can lead to a comatose state and having a stiff neck and high temperature. Such patients require urgent medical care and treatment.

■ What is a migraine headache?

I recently met a woman in my office who was in her 30s, was employed and a single mother of two children. She had a bandage around her head. Her face was very red and swollen, her eyes were half closed and were full of tears and she was not able to look at a bright light. She spoke slowly and quietly. Her headache started two days ago when she felt weak, irritable, depressed and with flashing lights in front of her eyes. She then experienced an intolerable headache on the left side of her head, which was followed by painful and unclear vision. She was not able to tolerate light and sounds around her. This was a classic description of a migraine headache.

The word migraine comes from words "half" and "head" which means that this headache was known even in Ancient Greece, several thousand years ago, because it often affected only one half of the head.

The cause of this headache is changes in the blood vessels of the brain or over sensitivity of the blood vessels of the brain to external stimuli. The most frequent stimuli or "triggers" of a migraine are: alcohol, especially red wine, cigarettes, some types of food such as cheese, dry meat products, spices and canned foods. Sometimes a migraine can be triggered just by an unusual smell and there are many other substances which can cause a migraine. There are two types of migraine headaches:

A classic migraine is characterized by warning signs that a headache is about to develop. These warning signs can include: different colored light flashes before one's eyes, vision of objects becomes deformed and one experiences blurred vision, double vision, change of smell, a feeling of burning on a certain part of the skin or muscle, irritability, unrest, bad mood and low work productivity.

Migraine triggers might be: coffee, drink, fragrance, food, emotions

A simple migraine can be preceded with no warning signs but can cause a loss of appetite, irritability and can sometimes also cause one to become talkative and full of energy.

Symptoms of this headache are usually pain on one or another side of the head (or sometimes on both sides) and a persistent strong pain with a feeling of pressure inside one's head. This headache is followed with painful tolerance of light or sound, confusion, feeling cold or being sweaty, a stiff neck, being overly sensitive to having one's head touched and a general feeling of weakness

A migraine headache usually lasts for hours and sometimes even for days. It's frequency can occur several time a year but sometimes it can also be experienced daily.

What are the stimuli or "triggers" of a migraine headache?

Besides the already mentioned causes, a migraine can also be caused by may other agents: strong smells, strong light or noise, weather change, change in barometric pressure, or when climbing heights, being overburdened at work or in the family, because of a disconnection between one's duties and one's achievements, disagreements with other people, dissatisfaction with oneself and with other people, skipping regular meals, not sleeping regularly, menstruation among women and many other factors.

■ **How can you stop or prevent a migraine headache?**

By avoiding all previously mentioned "triggers" and other possible stimuli which trigger this headache is the best prevention, but this is not always simple to do or always possible:

It's hard to reduce one's duties at work or in the family and to never have disagreements with other people. Even people who are near and dear to us always remind us that we have new duties about old problems.

How to prevent and treat a headache?

- *Leading a balanced, orderly life* with regular good nutrition, regular participation in physical exercise and activity and maintaining good relations with people are all basic prerequisites for preventing a headache. A majority of people who suffer from migraine headaches know what causes them and try to avoid these things. Elements of a healthy lifestyle include: regular and proper nutrition, avoidance of tobacco smoke, good organization of one's workday, regular rest and relaxation, entertainment, recreation and leading a peaceful life can not only prevent headaches but can also serve to prevent development of other diseases (12).

- *When a migraine begins* it's useful to go to a quiet, warm, dark room and place a cold pack on one's forehead, take only liquids and vitamins like B complex and vitamin C as well as several medications for pain: acetaminophen, Panadol, Advil, Motrin or Cafergot. If your headache doesn't go away after several hours or if it gets worse, it's advisable to visit your physician.

- *Secondary headaches* can be solved by treatment of main causes like problems with sinuses, eyesight, hearing, rheumatism or muscles in the neck.

- *A visit to your physician* has two main motives: to rule out the possibility of more serious diseases like inflammation of the brain meninges (membrane around the brain), bleeding in the brain or a brain tumor, and to ease and to stop the headache by use of stronger drugs against pain, through physiotherapy or by some other treatment.

Every form of pain, even a headache, is a symptom and a warning sign. It's an alarm that something is not right, that our biological balance has been upset and that we are not in tune with ourselves and with our community in which we live. We have a God given gift to recognize pain but also to prevent it and remove it.

An American writer John Patrick wrote in 1902: "Pain induces a person to think, by thinking a person becomes wise and wisdom makes us tolerant."

OBESITY IS AN EPIDEMIC

- Stomach obesity–increase in stomach girth
- What is stomach obesity?
- Misfortune rarely comes alone
- The consequences of stomach obesity
- It's easier to prevent stomach obesity than to treat it

Traditionally, a big fat stomach that protrudes out of the vest with a pocket watch on a gold chain is considered to be a sign of financial success and achieving a high position in government administration. With such a big stomach go a big round head with neatly slicked down hair, clean shaven look and an obligatory white shirt with a white collar. Such well recognized characters are the staple of comedies written by Oscar Wilde, George Bernard Shaw, B. Nusic, S. Sremac and Francois Moliere. Such a character usually carries a walking stick, top hat and always has a pipe or cigarette holder with a cigarette that never goes out.

Times change, however, along with structures of lower middle class society and vests are no longer popular. Not too many people carry a gold watch on a gold chain in their vest pocket any more. Smoking a pipe or a cigarette has been proven to be very unhealthy. However, our habits of eating good food still remain and have become even more prominent. Today, food is cheaper and available in greater quantity, and after lunch or dinner walks have become rare. Many people just take a nap after their meals or hop into their cars to go to a shopping mall.

After decades of studies, medical experts have concluded that many of our status symbols are not very healthy. And these symbols include general obesity, smoking cigarettes and more recently, stomach obesity.

- **What is stomach obesity?**

The definition of stomach obesity is a large increase of fat around the waist which damages health and leads to a higher risk of developing several serious diseases and dysfunctions. This problem is so significant that important world authorities agree about its existence and the need for a solution, however at the same time, they have different criteria about its meaning.

The World Health Organization considers circumference of the stomach around the waist of over 94 cm for men and of over 80 cm for women to be a sufficient indicator to diagnose obesity.

The European Group for the Study of Insulin Resistance has similar criteria used to define obesity, however, not everyone agrees about this.

One of the leading health organizations in the United States, The American Heart Association and their Panel for National Cholesterol Adult Education and Treatment is a little bit more liberal in their definition of obesity. Perhaps this is because many members of this Panel have a similar problem; they have defined obesity with a waist of 104 cm for men and 88 cm for women.

- **Misfortune rarely comes alone**

With stomach obesity come many other symptoms: high blood pressure, high level of cholesterol, high level of triglycerides, high level of blood sugar and a higher resistance to insulin (a hormone which lowers blood sugar level). What is higher resistance to insulin? It simply means that insulin is not performing the job it is designed to do.

The causes of stomach obesity

The causes of this serious dysfunction are:

An unhealthy lifestyle; or ingesting too many calories, especially of fat, starch and sugar contained in pastries full of carbohydrates, and food of animal origin like pork, chicken, beef, lamb etc., in quantities that are greater than we actually need to support our normal physical activity.

An insufficient level of physical activity; passivity, sedentary lifestyle, sitting in front of a computer or at one's office desk or on the couch without performing regular exercise of any active physical work.

Genetic predisposition toward obesity and diabetes that has been inherited from one's parents. However, it has been proven that these characteristics don't have to lead to obesity if a person leads a healthy lifestyle.

The aging process; this is a natural process which contributes to obesity, however, if it's combined with unhealthy nutrition and physical inactivity it occurs sooner, and often leads to stomach obesity and other unhealthy consequences for one's health.

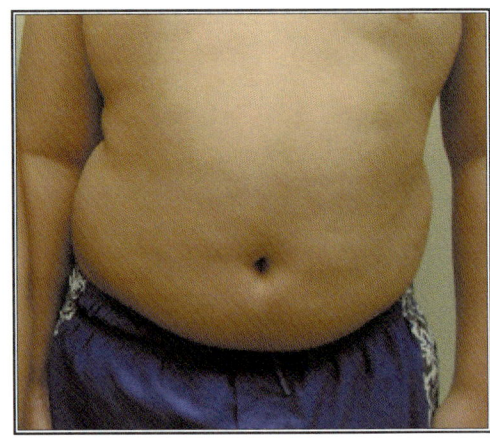

Apple shaped male abdominal obesity and pear shaped female is typical

- **The consequences of stomach obesity**

The syndrome of stomach obesity which is also called metabolic syndrome can be described on several levels: too much fat in the blood, a predisposition toward obesity or being diabetic, high blood pressure with all the negative consequences of damage to vital organs like the heart, the brain, eyes, and kidneys. There is also a predisposition to get cancer, especially breast cancer, uterine cancer among women and prostate cancer among men, as well as colon cancer in both sexes. Besides that, people with this problem have a high total level of unhealthy LDL cholesterol, high level of triglycerides, a low level of good HDL cholesterol, which is a particular risk factor, and these people often have an enlarged liver that's clogged up with fats, which is called fat infiltration of the liver. Women who have this dysfunction develop polycystic disease of the ovaries which leads to irregular menstruation and ovulation; they have a hard time getting pregnant and develop a hairy face and body.

- **It's easier to prevent stomach obesity than to treat it**

Stomach obesity, just like general obesity, has become, in the last several years, not only a problem of individuals, but a problem for physicians and for the medical system. It has become a big political problem in all the major developed nations because it damages the health of a great number of people, and at the same time, it overburdens the national budgets that are dedicated to health. It's estimated that in the developed countries of the west, including the United States, about 25% of the population has this problem. Prevention of stomach obesity is the task which needs to raise general awareness about health, good nutrition and the necessity of everyday physical activity (13). The majority of obese people often say that they don't eat too much and this is often correct. However, all these people eat, everyday, just a little bit more calories than they require, and in the course of several months or years, this leads to an increase in total body weight and to an increase in the circumference of one's waist, which seriously damages their health (14).

Recommendations:

- *reduce your intake of all sorts of fats to a level that's half the amount that you currently take;*
- *avoid white bread, pastries and potatoes because these foods contain starch which is converted into sugar or fat and hardly have any other nutritious qualities like vitamins, fiber and minerals;*
- *avoid cakes, pastries, ice cream, creams and other sugar loaded foods or reduce your intake of such foods to once a week;*
- *increase your intake of fruits and vegetables and grain based foods. Eat more peas, lentils, and green salads. It's ideal to consult a dietician who will determine the exact amount of calories and the type of foods you need to eat;*
- *begin a regular program of physical exercise or at least walk everyday for about 30 minutes. Consult your physician if you have any other health problems;*

- *participation in sport with your friends is better than exercising at a fitness club because you are socializing, laughing and playing with your friends;*
- *if you already have an increased circumference of your stomach or stomach obesity, it's probable that you already have complications like high blood pressure, high fat content of the blood and that you have borderline or well developed diabetes; and*
- *in that case, it's indispensable that you consult with your physician who will determine your need of medications, but who will also recommend various diet measures and physical activity, before he/she recommends that you should also take drugs, if this is absolutely necessary.*

Life contains many challenges and many temptations must be resisted if we are to keep our health. Most people agree: human beings don't live just to eat, but they eat to live and to achieve self-realization and their life's goals.

DIABETES: ARE WE TOO SWEET?

- What is diabetes?
- Types of diabetic disease
- Why is diabetes so harmful for human health?
- Chronic complications of diabetes

Diabetes or diabetes mellitus, as it's called in medical literature, is a common name used for several lifelong diseases which are characterized by higher levels of sugar in the blood and with dysfunctions of the metabolic system of energy creation in the human organism. This disease was already recognized in Ancient Greece, where the physician would taste with his own tongue the sweet composition of a patient's urine. That's where the word diabetes comes from; the Greek for "siphon" or to "go through" and mellitus as "something sweet".

Most frequently diabetes is associated with the pancreas which can be found in the center of the abdomen and is responsible for secretion of the hormone called insulin.

How many people suffer from this disease?

Over 30% of people in the general population on the North American continent are obese. One third of these people have diabetes. As the number of obese people rises, the number of people with diabetes also rises.

What is insulin?

Insulin is a hormone. It's a chemical substance which is normally created in the pancreas and which is indispensable in maintaining normal use of sugar in the blood. Insulin is associated with "receptors" on the surface of the cell membrane, especially in the liver cells, muscle cells and fatty tissue. These receptors are called insulin receptors. People whose pancreas doesn't produce enough insulin have a raised level of sugar in their blood (15).

- Types of diabetic disease

There are two basic types of diabetes

Diabetes, type 1, from which suffer about 10% of the total number of patients. This disease occurs among children and young people and is due to total lack of insulin and it manifests itself by large oscillations of concentrations of blood sugar. Such patients are predisposed to develop diabetic ketosis, which is very serious metabolic problem and must be treated with external injection of insulin. This type of diabetes can be due to genetic factors but also due to other factors such as: infections (mumps), toxins (like alcohol) and improper functioning of the pancreas.

Diabetes, type 2, usually appears among people older than 40 years, many of whom are also obese, who are more than 20% over their normal body weight as measured by body mass index of over 30 (normal level 19-27). The main characteristic of this type of diabetes is that the pancreas produces enough insulin but it's not effective because of lack of cell receptors or because of cell resistance to it. This form of diabetes is usually an inherited disease and includes over 80% of the sufferers of this disease. The cause is again, increased sugar level in the blood and all complications that originate from this (16).

This type of diabetes can be successfully controlled in a majority of patients by proper diet and by normalizing one's body weight. In difficult and well developed cases of this disease certain drugs can be applied which increase the secretion of insulin or the use of available insulin. In the most difficult cases of this disease, insulin must be injected externally. Besides these two basic types of diabetes, there also exists a form of diabetes that occurs during pregnancy as well as some rare forms of this disease.

Too much sugar in cookies is unhealthy for people with diabetes

Why are there so many people with diabetes?

Modern life, with its highly developed technology and high economic productivity has enabled people to lead a comfortable life with little physical labor. Food has become relatively cheap and is widely accessible. Many jobs are performed by sitting at an office desk with little use of physical energy. One of the cheapest pleasures is eating food. If muscles that are created for movement aren't used and exercised, then food energy that is created is not burned up and it accumulates in the form of fat, which eventually leads to obesity.

That's how we arrive at a paradoxical fact: our standard of living is measured by the food we eat, that we don't need, and we sacrifice our long term health to gain a momentary pleasure. The consequences of this are dire: obesity, diabetes, high blood pressure, high cholesterol, strokes, and rheumatic diseases (because joints are overloaded), more frequent infections, and what has been scientifically proven, higher rates of cancer.

Was there any sugar in concentration camps?

During the Second World War conditions were right to perform one unfortunate medical experiment which was conducted by a group of the world's physicians. Among the millions of survivors of concentration camps there was not even one obese person nor was there a person suffering from diabetes. Why? The answer is very simple; these people didn't even have enough food to maintain their basic survival or to overload their pancreas and to use up their stores of insulin. In other words, genetic predisposition toward diabetes is significant, but the main cause of diabetes is eating too much food. This shows that the solution rests in the hands of the individual. It depends on his/her awareness, culture and education, which includes wisdom to learn from mistakes, which we must admit, is not always easy or simple. How is a person to resist food when it's so easily accessible and near at hand? How is a person to avoid food when it is available in big quantities during celebrations, meetings and social gatherings? That's why awareness about health is so decisive.

■ Why is diabetes so harmful for human health?

There is an old proverb which says, "Moderation is the mother of all wisdom." This is not a secret, surplus of food for the organism is converted into surplus of sugar and such huge quantities of sugar are a poison for all living cells. Too much sugar especially harms the inside part of the capillaries and also represents a poison for the eyes, nerves, the heart, kidneys, the liver and all other vital organs which are rich in capillaries. Some patients experience pressure in their chest and blurred vision when their sugar level goes up! The body defends itself by converting part of this sugar (glucose) into alcohol (sorbitol) which is especially harmful to eyesight and to nerve cells. It's not an accident that one of the most serious complications of diabetes is permanent blindness!

In some patients, sugar is converted into acids like aceto-acid and acetone that are harmful for the whole body. The remaining surplus of sugar is converted into fats like cholesterol and triglycerides that accumulate in blood vessels and lead to clogging up of very small arteries and capillaries in the heart, kidneys or the brain and also lead to obesity.

What are the most frequent complications of diabetes?

Acute complications of diabetes are:

An exceptional rise in sugar (hyperglycemia) or an exceptional drop of sugar (hypoglycemia), diabetic coma and diabetic ketosis. Every one of these complications has its own symptoms and signs that are too detailed to describe here.

■ Chronic complications of diabetes

The most frequent complications of diabetes are damage or loss of eyesight, arteriosclerosis with diseases of the heart, heart attacks, strokes, gangrene in the feet, nerve damage and damage to brain cells (mental deterioration, paralysis and impotence) and kidney damage. Over 80% of patients who have artificial kidneys or are on dialysis suffer from diabetes. These complications lead to lowered capacity for productive work and disability. It takes a number of years for these complications to manifest themselves, but they are surely coming.

What to do in order to help oneself and other people?

There are three very important things that relate to this problem:

- the development of diabetes can be prevented by a good lifestyle and good nutrition in the majority of cases;
- if diabetes manifests itself, all complications of this disease can be prevented or significantly postponed; and
- people who suffer from uncontrolled diabetes have a lowered quality of life and lower longevity.

How to lower the risk of diabetes?

Learning more about your health is the best investment you can make and for which you will be amply rewarded. A healthy lifestyle takes into account adopting those habits that have been proved to be good for us and avoiding those habits that are harmful.

- Choosing a variety of healthy foods that are rich in complex carbohydrates (starches and cellulose), like cereals from whole grains like beans, peas, a variety of fruits and vegetables, and taking in a reduced level of fats and using unsaturated fatty acids contained in canola, sunflower and olive oils).
- Eating smaller meals more frequently during the course of the day so that the concentration of sugars oscillate less and remain at normal levels.

- Participation in a regular program of exercise and physical activity. You should exercise for at least 45 minutes to one hour at least three times per week. The type and level of this activity depends on your age, occupation and health status, but also depends on your personal preference.

- Maintenance of your normal body weight according to normal levels of body mass index (20-27). You should consult your physician about this.

- Unburdening yourself from stress at your place of work, in the family and social community where you live and work.

- Getting regular sleep and rest, along with emotional and psychological recovery and regeneration, as well as mental development in healthy micro-social conditions, are a basic need for every human being.

- Avoiding harmful habits and effects especially toxic substances like: alcohol, tobacco, unnecessary drugs and eating too much unhealthy foods such as fats and concentrated sugar contained in candy, cakes, ice cream and pastries.

A patient is educated for self sugar control from the fingertip blood drop

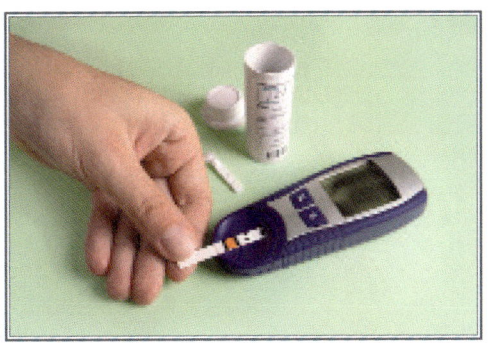

- If you suffer from diabetes, consult your family physician and dietician. Also undergo a detailed examination, and a detailed history of their disease should be made. Various biochemical markers like daily oscillation of sugar in the blood, HbA1c level that maintains concentration of sugar in the blood for the last 3 to 4 months, and cholesterol and triglyceride levels can be determined. It's also important to determine if there has already been damage done to the heart, blood vessels, kidneys, eyes and the nervous system.

Sometimes it's hard to refrain from small but potentially dangerous pleasures in the long-run in order to achieve our goals, but it will pay off in the end. Wisdom in life doesn't only consist of what we can accomplish during the course of our life, but also, which is even more important, in what we can still do in our sunset years. Suffering from uncontrolled diabetes, obesity, or being a smoker of cigarettes who has high blood pressure, is similar to being a passenger in a fast train which has lost its driver and is fast approaching an abyss without the passengers even being aware of this. This is another reason why we need an awakening of awareness about health and more learning about important diseases among the general public.

HIGH CHOLESTEROL–AN INSIDIOUS ENEMY

- Cholesterol is a risk factor in diseases of the heart and blood vessels
- Where does cholesterol come from and what is its role in the body?
- What are different types of cholesterol and are all of them harmful?
- How to lower and maintain cholesterol?

Diseases of the heart and blood vessels or arteriosclerosis, are the leading causes of disease and mortality in Canada and in other developed nations. Heart attacks or infarcts and strokes in the brain are the most frequent forms of these diseases and most often affect people who are middle age or older.

Here is a short story from my life. I knew a wonderful man, who I was friends with from our early childhood. We sat together at a school desk in the classroom, we played together in the field, and then we both grew up. He was full of life, happiness, humor and laughter! There was always happiness around him. He finished his schooling, got married and had children. He started to get ill after he reached 30 years of age. After forty years of age, he suffered a heart attack and had several "by-pass" surgeries to repair blood vessels. His cholesterol level was extremely high at 25. He loved life, loved people, in the best way: he was always ready for humor, song or play. He had a hard time resisting good food, a glass of good wine and a cigarette. It became impossible to control his high level of cholesterol. He left us, too early.

- Where does cholesterol come from and what is its role in the body?

Cholesterol is a complex chemical substance which is created in the liver or is ingested with food. Cholesterol is the building material of many body tissues and organs such as nerve cells in the brain, bone marrow and liver. It also serves in the creation of important hormones such as sex hormones like testosterone in males and estrogen and progesterone in females, as well as adrenal hormones such as cortisone and androgen.

These hormones play an important role in the maintenance of vital body functions like: temperature, creation of energy, growth of tissues and cells and they play a role in reproduction or creation of our progeny. The greatest amount of these hormones is created in the reproductive period in women and men between 15 to 45 years of age. After that age, the amount of these hormones begins to slowly decline and disappear.

With this lower production level of hormones, there remains a greater amount of unused cholesterol. If our food intake continues to increase and we don't burn up extra energy that is created as a result of this, than there is a surplus level of cholesterol that's created which damages human health.

An increase in cholesterol may be acquired and inherited

- What are different types of cholesterol and are all of them harmful?

There are several types of cholesterol: total cholesterol, low density lipoprotein (LDL) and high density lipoprotein (HDL). Total cholesterol is a combination of two types of cholesterol in the blood and its high normal value of cholesterol in the blood needs to be less than 5.2 mmol/L. LDL cholesterol needs to be lower than 3.4 mmol/L and HDL cholesterol needs to be higher than 1.1 mmol/L.

Desired values of cholesterol are even lower for those who have risk factors like high blood pressure and diabetes or who have already had heart attacks. These people should be regularly monitored by their physician.

LDL cholesterol is very harmful if your level is high. In the words of one of my professors, LDL cholesterol is like a small spoiled child who walks around the house with dirty hands. Everything that he touches is soiled. LDL cholesterol sticks to inner walls of blood vessels and gradually clogs them up so that normal blood flow is lessened.

HDL cholesterol is a good natured cholesterol like a clean, neat little girl that goes around and cleans up after her younger brother, LDL cholesterol (18).

Besides cholesterol, there exist simple fatty acids and triglycerides that play an important role in the transfer of materials in the body. In chemical structure, triglycerides can be saturated fats that are harmful and also unsaturated fats that are a lot less harmful! It's extremely useful to read food labels to be informed while you are buying food. Ideal foods don't contain saturated fatty acids! The terms used here like saturated and unsaturated are not indicating that you will satisfy your appetite but are indicating chemical structure of all free chemical bonds on the carbon molecule which are connected with hydrogen.

All types of meat are high in cholesterol

What leads to the rise of cholesterol in the blood?

Unhealthy nutrition, big meals full of fat; animal fats, sugar, cakes, and concentrated foods full of calories are the main reason.

Physical inactivity, a sedentary lifestyle, and lack of movement and regular exercise, in combination with a disproportionately high intake of calories will lead to the rise of cholesterol in the blood.

There is incontestable proof that smoking cigarettes and drinking alcohol leads to damaged blood vessels and an increase in accumulation of cholesterol inside blood vessels. Smoking cigarettes should be completely avoided and alcohol should be taken in moderation (one to two glasses of wine is enough).

Diabetes, obesity and diseases of the liver and kidneys are often a cause of high levels of cholesterol. Over 60% of patients with diabetes also have increased levels of cholesterol and triglycerides.

A familiar increase in cholesterol appears in 15% of patients and often leads to early complications, diseases and can lead to death before 30 years of age.

It's possible to effectively lower cholesterol levels through healthy nutrition, regular exercise and avoidance of tobacco.

What is healthy nutrition in order to have low cholesterol levels?

This healthy nutrition consists of plant based foods which contain lots of fiber, vitamins and minerals and don't even have one gram of cholesterol!

The main sources of ingested cholesterol are meats, processed foods with lots of fats and milk products (if they don't have a reduced level of cholesterol).

■ **How to lower and maintain cholesterol?**

- *Use breads and grain based foods made of whole grains:* whole wheat grain, barley, oats and brown rice. These foods contain soluble fiber materials which lower synthesis and help excretion of already existing cholesterol. It's also recommended that one drink a lot of liquids (water), and supplement with minerals such as calcium, magnesium and zinc.

- *Eat a lot of beans, peas*, lentils, and soybeans which are all rich in proteins and contain vitamins, fiber materials and minerals. Prepare such foods with other liquids and combine them with other foods.

- *Drink fresh natural fruit juices* especially carrot, tomato, celery and apple juices. Carrot juice serves to "clean out" fats from the liver and thus lowers cholesterol levels and besides that, it contains vitamins A and C.

- *Apples contain pectin* which binds up cholesterol and increases the secretion of cholesterol through the large intestine (colon). Bananas, grapefruit and garlic also have similar properties.

- *Garlic dissolves fats,* protects the blood vessels, lowers sugar level in the blood and has an antibiotic effect. However, if the smell of garlic is neutralized then it loses this effect.

- *Vegetable oils.* Instead of animal fats, use vegetable oils, such as olive, canola, flax and sunflower oils.

- *It's recommended to periodically take vitamin* supplements, especially vitamins B1 and B3, vitamin C, inositol, granules of lecithin, and Omega 3.

- *Lower all sorts* of fats from one's diet such as saturated fats, hydrated fats (margarine), solid fats and butter.

- *Participate in a regular program of physical exercise:* One of the best ways to raise one's levels of good HDL cholesterol is through regular physical activity and exercise.

- *Drugs used to lower cholesterol levels:* If after using healthy nutrition, regular physical exercise and avoiding tobacco, the cholesterol and triglycerides levels are still not normalized after 6 months, then certain drugs can help to treat high levels of cholesterol in the blood. Consult with your physician about which of these drugs to take.

SMILE, YOUR TEETH ARE SHOWING

- **Eyes and teeth are the most prominent features on our faces**
- **How to save your healthy teeth?**
- **Healthy teeth save us from many diseases**
- **Foods you have to be aware of**
- **Why does Mona Lisa stay silent?**

What is the first thing that you notice about the person you are talking to? The importance of healthy and beautiful teeth by far exceeds the look and appearance of an individual.

Teeth and the mouth are the door for some of the most important diseases that affect modern man: too much unhealthy food, obesity, diabetes, high blood pressure and arteriosclerosis, clogging up of arteries, stomach diseases, kidney and gall stones, premature aging and depression (19).

Several days ago, I met a woman in my office. She was skinny, weak looking, middle aged, with deep set eyes, a wrinkled face and did not have a single tooth in her mouth. She said that she was feeling unwell, that she wasn't able to eat, that she was losing weight, that she had stomach pains, was suffering from sleeplessness, had irregular menstruation, and pain in all her joints especially when she woke up in the morning. She said that she needed the whole morning to become fully awake.

She looked like a 60 year old woman. Of course, she was only 38 years old. A disorganized life combined with unhealthy nutrition, lack of regular dental work, smoking for several years, and stress, all left negative consequences on this unfortunate woman's health.

Treatment and recovery from such a state is a long term process and demands, before anything else, a change in bad habits and lifestyle. She also needed to live under better conditions, which begins with healthy and proper nutrition. As well, she needed to visit a good dentist to treat her inflamed mouth and replace her missing teeth.

- **How to save your healthy teeth?**

Eat food in smaller portions, chew it slowly and for a sufficient amount of time, avoid strong spices, food that's too sour, too hot and too salty. Also avoid food that is too hot or too cold. Teeth enamel is very thin, and is made up of a shiny protective covering that is very sensitive to the above named physical and chemical materials. Eating smaller meals more frequently during the day makes digestion easier.

After a big meal a person will feel tired and sleepy because all the blood rushes to the stomach. This can lead to the speeding up of arteriosclerosis, diseases of the liver and other diseases.

- **Healthy teeth save us from many diseases**

Brushing your teeth with a good toothbrush after breakfast and before you go to bed and ideally after every meal, is the recommendation of professor Hazel Harper of the University of Washington. A good toothbrush should be soft, elastic and with short bristles and changed frequently. When you brush your teeth, you remove food particles, bacteria and plaque created by mucus and mucus cells and by leftover particles of food. This plaque is a good environment for bacteria and for creating tartar which begins to be formed that same day. According to the latest medical research, tooth plaque can be partially absorbed by damaged capillaries in the mouth, which can stimulate development of arteriosclerosis. This can lead directly to heart attacks, strokes and other negative consequences for human health (20).

There is no ideal method to brush your teeth. Dr. Harper recommends using a combination of horizontal brush strokes that only encompass three teeth at a time and then using vertical brush strokes from gums to the top of teeth in order to thoroughly clean the surface of teeth and gums. Slow circular action also helps when cleaning your teeth and you always need to be careful about your gums. If your gums bleed whenever you brush your teeth, see a dentist or a specialist for gum disease. In regard to what type of toothpaste to use, consult with your dentist. Your choice depends on the presence of plaque, tartar, condition of your gums and color of your teeth.

*Healthy teeth are not only a sign of beauty–
but also a sign of good health*

Using floss to clean your teeth at least twice a day, beginning in early childhood, is indispensable in order to maintain the long term health of your teeth. By flossing, you remove those food particles and plaque that aren't removed when you brush your teeth.

Regular visits to your dentist, once or twice a year, is vital to the growth and condition of your teeth. Visit a good tooth hygienist every six months. This is a minimum requirement in order to have healthy teeth (21).

Rinsing your mouth continuously pays off! Rinsing with water is a very useful way to remove most food particles after meals, especially when you don't have a chance to brush your teeth.

The best dessert to use after meals–cheese!

Ancient Romans had a proverb; "From the egg to the apple" (Ab ovo usquae ad mala) because they started their main meal about 6 pm with one boiled egg and finished with one apple at midnight because they believed that an apple cleaned their teeth. This proved to be false because an apple contains a lot of acid, which damages teeth enamel.

A better dessert is old, hard cheese which cleans teeth very well. It reduces the chance of cavities and destroys mouth bacteria. In some cultures this has been a tradition for centuries. Of course, this is the last resort, if you are not able to brush your teeth.

- **Foods you have to be aware of**

Everything that sticks to teeth can stimulate tooth decay. That includes sugar, cakes, chocolate, dry fruit, figs, plums, hot bread and many foods made from flour. If you are not sure that the food is sticky or not, simply brush your teeth after your meal and everything is solved.

Tobacco smoke from cigarettes contains hundreds of poisonous materials that damage not only your teeth, but also damage your gums, mucous covering of your mouth, your tongue and can lead to chronic inflammation, and even cancer inside the mouth.

Coffee is also damaging because of high temperature and because it contains caffeine which discolors and damages tooth enamel.

- **Why does Mona Lisa stay silent?**

Mona Lisa was a famous painting by Leonardo Da Vinci that was painted in the middle ages. In this painting Mona Lisa has a sly smile, and many people have tried to find the meaning of this mysterious smile. One explanation is very simple: the dental explanation is that Mona Lisa is only smiling and is not laughing with her mouth open to reveal her missing teeth as this would mar her beauty.

This mystery will never be fully solved and we will never know the truth about Mona Lisa's teeth, however, we can see our own teeth very simply. Just look at your teeth in the mirror. If you have any doubts about their health and appearance, see a good dentist for a consultation and help.

Healthy teeth have a very important role to play not only in our appearance and beauty of our face but also to prevent diseases of digestive organs, the heart and blood vessels. Healthy teeth raise our quality of life and prolong our life.

All sweets and sticky food are unhealthy for the teeth

Key recommendations:

- *have regular, smaller meals, 3 to 4 times per day;*
- *avoid food that's too hot or too cold. Such food damages teeth enamel;*
- *avoid food that's too spicy and sour for the same reason;*
- *smoking cigarettes and drinking coffee, not only damages your teeth, but also speeds up the aging of your gums;*
- *avoid all food that easily sticks to your teeth, because such foods damage your teeth and also damage your blood vessels;*
- *brush your teeth with good toothpaste at least three times per day and floss regularly;*
- *visit your dentist at least twice a year; and*
- *in case you have a toothache, bleeding of your gums, appearance of cavities and other problems, see your dentist more often.*

WHAT'S BUGGING OUR LIVER?

- The liver is one of our life's most important organs
- The liver is a factory for the production of important substances
- Most frequent causes of liver disease
- Key approaches to saving your liver

There is a common saying which states, "You are getting on my nerves" but also "You are "bugging" my liver" with medically justified reasons for this saying: when a person is under a lot of psychological stress and if he or she is consuming too much food and alcohol they can get a sharp pain under the right side of the ribcage because of a spasm of the liver, gallbladder, and gallbladder passages.

Without a doubt, the liver is a vital organ. Those people whose liver is unable to perform its basic functions usually manifest serious signs of acute or chronic disease. In most serious cases of liver malfunction, death is the result.

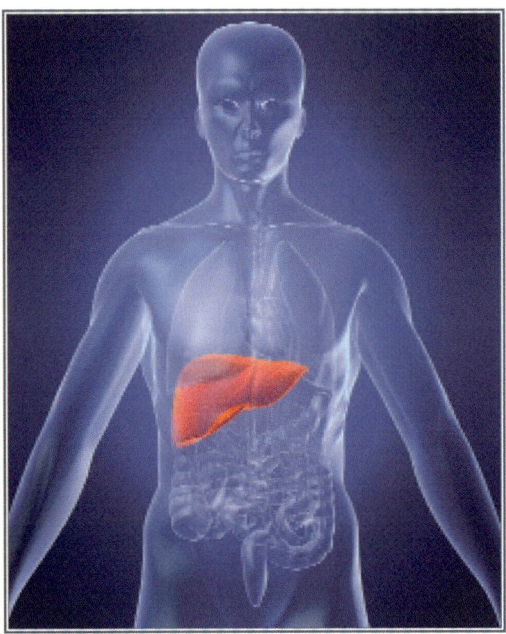

The liver is a vital organ with multiple essential functions

- **The liver is a factory for the production of important substances**

The liver is a big gland organ which usually weighs about 1,500 grams and is composed of two large lobes. The liver is located under the diaphragm under the right ribcage in the upper corner of the stomach cavity. On the top part of the liver rests the lower part of the right lung, and toward the stomach the liver touches part of the stomach and duodenum. The right kidney is located under the liver. The liver is richly supplied with many blood vessels. All the food which we eat is absorbed by the intestines and is transported to the liver. The liver creates many life sustaining substances. It is the main factory but also a storage place for many important substances which serve to maintain the balance of our internal state, and to maintain efficient circulation to all other tissues.

- **The liver makes bile,** a green/yellow liquid that is indispensable in digestion and absorption of fats in our ingested food, but it also neutralizes and eliminates a number of toxic substances that are continually created in our body.

- **The liver makes proteins:** albumin is contained in our blood and helps to bind liquids and salts so that they don't seep out of our blood vessels; fibrinogen is an important factor for blood clotting, as well helping to heal wounds and creation of immunity maintaining antibodies, which help the body to defend itself from infections.

- **The liver is a storage place for glycogen** (complex sugar which is created from our intake of simple sugars and other substances) and serves as a storehouse of energy.

- **The liver makes cholesterol,** which is a basic substance used in the synthesis of many hormones (estrogen, testosterone, adrenal gland hormone) that help to transfer other fatty substances through our circulatory system. In the second half of our life, when our need for hormones is less, if the level of cholesterol is not reduced, this may be a big factor in the risk of developing arteriosclerosis, which is the number one cause of disease of the heart and blood vessels.

- **The liver serves to detoxify the body;** it reduces and eliminates a great number of potentially toxic substances like alcohol, and various chemicals which we ingest with food and when we take drugs.

■ Most frequent causes of liver disease

Overeating, especially excessive intake of fats and sugar serve to overload the liver and cause a rise in cholesterol and triglycerides. These fats cause damage to our blood vessels and impair our blood circulation. On the other side, they lead to fatty liver infiltration which, all by itself, leads to pathological obesity, which is a big risk factor for causing various problems of circulation, heart and blood vessel disease, diabetes, rheumatism and many other disturbances. Today, about twenty five percent of Americans have fatty infiltration of the liver which is not caused by alcoholism and many of these people with these changes will develop cirrhosis of the liver or diabetes, or both (22).

Alcohol is well known as a cause of chronic disease of the liver in the form of fat infiltration or alcohol related hepatitis that slowly but surely develops into cirrhosis of the liver (change of the liver into scarred tissue), which is the last stage of liver disease with an unpleasant result. It's often said that people in France suffer the least from heart attacks but it needs to be said that France is a country where most people die from cirrhosis of the liver because wine has been declared to be a nutritiously beneficial substance, and people drink enormous quantities of wine (23).

Viral infections, especially hepatitis A, hepatitis B and hepatitis C are among the most frequent infectious causes of diseases of the liver. Hepatitis A is an illness transmitted by dirty hands, tainted food and improper preparation of food. Hepatitis B is a much more difficult infection which often permanently damages the liver and is transmitted through direct contact with body fluids, sexual contact or by sharing of needles when injecting recreational drugs. Hepatitis C is a very serious illness which is also transmitted by using dirty needles or during blood transfusions. For virus type A or B there is now a very effective vaccine, while we are still awaiting development of a vaccine for virus type C.

Psychological stress, tenseness, anger, depression are all significant contributors in the development of diseases of the liver and bile passages. Even Ancient Greeks knew 2,000 years ago that bile function is connected with our moods and that an unhappy man secretes dark gray bile. That's where our term "melancholy" comes from. A life spent under stress, worry and often excessive anger, have a significant effect not only on the bile duct, but also on the liver. A person who is depressed has a poor appetite, bad digestion and stomach bloating, among other symptoms.

Drugs are a significant cause of diseases of the liver. These drugs include: Acetaminophen, Aspirin, Ibuprofen, Tetracycline, Steroids and antidepressants, as well as many other drugs, are broken down and disintegrated in the liver. Acetaminophen is the most frequent cause of acute narcosis of the liver of 40% of patients admitted to American hospitals in the last three years, which was reported in a recent study. This drug in the form of the popular brand Tylenol is often taken for all sorts of pains, for high temperature and flu and many other applications. Taking Tylenol is OK, but it must be taken in moderation and must not be overused. Don't take more than the recommended dose, in this case not more than 4 grams per day if you are healthy, if you have a good liver, and if you are not taking other drugs. If your liver is damaged because of alcohol, fat, hepatitis or any other disease, even half the recommended dose can damage your health and your life.

A part of unused fat and sugar is deposited to the liver

■ Key approaches to saving your liver

- Healthy lifestyle, moderate food intake, balanced private and career duties, regular exercise and recreation, a well developed social life, dynamic psycho-emotional and mental balance, are all vital components of a healthy body and a healthy soul.

- Alcohol–in moderation. According to The American National Institute, moderate consumption of alcohol for people younger than 65 years of age is two glasses of wine (150 ml) or one glass (50 ml) of hard liquor per day, two or three times per week. For women this quantity is a bit smaller and for people older than 65 years the quantity is half of the recommended dose. If you haven't consumed alcohol until now, don't start.

- In relation to our food intake, consume limited quantities of fat, preferably use vegetable based oils, with lots of fresh vegetables, whole wheat bread, and reduce our consumption of protein, like meat, to 80 to 90 grams per day. Have smaller meals more often in order to digest our food easier. Prevention and reduction of obesity, diabetes type II, reduction of our caloric intake, regular exercise, and maintenance of normal body weight.

- Drugs need to be taken with caution, with physician's and other health worker's approval. Special care is needed with people who take multiple drugs, have serious chronic disease of the heart, lungs, liver and kidneys, small young children and older people.

- Prevention of stress: Defining our priorities, balancing our personal and professional duties and needs, and systematic planning of our duties is a complex but essential process, which serves to maintain and to ensure our psychological health. The stress coping skills for mutual misunderstandings, personal incidents, illnesses and unfortunate events, all represent an important dimension in every person's life. Techniques of relaxation through deep breathing, meditation and focusing our attention on a particular problem, are all good approaches toward reduction of acute stress.

- Chronic stress is very complex, it occurs because of being overloaded over a long period of time, on the job, in the family or in our community where we live and work. It's often a result of being overloaded with duties, unrealized expectations, poor organization or lack of support.

Life in our modern technologically and highly developed society places significantly higher demands on people than in the past. If a person is to fulfill all of these demands, save his/her health, and maintain personal and family good health and a high quality of life, it's necessary for a person to continue their education, gather new information, organize and improve themselves and their local community. Health is the corner stone on which we build all of our successes and accomplishments. Our care to maintain our liver health is only one ring on the chain toward good health.

WARNING: KIDNEY STONES

- Over 10% of people in the general population develop a kidney stone
- What is a kidney stone and how is it created?
- A kidney stone manifests itself by acute abdominal pain
- How to prevent an attack and appearance of a new kidney stone

One of the most frequent pains that are described in medical books is pain caused by a kidney stone. Often this type of pain is more intense that pain of broken bones or pain during childbirth. Every year in the United States there are over a million patients who register with an acute attack of kidney stones. It's estimated that 13% of people in the general population suffer from kidney stones during the course of their life. This type of disease often affects men (80% of cases occur in men). People who experience an attack of kidney stones have a 50% chance that they will suffer another attack during the next 5 years (24).

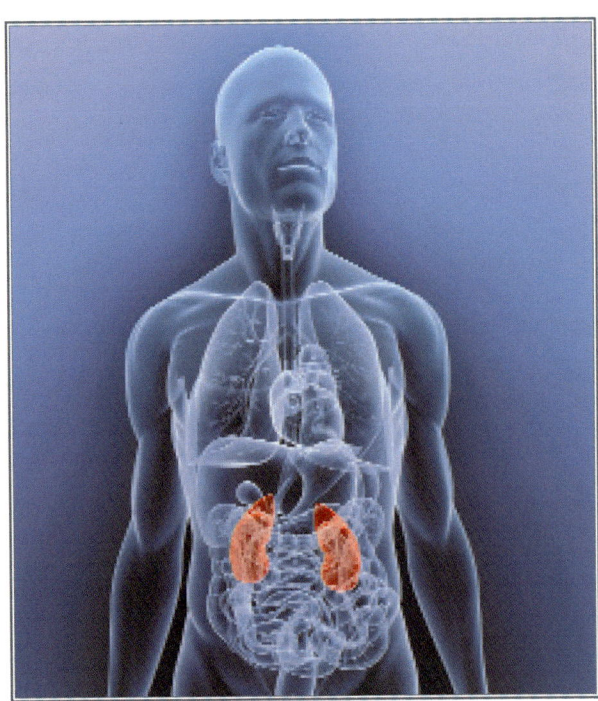

Kidney stones are made from insoluble salts

- What is a kidney stone and how is it created?

A kidney stone is a solid lump of crystallized salt which can't be dissolved with water and which is created in the kidney from components of urine. It can be the size of a sand grain or up to the size of a golf ball. Usually a kidney stone is round in shape but can also have an irregular shape in the form of a burdock with thorn like structures. It's usually located in the kidney cavity but can also be located in hard kidney tissue. If the stone is 10's of millimeters in size it can usually be eliminated during urination. However, stones that are deeply embedded inside kidney tissue can't be eliminated by natural means.

A calcium kidney stone is composed from 70% of calcium that's combined with oxalates and phosphates that are a normal part of food.

A struvite stone is a less frequently occurring type of stone in 15% of patients. Struvite is composed of crystals of magnesium, ammonia and phosphates. This type of kidney stone is most often found in people who suffer from more frequent urinary infections and is mostly found in women.

A uric acid stone is found among 10% of kidney stones and is made from urine acids which are a decomposing product of proteins, and appears in people who are predisposed toward gout, or one type of rheumatism or arthritis. Because the same type of crystals accumulate around the joints they can lead to inflammation of joint structures.

A cistein stone is the rarest type of kidney stone and is composed from amino acids of cistein and is usually an inherited dysfunction because of a surplus production of cistein.

Different factors individually, or in combination, favor the development of a kidney stone. First of all, it's the amount of calcium, oxalates and uric acids in the urine, as well as acidic urine that is created with a surplus intake of proteins, above all, meats. A reduction in some protective materials like liquids, water or citrates, can also facilitate the appearance of a kidney stone.

There are whole numbers of diseases where a kidney stone is more easily developed. These diseases include: disease of para-thyroid glands (small glands behind the thyroid gland responsible for the regulating of metabolism), calcium, diseases of the kidneys, sarcoidosis and others.

■ **A kidney stone manifests itself by acute abdominal pain**

Most frequently a kidney stone manifests itself with a sudden, strong attack of stomach pain, usually on the left or the right side. These pains from a kidney stone are called kidney colic, and appear in very sharp waves of pain and cramp-like stabbing pain in the upper side of the abdomen. Such pain often passes over the groin toward urinary passages and can be accompanied with nausea and vomiting. If the kidney stone is moving through urinary passages toward the bladder, this can lead to frequent urination and appearance of blood in the urine. If there is, at the same time, a rise in temperature with fever, this can be a sign of the presence of infection.

The treatment of a kidney stone attack is aimed at reduction of pain and prevention of an attack with drugs that reduce a spasm or cramp of urinary passages and with other options that reduce pain. Treatment also consists of a large intake of liquids by mouth or intravenously if the patient is unable to drink or is too nauseated and inclined to vomit. In the vast majority of cases (over 90%) this type of approach ensures significant easing of symptoms and then facilitates the elimination of the stone through urination.

Permanent removal and healing. If the patient is unable to pass the stone by urination for whatever reason (it's too big or it's embedded into kidney tissue), then a way must be considered and chosen for its permanent removal. There are several techniques that are used to remove kidney stones:

Lithotripsy means the disintegration of the stone through the use of a special apparatus that creates strong ultrasound waves which have the capability of breaking up and disintegrating the stone without damaging healthy surrounding tissue. Once the stone is broken up into small pieces, it can be eliminated through urination with the help of a large intake of liquids.

Percutaneus nephrolithotomy is the approach to the kidney through the skin in the region of the diseased kidney, where an instrument is inserted through the abdominal wall and into the kidney with the guidance of ultrasound and a scanner. This method successfully removes the stone.

Urethroscopy is a less invasive method of treatment by insertion of a fiber-optic instrument through the urinary tract with which a urologist or a radiologist can follow, recognize and remove the stone from the lower regions of the urinary passages.

Open surgery is the classic surgical approach when the abdomen is opened up and then the kidney and the stone is localized and removed.

The choice of these methods of treatment and their application depends on the type and location of the kidney stone. Usually the physician, in consultation with the patient, will choose the least invasive and most effective method of treatment.

- How to prevent an attack and appearance of a new kidney stone

Attack of pain in the kidneys: take up a position on the bed which irritates the affected region the least, place a hot compress on the side you are experiencing pain, take plenty of liquids, especially tea and take a drug from the group NSAID like Indocin 50mg, two to three per day. Carefully examine the urine for signs of blood, but also for a sign that the stone has been passed, if it's smaller than 8 to 10 mm. If the above methods don't help, see your physician or go to the nearest hospital to seek help.

Healthy nutrition with a lower intake of proteins and salt reduces the chance of developing a kidney stone. It was believed for a long time that an increased intake of calcium was one of the most responsible causes for creation of a kidney stone, and that's why physicians for decades in the past recommended patients reduce their calcium intake if they had a predisposition toward a kidney stone. However, recent exhaustive research in the last few years shows that lowered intake of calcium not only doesn't reduce your chances for a kidney stone, but also increased your chances of having other diseases, like developing brittle bones and osteoporosis. It was discovered that among patients who already had a kidney stone, those who lowered their intake of meat and salt for five years, reduced their chances of developing new kidney stones by half over those who only reduced their level of calcium in their diet.

Intake of liquids. One of the most important steps in reducing conditions for the development of a kidney stone is increased intake of liquids and greater creation of urine. An average person usually urinates about one and a half liters of urine per day. To reduce the risk of a kidney stone this amount should be doubled. This means drinking 10 to 12 glasses of water or other liquid (not including beer or any other alcoholic drink). Increased intake of liquids also reduced the possibility of infection of the urinary passages. Another recommendation is to reduce the intake of high protein foods, especially meats. This especially applies to people that have a tendency to create a uric acid stone. These people need to lower their salt intake. For people with oxalates stones, they need to lower their intake of food with oxalates such as chocolate, beans, spinach, and eat a moderate amount of green salads (25).

The human body like the human soul is an especially sensitive and complex organism. It's necessary to be in tune with it, to carefully listen to its inner messages and impulses, and to pay heed to early messages and warnings that our body is sending us. This is the most reliable way to maintain your health and to preserve it, so that you can continue to experience all the happiness and beauty that life has to offer.

Increased intake of fluids enable faster kidney stone excretion

CANCER IS PREVENTABLE!

- Lung cancer, breast cancer, and colon cancer are leading cancers among women
- Why is cancer a malignant disease?
- What are the most common causes of tumors?
- How to prevent the development of many types of cancer?

Into my office walked a very skinny woman in her 50s, with a tired walk, sunken eyes with evident dark shadows under them. She was noticeably sad, with deep wrinkles and look of worry on her face. She sat down without being asked, sighed deeply several times, looked up and said, "I don't feel very well. I am weak and skinny. I don't have any appetite and I've lost over 10 kilograms in less than two months."

When I saw that she had traces of blood around her eyes and several bruises on her face, I asked her if she had any other complaints. "Oh, yes" she said sadly, "Two to three weeks ago, I started with small nose bleeds, which got worse, bleeding from my gums, bleeding from bruises on my skin, blood in my stool and after a pause of two years; I have started to menstruate again."

She continued her story with small pauses, and with my encouragement, she started to reveal the tragic story of her life. She finished her university education more than 25 years ago; fell in love and married a somewhat older man who was her colleague while she was studying. She started to work, had children, a son and a daughter. Her children grew up, they were good students and everyone in the family was happy. Her son finished his university studies, served in the army, and then came home where his girlfriend was waiting for him. Preparation was made for a wedding. It was spring, with lots of sunshine and the scent of flowers in the air and birds' singing. It was Saturday noon. Everyone was busy with their small chores.

The woman paused at this spot, she was wiping tears that were falling from her eyes. Her young son was repairing the car in the garage. Then all of sudden a horror happened: an electrical short-circuit, a loud bang and her young man's heart stops. A scream! Weeping! First aid arrives! All in vain.

She experienced stress, terrible stress, the greatest possible stress. Everything completely changed, her life stopped, it's meaning lost. High stress due to losing a loved one carries with it many consequences. One of the consequences is a drastic fall in immunity and being prone to catch infections and develop malignant diseases.

After I finished a history of her disease and conducted a detailed examination, I discovered that the unhappy woman was suffering from acute leukemia. This was probably due to all the stress that she underwent.

The above true story serves to illustrate one of many causes of malignant disease and cancers as it's described in medical circles and among patients.

What is cancer?

Cancer is a common name for a whole series of malignant diseases that can have lots of different causes and can appear in different parts of the body.

- Why is cancer a malignant disease?

There are several reasons for this. First, this disease begins to develop from one affected cell, often for example, in the lungs, breast or uterus among women, or the prostate gland, lungs or colon among men. It's believed that these malignant cells continue to grow and to multiply for one or two years before they can be discovered.

Another reason for cancer cells' malignancy is that they continue to multiply in an uncontrolled manner and can't be controlled through a natural mechanism of growth which applies to healthy cells of all body tissues.

The third and maybe the most dangerous reason for their malignancy is because these cancerous cells quickly outgrow the locations where they find themselves, for that reason they don't have enough nourishment, and some of them die and disappear. However, many of these cells enter blood circulation, and are carried by the blood stream and enter many other organs, where they continue to multiply, spreading the disease further, most often into the lungs, liver, bones, the brain and other vital organs. This spread of malignant disease occurs in many ways and affects distant tissues and organs. This process is called metastasis. Some types of cancers metastasize relatively early while the primary tumor is very small and can't be discovered.

What are the most frequent signs of malignant disease?

The beginning of a malignant disease is difficult to determine because malignant cells multiply and grow a lot sooner than the patient experiences any type of complaints. In other words, there is a quiet, latent period of the disease which can last several months to several years. This depends on the speed of the multiplication of malignant cells and on the strength of the immune system which is successful in fighting the tumor.

When general symptoms begin to manifest themselves, they are usually of a mild variety. They include: weakness, loss of appetite, losing weight, lowered capacity for productive work, irritability, depression, and sometimes high temperature. In this phase of the disease, specific symptoms begin, depending on which organs are affected:

When lungs are involved, there can be a persistent cough, or changes of one's usual cough, pain in the chest, spit, gagging and lack of air.

In the breast there is an increase of the sensitivity of the breast, deformation, redness of the skin above the tumor, a tangible lump, secretion of serious liquid or blood from the nipple and sometimes an increase in size and sensitivity of lymph nodes.

With colon cancer the development of the disease depends on which side is involved, the left or right side, since if it involves the right side, the situation is significantly worse, because there are no complaints that appear for a long time or only signs of weakness appear. A tumor located on the left side of the colon can develop with left abdominal pain, bloody diarrhea, occasional constipation and problems in stool elimination.

Prostate cancer leads to problems with urination and emptying of the bladder in males, a burning sensation and insufficient urination, and pain in the lower parts of the abdomen and back.

With patients suffering from leukemia, the most common signs are significant blood anemia, weakness and bleeding from the skin and mucous membranes in the nose, in urine and stool, and lowered immunity and predisposition to catch infections. Other types of tumors can have similar or completely different symptoms.

■ **What are the most common causes of tumors?**

Different toxins and poisons, such as pollutants and exhaust gases from industrial plants and gasoline engines, tobacco smoke from cigarettes, chemicals, asbestos, chromium, paints, varnishes, some drugs, excessive x-rays and some viruses are some of the common causes of tumors. It's believed that excessive food intake, above all excessive intake of fats, fried foods, lack of fiber in the food and irregular elimination from the intestines, all significantly increase the risk of developing colon cancer and cancer of some other organs. There is good documentation about some genetic factors of different tumors. For example, a woman whose mother or sister had breast cancer has three times the greater chance of developing breast cancer than a woman who lacks this genetic component. Similar findings exist about colon cancer and some other localizations of cancer.

What can you do to lower your risk of cancer and prevent it?

The standard of life in developed nations is at such a high level that a majority of people can enjoy a high quality of life. But above all else, people need to be informed and educated about a healthy lifestyle, healthy nutrition, and avoidance of dangerous materials like tobacco smoke, alcohol, chemicals and drugs (26).

■ **How to prevent the development of many types of cancer?**

Modern medicine has devoted an increasing amount of attention to preventing the development of tumors and its early detection. Many studies have been conducted and more is known than 10 to 20 years ago. There is very effective protection against a large number of very dangerous cancers. These cancers include:

- **Lung cancer** which in 80% of patients is the result of smoking of tobacco cigarettes. Waste products from burning tobacco contain over 800 cancer causing materials, which sooner or later, in about 35% of smokers, cause lung cancer. Why only 35%? Because genetic predisposition of different people is different, and because there exist other genetic and ecological factors. Just smoking one cigarette causes 10 thousand genetic debris, which are a prerequisite for cancer. A healthy immune system recognizes all that debris and destroys it before it causes cancer. But if only one mistake occurs in the immune defense system then cancer begins to develop. Smoking cigarettes also causes the development of cancer of other organs such as the pancreas, colon, uterus (in women), pharynx and larynx (27).

It is believed that about 80% of lung cancer is linked to smoking

Recommendation: Avoid tobacco smoke and smoky places, industrially polluted air, released gases from car exhaust and other forms of air pollution.

- **Colon cancer** can be prevented by the use of food with plenty of fiber and cellulose materials. These materials are contained in grain based foods and dough made from whole grain and in fruits and vegetables. On the other side, food containing a lot of fats such as fried meats, grilled and barbecued meats and dry meat products are all rich in cancer causing substances. These foods lead to irregular elimination of waste which raises the chances even higher of developing cancer. The question of proper nutrition is of great significance because of prevention of cancer and diseases of the heart and blood vessels and because of preservation of good health in general (28).

- **Cancer of the cervix** among women is a virally spread infection which is transmitted sexually and can be prevented very successfully with the use of a condom. This simply means that use of "anti-baby" birth control pills only prevents a pregnancy while the use of a condom (for the male or female) at the same time prevents the spread of viruses that cause cancer and also prevents the spread of other diseases. A regular pap test in consultation with your physician for women is the most popular method for early detection of this cancer.

Fibre rich food may reduce the risk for colon cancer

- **Cancer of the uterus** among women can be prevented by following the regularity of monthly menstruation and by the prevention of an excessive secretion of estrogen (caused by birth control pills and HRT), which raises the risk of cancer of the uterus and of the breast as well. With every irregular, excessive and unusual menstruation in women, a physician needs to be informed and their help and advice should be sought. Obesity is a big risk factor because obese women have more estrogen hormones which are potential carcinogens.

- **Breast cancer** is complex because it's tied to genetic predisposition, especially if a woman has a mother or a sister who have had this cancer. Other causes are: excessive secretion of estrogen, smoking cigarettes, inflammatory processes and cysts in the breast. Women who don't breast feed their babies have a greater risk than those that breast feed. Education about self-examination, avoidance of excessive estrogen stimulation and regular monitoring by the physician can significantly lower the risk and help in early detection of breast cancer (29).

- **Liver cancer** (primarily the one that originates inside the liver) is prevented in the majority of cases with successful vaccination against Hepatitis B, since persons with chronic Hepatitis B often suffer from liver cancer.

- **Stomach cancer** today, can miraculously, in great part, be prevented by antibiotic therapy of the inflammation of the stomach or stomach ulcer which is caused by bacteria called Heliobacter pylori. Such a treatment can be applied successfully in consultation with your physician.

The above named discoveries about cancer represent a significant advance of practical medicine in the last few years. Good health is in our hands and with a little care, effort and education about these questions, every human being can significantly contribute to their own health. Through active prevention of cancer, we can preserve and maintain our own health.

HARD BONES FOR A LONG LIFE

- Brittle (soft) bones or osteoporosis often cause problems in later years
- Confirming the presence of osteoporosis
- The most important factors for the risk of developing osteoporosis
- How to prevent the development of osteoporosis?

Every fourth woman and every eight man have a chance to develop osteoporosis which is a disease of soft bones during the course of one's life. This problem becomes an ever more significant cause of illness and leads to physician visits and hospital stays.

Bones are composed of special types of connecting tissue and collagen that create a dense net of pores with small openings in which is deposited calcium, carbonate, phosphates and other materials. Bones continue to grow until we reach our full adult maturity. This maturing process of bones usually ends between 20 and 25 years of age among men and a bit earlier among women.

The main factors that ensure proper development of bones are healthy nutrition with a sufficient quantity of proteins, vitamins, especially Vitamin D and A, minerals and, above all, calcium, phosphates and magnesium.

Another significant factor is physical activity and exercise. Movement assures renewal of bones and daily deposits of minerals into bones. A great number of people in contemporary society work 8 to 9 hours daily by sitting behind an office desk or in front of a computer and then take breaks or rest by sitting on an arm chair or couch in front of the TV set, or again in front of the computer. The remaining third of the day is spent in bed, so that the amount of time devoted to physical activity is reduced to a minimum.

It's well known that the process of gravity plays a determining role in the process of mineralization of bones. It was discovered that among astronauts that spend a long time in space without the benefit of gravity, there is a loss of minerals in their bones, their bones get softer and this also leads to an intensive development of osteoporosis.

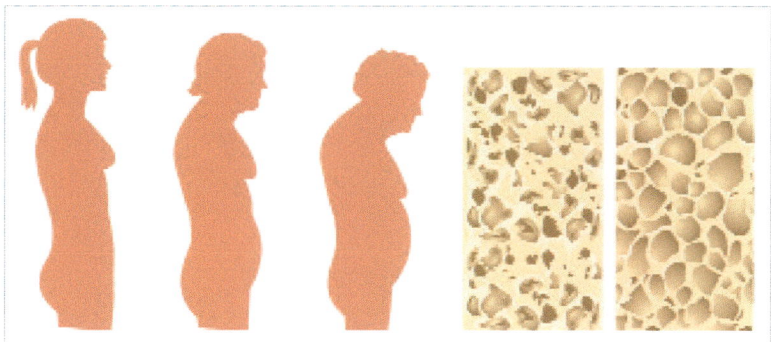

Reduced bone density may lead to severe spine deformity.
Dairy products are a good source of calcium

The third factor that prevents weakening of bones is avoidance of potentially toxic material such as alcohol, tobacco smoke, and coffee. Everything above two cups of coffee per day is probably unnecessary. Caffeine from coffee speeds up the secretion of calcium from the organism through urination. This means that those who drink a lot of coffee lose a lot more calcium than those who don't. It has also been confirmed that smoking not only raises the risk of softening of the bones but also facilitates easier development of serious diseases of the bones and joints like rheumatism.

These above named factors are a lot more evident among women, especially among those going through menopause (cessation of menstruation) which usually takes place around 50 years of age.

■ **Confirming the presence of osteoporosis**

Osteoporosis is diagnosed through special tests of which the most reliable is bone mineral density test. This test determines the mineral density of bones (bone mineral density). This test is conducted with an instrument that works on the principle of x-ray radiation. This radiation is ten times less than routine x-ray examination of the lungs. Most often the bone density is determined in the vertebral bodies of the lumbar spine, in bone above the knee joint or in femur bone.

Ultrasound examination of the bone in the heel can also be used to diagnose serious deterioration of osteoporosis, especially if there is the presence of a break of a spinal disk which is often seen among elderly patients.

■ **The most important factors for the risk of developing osteoporosis**

- **Insufficient movement** or lack of exercise has been proven to be one of the main risks factors which occur from an early age. A large number of children spend a majority of their time inside, sitting in front of a TV set or playing in front of a computer and so, lack invaluable benefits of playing outdoors, running around and playing with their friends in the clean outdoor park air or on the playing field. All forms of exercise and work, involving lifting of objects, has a positive effect on strengthening of bones and should be applied at least 4 to 5 times a week (30).

- **Nutrition that contains sufficient levels of protein, minerals and vitamins** is decisive as a source of building materials for healthy and strong bones. The best source of calcium is milk and milk products, but these foods can contain too much fat, especially saturated fats, so older people with serious diseases such as diabetes, high blood pressure and high level of cholesterol, should use fresh fruits and vegetables rather than using milk. Women going through menopause after 50 years of age should take regular supplements of calcium (1 to 1.5 grams daily) and Vitamin D (800 units daily) as a good preventative measure against osteoporosis.

- **Alcohol** in larger quantities than 1 to 2 drinks per day speeds up the loss of minerals from the bones and among men is the greatest cause of developing osteoporosis and breaking bones in middle and later years.

- **Smoking cigarettes,** especially among women, significantly contributes to the development of osteoporosis. Women who smoke cigarettes stop menstruating earlier and in such a way, contribute even more to the risk of softening their bones (31).

- **Family predisposition** toward osteoporosis has been observed in many families and probably contains a genetic component. Families that have someone with a broken back, hip, or other extremities should devote even more care to these named factors.

- **The presence of other diseases** such as disease of the thyroid gland, para-thyroid gland, sex glands, diabetes, kidney disease and liver disease can significantly speed up the above named dysfunctions and can lead to softening of the bones.

■ How to prevent the development of osteoporosis?

- **A higher intake of calcium** can prevent and slow down softening of the bones among both adult men and women. Studies have been done which have proved that those who regularly take sufficient quantities of calcium lose less bone density (0.5% less per year) which over a long term, say 20 years, makes 20% and represents a huge difference in bone density and inclination toward serious bone breakage.

- **Regular supplements of Vitamin D (800 units)** per day enable a deposit of the above named calcium in bones and prevent predisposition toward bone breakage.

- **Healthy lifestyle:** Healthy nutrition and maintenance of normal body weight and regular exercise are the basic, unavoidable prerequisites of good health. These measures prevent not only osteoporosis but also other diseases, such as high blood pressure, diabetes, heart diseases and blood vessel disease, and help in maintaining mental stability, and in avoiding malignant diseases and many other diseases as well.

- **Avoidance of smoking cigarettes and moderate intake of alcohol** are significant factors in the prevention of osteoporosis. Moderating and controlling your intake of coffee is also an important factor in preventing osteoporosis.

Today, treatment of osteoporosis is a lot more successful than it was two or three decades ago. We now have several groups of drugs with which we can treat osteoporosis. The most common treatment involves hormone replacement among women. Other chosen drugs are also used, such as Bifosphonates and Calcitonin. There is also the use of selectively changed hormone preparations and other drugs that have been proven in clinical studies to be effective in a majority of patients with osteoporosis. The decision about the type of treatment and drugs to be used is best determined on an individual basis for every patient, in consultation with the family physician. The physician will conduct a thorough examination and will gather detailed data and conduct a basic analysis to determine the best treatment to be used.

Sun exposure increases vitamin D in the skin and strengthens the bones

JOINTS AND ARTHRITIS, ACHES AND PAINS

- C-reactive protein (CRP) in the blood can indicate an inflammatory reaction
- A higher level of CRP can define a risk for heart attack and stroke
- Using healthy nutrition against arthritis and created proteins!
- Too much fat and meat

People who have a chronic inflammation process in the body, such as chronic inflammation of the sinuses, the lungs (bronchitis), kidneys, the liver, joints (arthritis) or any other type of chronic inflammation, have a much greater chance of getting high blood pressure, arteriosclerosis (clogging up of the blood vessels), heart attack or a stroke, than those people who don't have this chronic inflammation. This also applies to people who experience inflammations in the lungs and other organs or who have many colds and allergic diseases.

The leading American medical journal, *JAMA (Journal of the American Medical Association)* published a study with about 40 thousand women who were older than 45. This study was based on testing the blood with a special test called C-reactive protein (CRP). This is the test that is used to diagnose some rheumatic diseases. It became evident that the presence of this type of protein in the blood was of deep significance. The women in this study were followed for a period of 8 years and their levels of this protein were divided into three groups: up to 1 mg/L; up to 3 mg/L; and over 3 mg/L.

If one has the flu–stay home

By observing these women, it was discovered that all the ones who had a level of C-reactive protein over 3 mg/L, had a significantly higher chance of developing high blood pressure and arteriosclerosis of the blood vessels, even if their blood pressure was very low at the beginning of this study.

Besides detecting higher levels of C-reactive protein, this study also followed other parameters which were responsible for high blood pressure and heart diseases. These parameters included: body weight; higher level of cholesterol; smoking; diabetes; and the level of physical activity. It became evident that the higher level of CRP was an independent risk factor but at the same time it has a higher effect in the presence of other known proteins.

What is the lesson that we can learn from this study?

- Above all else, every inflammatory process needs to be treated carefully and, when necessary, to spend time in bed and allow the body, and especially one's immunity, to recover.

- Second, it's necessary to consistently take prescribed drugs and to ensure care and monitoring by the physician and other health personnel.

- Third, which is of special significance, is the need to follow a healthy diet.

- Top physicians at Harvard University and other famous health institutions recommend the lowering of body weight, using healthy nutrition, participating in a regular program of physical exercise, and avoidance of cigarette smoking.

■ **Using healthy nutrition against arthritis and created proteins!**

Diseases of the bones and the joints have many forms but most often appear as two types: degenerative arthritis and rheumatoid arthritis. Besides the influence of lifestyle, occupation, physical effort, and injuries of knees and palms, nutrition plays a significant role in the development of these diseases.

Eating huge servings of food during meals!

You were probably surprised by a huge portion of food that was served to you the last time you had a meal at a restaurant. The restaurants seemed to be competing to serve you the biggest plate of food possible! The market place battle for the consumer dollar shows no mercy. Next time that this happens, feel free to divide your meal with someone else.

Too much saturated fat stimulates both inflammation and aging

■ **Too much fat and meat**

Food that causes inflammation of joints. Ingestion of food that contains lots of organic acids such as red meat (beef, pork or chicken), releases lots of ammonia acids and other organic acids which are considered to contribute to more inflammation of the joints, ligaments and cartilage. At the same time, the above named foods contain saturated fatty acids which contribute to prostaglandin inflammation that plays a role in the increase in inflammation process. A steak weighing approximately 250 grams is too big. What we need is about one third of this (32)!

Food which can prevent inflammation. Healthy food such as fish, especially salmon, cod, and tuna, bread and dough made from whole wheat grain with lots of fresh fruits and vegetables, all contain less acid products and contain unsaturated fatty acids, which enable the creation of anti-inflammatory prostaglandin. This type of nutrition can not only prevent the worsening of existing arthritis but can also speed up recovery of joints and bones (33).

How to determine an appropriate level of exercise and movement?

The reduction of body weight and a moderate amount of physical activity are the main components of a healthy lifestyle. However, this is not always simple to do. People who have arthritis need to exercise or at least take regular walks, in order to lower their body weight (which overburdens their joints), but they can't take walks because their joints hurt.

However, there is a solution to this: lowered intake of calories and exercise of an isolated part of the body in a prone position when you are lying down. Another possibility is water exercise or swimming because this type of exercise places minimal pressure on joints in obese people. Useful instructions about these exercises can be obtained from a physiotherapist who can advise you which exercise is best for individual possibilities and needs.

SAVE YOUR EYES!

- Eyesight and vision play a central role in human psychology
- Saving your eyesight and healthy eyes
- Cataracts, glaucoma and macular degeneration
- Diabetes is the main cause of eye disease and blindness

Sparkling eyes, happy eyes, sad eyes, wandering eyes and mischievous eyes. All these expressions have been used by poets for centuries to describe the mirror of the human soul. The eyes have become more than just one of the senses or the means to recognize forms, colors, pictures, people, plants, nature and everything that surrounds us. Vision or sight has a direct or indirect figurative meaning: a person can have insight, an inner vision, perception, view, supervision and–a look.

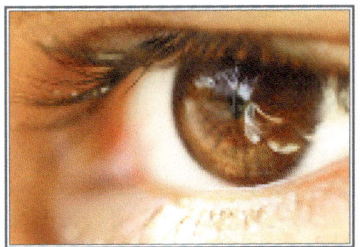

- **Saving your eyesight and healthy eyes**

Besides expressing psychological states and feelings, the eyes can be the mirror of physical health. Damaged eyes and eyelids, eye infections, hollow eyes, unclear eyes, jaundice in the eyes and goggle (an expression with wide-open and protuberant eyes) eyes, are all signs that reflect different health states and diseases that often include the whole body. The most common eye diseases are cataracts, glaucoma and macular degeneration.

Eyes are the mirror of the soul

- **Cataracts, glaucoma and macular degeneration**

Cataract or the clouding over of the eye lens is often seen among older people after 65 years of age but can also occur earlier and is seen as a sign of aging.

Cataracts can occur earlier in people with diabetes, kidney disease, and metabolic disease which leads to an accumulation of unsecreted materials into the lens. Cataract development can also speed up due to frequent infections of individual structures in the eye or due to eye injuries and excessive exposure to strong light and bright sunshine. Some drugs like steroids, fenotiazin and some anti-rheumatic drugs can also contribute to cataract development.

A cataract manifests itself through the gradual, painless loss of sharpness of vision, and sometimes with the appearance of a halo around light at night.

It's extremely important to use measures to prevent and slow down the development of cataracts, such as healthy nutrition, not smoking cigarettes, control of kidney disease, diabetes and other diseases which affect the whole body.

Cataracts today are treated by the surgical removal of the cloudy part of the eye lens and replaced with a new lens which normalizes the eyesight in the majority of patients.

Glaucoma is a disease of increased pressure inside the eyeball of over 21 mm which is measured by a tonometer, a special instrument used for this purpose. Besides genetic factors which we can't change, other causes of glaucoma which we can influence are: high blood pressure, smoking, diabetes, nearsightedness, frequent eye infections and use of steroids, eye injuries and other dysfunctions. In its early development, glaucoma can be without symptoms, and then there is eye pain, nausea and vomiting, weakening and loss of eyesight, typically loss of peripheral vision, which can remain undetected. If this is not treated, there can be loss of central vision (34).

Glaucoma is treated by control of high blood pressure and diabetes, by living a healthy lifestyle and by quitting smoking. The long term application of drugs can also be used to lower pressure inside the eyes.

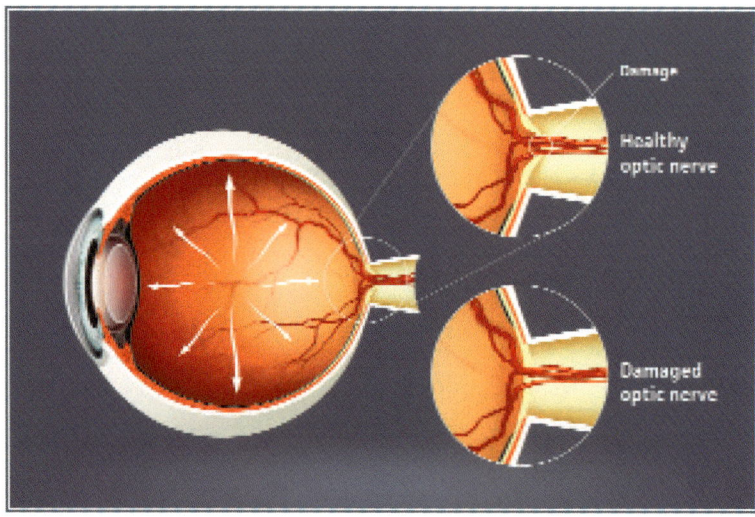

Macular disease is the disease of the macula which is the region of greatest visual acuity in the retina. Damage to this region of the eye can lead to serious damage of the eyesight and can also lead to blindness. This disease is the most frequent cause of blindness in people over 65.

The macula is composed of deposits of collagen and yellow/white fats under the retinal membrane. These changes are often complicated by bleeding in the retina, separation of the retina, deposits of pigments on the optic nerve and loss of eyesight.

The main causes of macular disease are high blood pressure, diabetes, a raised level of fats in the blood and smoking. It occurs more frequently among women and older people (35).

Macular disease manifests itself by distorted vision and by loss of sharpness of vision. It gradually leads to a loss of vision which is difficult to stop.

It is treated by laser cauterization and improvements can be made by taking Vitamin E contained in fresh vegetables like vegetable oils, spinach, carrots and sweet potatoes; Vitamin C in lemon, green peppers, broccoli and tomatoes; and zinc contained in pumpkin seeds, whole wheat bread and seafood.

- **Diabetes is the main cause of eye disease and blindness**

Diabetes is the most frequent cause of damage and loss of eyesight and blindness. A surplus of sugar is toxic for the whole body and is especially dangerous for small blood vessels and the eyes. Uncontrolled diabetes leads to the majority of eye diseases, such as damage to circulation in the capillaries of the fundus or back of the eye, damage to the optic nerve, separation of the retina in the back of the eye, bleeding of vitreal body behind the eye lens and other diseases.

Research studies have shown that the best way to prevent these problems is through regular control of diabetes by healthy nutrition, the taking of necessary drugs and through regular monitoring by your physician.

Besides the above mentioned diseases, there are also many other diseases of the eyes and of eye structures.

People who use contacts often experience problems: especially if they don't wash their hands or if they forget to take out contacts overnight. This can cause damage to the cornea (which is the transparent membrane in front of the eye socket) and can also lead to infections, ulceration and other serious eye complications. It's extremely important to keep your hands completely clean and to keep your contacts clean during and after they are used.

Unhealthy lense handling is a frequent source of eye infections

Emergencies which require immediate attention of a physician are: eye injuries (particularly the presence of a foreign material in the eye), obvious eye infections with the presence of pus in the eye and with bleary eyes in the morning, chemical eye injuries, eye burns and the presence of acute eye pain which can indicate increased eye pressure and glaucoma. Sudden loss of vision or loss of vision in certain parts of the vision field, the appearance of waves and curtains in the eyes, double vision and rapid clouding over and distorted vision, are all cases where immediate medical attention should be sought.

A large number of drugs can cause major changes in the eyes and can cause eye damage. These drugs include: contraceptive birth control pills, antibiotics, drugs used for the heart and for control of high blood pressure, drugs used to treat rheumatism, steroids such as Pronison and taking too much Vitamin A and D. That's why it's so important to take these drugs under the supervision and advice of your physician, and if any changes or dysfunctions occur in the eyes, it's necessary to immediately consult your physician, taking to him/her a list of drugs you are taking for other diseases.

The German poet Goethe said, "So you think that you see, just because your eyes are open!" This short proverb contains a deeper meaning. What we see may not be what we think it is, but can be something completely different and contrary to what we believe that it is. That's why we need the higher functioning of the frontal cortex brain cells so that we can conclude on the basis of our experience and knowledge what the true meaning is of things that we see.

V

SOME ASPECTS OF MENTAL HEALTH

The roots of our behavior are in our upbringing, education, genes, family and society influence

PSYCHOLOGICAL ASPECTS OF MENTAL HEALTH

- Why are people renouncing their own common sense?
- Confrontation with reality is not always pleasant
- Why do people consciously spend more money than they have?
- Are children more important than parents?
- How much is human experience worth, if it's not used?

Common sense is a basic characteristic of a normal and calm person who has attained maturity. For centuries, people have lived by following their sense of fairness (justice) and by using their common sense, their senses, judgment, experience and the experience of other people, not only to maintain their own health and their life, but also to help other people.

According to this same common sense, it was logical if it was raining to seek cover, if it was cold, to dress accordingly, and if one was hungry, to eat a moderate meal and satisfy one's hunger.

According to this same common sense, parents were responsible for taking care of their children and children obeyed their parents, not just until they reached 16 years of age, but until they were capable of taking care of themselves.

Many people today talk about their rights but often forget about their responsibilities. Is it possible to expect people to be responsible for others when they are still irresponsible themselves?

- **Confrontation with reality is not always pleasant**

Real life is very complex and multifaceted and this is what makes it charming. Life consists of an endless process of change, both within ourselves and in our surroundings. We assure our survival by adapting to these changes. From early childhood onwards, with constant changes in our life, we experience many joys but we also learn many painful truths.

Everyday life places before us many new situations which pessimists call problems and optimists call challenges. There is a significant difference in this interpretation. A pessimist views a problem as something that shouldn't happen to him or her, that is irritating, and that should be solved by someone else.

A challenge is something that serves to inspire us and that spurs us to do something new for ourselves, for our loved ones and for the community in which we live.

When I was approaching one of my rooms in my office, I heard the yelling of children who were shouting at the top of their voices. There were four children in the room, and they were trying to take away each other's toys and they didn't even notice me as I entered. Their helpless mother tried to tell me that two of her four children were ill. These children were very beautiful, they were real angels, but it was evident that they were spoiled. Their ages were from three to eight years old. When I asked about their father, I learned that he had left them because he couldn't cope with this situation. "He couldn't take it anymore," said their mother.

These children needed to be approached with common sense. They needed love, support, play time and a proper upbringing provided by two full time parents. What the mother needed was understanding and help. I encounter similar situations like this almost everyday.

- **Why do people consciously spend more money than they have?**

Life in contemporary society implies our willingness to work, learn, exercise self-discipline and take responsibility for ourselves. Only after fulfilling these things can we expect to enjoy big and small pleasures. Survival in our modern world is only possible with an endless stream of money, which means gainful employment. Many jobs today enable people to earn more money than they need for basic survival. But despite this, many people want to earn even more money in order to buy new things, such as an additional car, house or apartment, TV set or computer and more new clothes. A lot of these additional things just gather dust and go unused. Take a look in your cupboards, garages and drawers. When was the last time that you moved? Did you notice mounds of things that just sit around unused for months or years? Eric Fromm is a modern psychologist and sociologist who wrote a very good book 40 years ago called, To Have or to Be? This book describes, in a very persuasive manner, modern man's obsession with material wealth, and shows how it is much more beneficial to us to devote ourselves to learning and education for ourselves and our children. Happiness comes from traveling down the road toward our goal, and not from the chaotic acquisition of material goods and spending of money.

A big house and luxury car–a status symbol

- **Are children more important than parents?**

In healthy families, parents are responsible for the family's survival. Parents ask themselves who, how and when, is one or both parents to work, of course with the agreement of the children. However, in many families, children learn very early on how to avoid responsibility and seek out unhealthy pleasures. Such unhealthy pleasures include; eating too much food, spending too much time watching television or in front of the computer, driving while underage, and the use of alcohol and drugs without the parents knowledge. These unhealthy habits and pleasures result in negative consequences, which are registered in the physician's office or at the police station. Modern psychologists call such families, "dysfunctional." In such families, all the family members are physically present but rarely or properly communicate with each other. They live under the same roof but children are not behaving in a mature and responsible manner. These children are avoiding their responsibilities but they are well aware of their rights and they know how to take advantage of these rights (1).

In one week I saw a girl, 15 years old, who came to tell me that her menstruation was late by one week. This girl lived with her single mother who worked and had a boyfriend. A test which was done in several minutes showed that this girl was 6 to 7 weeks pregnant. When I told her this, she blushed and then turned pale and couldn't speak. I asked her several more reassuring questions and offered her a glass of water. It would be common sense to inform her mother about this pregnancy (the girl didn't know where her father was). However, according to the law, which doesn't function according to common sense, I am not allowed to inform her mother. I can offer this girl social assistance and three solutions to her pregnancy, which include; termination of the pregnancy, carrying on with the pregnancy and keeping the baby, or giving the baby up for adoption. How is a girl, 15 years of age, to go through these psychological and physical traumas? What will the consequences be of this situation on this girl's health? How is this child going to grow up after giving birth to another child? The main theme in schools and physician's offices in regard to sex education is to stress the use of contraception and avoidance of sexually transmitted diseases. However, little is spoken about sexual restraint and abstinence for these sexually active teenagers. Parents of these teenagers are either absent or don't have enough time to talk about this to their children. Proper upbringing and responsible behavior are words that are rarely used today. What is important for teenagers, is to be "cool" and accepted.

Parents who spend time with their children in order to give them a proper upbringing, to educate them and to establish healthy, human and normal relationships with their children, are making the most important and the greatest possible investment of their life. This investment of time and effort spent on one's children will pay off in the long run. Such an investment is more important than any other in life.

- How much is human experience worth, if it's not used?

Someone said a long time ago that history keeps repeating itself because we fail to learn its lessons. A generation gap is often mentioned as being proof of our inability to find common ground between older and younger people. In our childhood, the majority of adults had a chance to grow up in the presence of both of their parents, but also with the presence of grandfathers and grandmothers. In modern society many parents are divorced, children often grow up on the street and their grandparents are placed in homes for the elderly.

Every person is given intelligence to wisely plan their life and their future, and their children's future, and thus to influence the course of future generations. Why is this intelligence and responsibility often lacking?

A peace of grain from the physician's brain

Another research study discovered that children who watch more than 2 hours of television per day begin to be sexually active much earlier.

Here is a common sense question: Do we really need these studies to see what's evident, even to those who are completely illiterate? If children spend hours every day watching scenes of brutality and unrestrained sexual conduct, they will come to accept that this is a normal form of conduct. We have forgotten that children are best brought up and educated not by words but by deeds that they observe in others.

HOW TO DEVELOP AND APPLY YOUR OWN MIND?

- The brain or central nervous system is the most important and vital organ
- The brain is the control and coordination center for all vital functions
- All of our basic mental functions originate in the brain

The structures of the brain and brain functions were poorly understood for a long time and were the least explored region of the human organism, mainly because they were hidden from view and were inaccessible. The brain is composed of very sensitive material of brain tissue and this also prevented its exploration.

The human brain is composed of about 100 million brain cells that are all individually interconnected by an extremely complex net of thin cell extensions called dendrites and neurons. These cell extensions contain, on its ends, very sensitive receptors which touch each other in the form of a synapse. In these small synapses, originates everything that we think, feel and do. These synapses are very lively and are undergoing an endless process of change. Establishment of connections between synapses serves to form all of our memories and erasure of these synapses means that we will forget these memories.

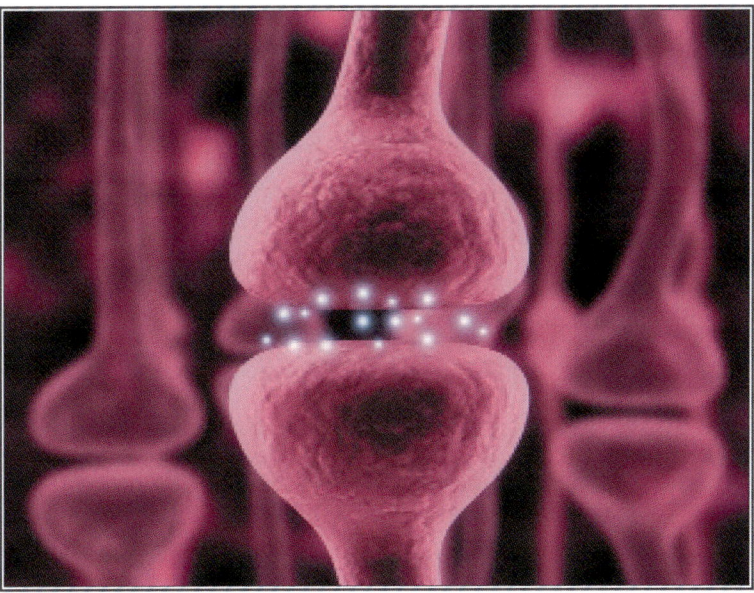

Synapses–a contact of nerve endings and a place of significant happenings

It was believed for a long time that thousands of these brain cells die every day (which is correct). However, since they are so numerous, the overall impact of this process is negligible. What has been proven in the last few years is that by specific stimulation of these brain cells, they can be made to multiply and to establish new synapses, and this means that new functions can be created (2).

Use it or lose it! This principle applies to all organs and tissues in the body, and particularly to the brain. The more we use our brain and other organs the more they develop and become more efficient. The greater and more complex functioning of the brain enables the creation of so-called neurotransmitters, which are special substances located between cell extensions or synapses.

The proof about the dramatic increase of the number of brain cells and their synapses has been discovered in the part of the brain called the hippocampus. This is an extremely important part of the brain responsible for memory and storage of long term memories.

■ **The brain is the control and coordination center for all vital functions**

Key factors in regards to the development and maintenance of mental acuity, clarity of thought and long term memory are learning and education, physical activity and emotional well-being.

Learning, curiosity and mental training promote critical thinking skills, contribute to plasticity and flexibility of memory, help to increase the number of brain cells and to improve the stability of their connections or synapses. Creative memory games, toy making or the making of useful implements and word games all serve to increase the work and quality of our brain functioning. All these processes represent a challenge for our brain functioning and serve to stimulate better blood flow in the brain. It was discovered that people who have higher levels of education and are more creative suffer less from dementia (which is a disease that leads to lower mental functioning and loss of memory) in their later years. Computer and video games which preoccupy the time of many children and young people have not yet been proven to have a positive effect on the development of their psyche or their brain.

By creative play, children grow both mentally and physically

Physical activity significantly increases blood flow into the brain. The brain is a big user of oxygen. Even though the brain represents only about 1.5% of the total body weight, it uses about 25% of the oxygen that is taken in through the lungs. That means that a working brain requires 25 times more oxygen than any other body tissue. Knowing these facts it's not surprising that regular exercise, physical activity or work and recreation all serve to increase blood circulation and to provide the brain with blood. By staying physically active you also contribute to brain growth, its development and proper functioning. That's not all, with better blood circulation there is faster elimination of unneeded substances from the brain such as carbon dioxide.

Emotional stability and balance. The purpose of life, existence of healthy and acceptable value principles, self-confidence and trust toward the family, relatives, friends and those that one lives with, provide a feeling of security, meaning and purpose. Sympathy, respect, understanding, support and love are all essential emotions, which are necessary if one is to lead a healthy and productive life. A good sense of humor and telling jokes, meditating, religious rituals and beliefs contribute toward emotional and mental stability. If we add to this, fulfillment of the basic problems of existence, such as proper accommodation, regular and healthy nutrition, continuous employment and a relatively stable financial situation, the conditions for the development of brain cells are assured.

■ **All of our basic mental functions originate in the brain**

Besides using previously mentioned mental stimulation to sharpen one's mental powers, such as learning, work, various exercises and through positive emotions, it's also possible to do this by paying attention to certain aspects of a healthy lifestyle.

Healthy and adequate sleep time. Sleep is an essential need of the whole body and, especially for the brain. People have different sleep needs and these needs will vary from person to person. However, the majority of people will feel refreshed and rested after sleeping for about 7 to 8 hours. In older people the need for sleep drops to about 6 hours. It has been proven that students, physicians and nurses who work late at night or during night shifts and other people who are unable to get sufficient hours of sleep, are less mentally alert and have a lower level of ability to concentrate, which means that their ability to perform productive work is also lowered.

Healthy nutrition. Eating a variety of healthy foods, that contain the proper quantity and balance of ingredients, contribute significantly to the development of our mental powers and intelligence. A healthy diet contains foods made from whole grains, a wide variety of vegetables and sufficient levels of proteins, carbohydrates, minerals and vitamins. Despite the fact that 90% of the brain is made up of complex fats, it's necessary to avoid foods containing a lot of fats from animal origin, to avoid saturated fats (read food labels!), and to avoid foods that are high in cholesterol. These fat loaded foods contribute to clogging up of the arteries and weaker blood circulation in the brain. The most important vitamins for the brain are from a group of Vitamin B, such as B1, B2, B6, B12 and folic acid because they are needed for increased growth and maintenance of brain cells. Vitamin C raises the stability of blood vessels and Vitamin E plays a very important role as an antioxidant, in order to reduce toxins in the blood.

Wheat is an important source of B vitamins

Stress coping skills. Long-term stress, tension, restlessness and anxiety lead to an increase of cortisone and adrenaline in the blood. These hormones serve to raise blood pressure, heart rate, muscle tension and lead to tiredness and pain in the muscles. They can block the development and growth of brain cells and thus inhibit and lower the effectiveness of mental functions, leading to the lowering of our capability for productive work, learning and memory. The most effective way to deal with stress is by learning and by being prepared to cope with life's challenges, duties and responsibilities. A deep breathing technique, relaxation and concentration toward solving problems, will all help to reduce the level of stress. Regular exercise, meditation, yoga, and muscle relaxation will help to reduce the level of surplus hormones. Consultation with an understanding friend, psychologist or a physician can also go far toward a real solution to one's problems.

Moderate use of alcohol and coffee. Alcohol is easily dissolved in the brain. Frequent use of alcohol can destroy a large number of brain and nerve cells, which can lead to very serious mental and neurological problems with long term negative consequences. Memory loss or memory damage, paralysis of nerves and certain parts of the body, damage to eyesight or hearing, loss of balance and depression, are just a few of these negative consequences.

The caffeine in coffee temporarily serves to increase the level of alertness and ability to concentrate but it does not lead to effective long-term learning and memory. High amounts of coffee (over three cups per day), increases irritability, creates confusion, leads to an inability to sleep and to secretion of stomach acids, and produces heartburn. Too much coffee also speeds up the loss of calcium from the bones, through the kidneys.

Smoking cigarettes is very damaging for brain cells and for blood circulation in the brain.

Limit time spent watching television. There are many scientific research studies which prove that watching television negatively affects our ability and process of thinking, and impairs our ability to be mentally creative. This is particularly true with pre-school children and school aged children.

Avoid routine-like behavior. Small changes in our daily routines such as writing or brushing your teeth with your left hand if you are right-handed, kicking of the ball with your other foot and memorizing telephone numbers, can help to improve your concentration and sharpen your mental powers. Learning to play a new musical instrument, learning a new language or listening to new music are just a few of new beneficial approaches to stimulate and to develop your brain cells and your memory.

A person will remain young at heart as long as they are motivated to learn new things, acquire new skills, habits and make new friends. In such a way they will ennoble their life and their thoughtfulness, and the lives of people around them. It's better to add life to your years, not add years to your life.

DEPRESSION–RESULT AND PRICE OF TECHNOLOGY?

- **Depression is a frequent chronic disabling disease**
- **What are the causes of depression?**
- **What are the symptoms of depression?**
- **How to help a depressed person?**

It is estimated by medical experts that at this moment in Canada there are 1.3 million people who suffer from depression. About 40,000 people are lost to the workplace because of depression and the price of treating depression is over 3 billion dollars. After physical injury, depression is the second leading cause of disability among employed people in this country. It's estimated that half of all people who have symptoms of depression don't seek medical help, and in this way do great damage to themselves, to their family and to their community. Today, depression is a disease which can be treated and controlled with much greater success than was the case several decades ago.

- **What are the causes of depression?**

There are many causes of depression. Personal psychological mechanisms, such as conditions of life and lifestyle, especially stressful factors like serious traumatic experiences in childhood or later on in life, have a significant role to play in the appearance of depression. It was discovered that people who live under difficult conditions, who were abused, (either psychologically, physically or sexually), show signs of serious depression in high percentage levels. People who have had traumatic experiences, such as a difficult illness, the loss of a loved one, divorce, death in the family, loss of a job, sooner or later show signs of being in a bad mood or of being depressed.

Life in dysfunctional families with constant arguments, misunderstandings and mistreatment, often leads to the appearance of depression and turning to bad habits, like drinking alcohol or the use of narcotic drugs. Depression occurs more frequently in some families mainly because of genetic causes, and partially because of the formation of one's personality in an unhealthy environment.

Social factors such as social isolation, loneliness, unemployment, lack of social contact or communicating with people, are all considered to be significant moments in the beginning of depression. Break-up of the family, the race for material goods, money and wealth, which lead to distancing from other people, cool emotional relations and the loss or reduction of the quality of life, are all contributing factors of depression.

The high level of technology, which overwhelms modern man, contributes to the development of depression. This technology includes television, computers, telephones, e-mail, high traffic congestion and public media, which offer us more information but less personal contact with other people. Children, as well as adults, spend hours at a time sitting in front of the television set or the computer, and have less and less time to spend with their friends, family or to go to social gatherings. The paradox is the fact that more exchangeable information leaves a person feeling less satisfied than they would be after a warm talk with a dear friend that understands and respects them. This is the crux of the problem. A person needs human contact, dialog, spoken words, an exchange of feelings, respect and recognition of human qualities, and these things can't be obtained from technology.

The biochemical base of all changes in depression is the breakdown in creation of certain chemical substances in the brain. These substances are called biogens amines or mediators. Neurotransmitters like serotonin, noradrenalin, and dopamine are created in sufficient quantity, but the whole process of chemical creation and dissolving of these substances in the body is happening in an abnormal manner. Most drugs that are applied to treat depression base their effect on correction of these mediators or substances which serve to produce a good mood.

There are several types of depression but the two most common types are, isolating depression, and depression that occurs in cycles and alternates, with a high level of activity with elements of abnormal behavior.

■ **What are the symptoms of depression?**

Symptoms of depression include; being in a bad mood with a feeling of loneliness and expression of sadness, being uninterested in most things about the external world, feelings of hopelessness and meaninglessness, as well as a feeling of personal worthlessness.

Depression manifests itself by a loss of interest in things, work or events that a person was previously interested in, such as contact with people who are close to them, with family members, co-workers, a failure to complete one's duties, and being late or avoidance of work or school.

The disturbance of sleeping patterns, in the form of too much sleep, or lack of sleep and insomnia. This shows up with the inability to fall asleep or to remain asleep for any extended period of time.

The disturbance of one's appetite usually manifests itself with a general loss of feeling for food and loss of weight, but can also be manifested by an excessive appetite and obesity, as a consequence of depression.

Loss of energy in the form of a feeling of weakness, reduction in work capability, and a presence of a constant feeling of being tired, even when one gets a full night of sleep.

Loneliness may be both the consequence and cause of depression

Having a difficult time concentrating and mental activity, which is reflected in being confused, making frequent mistakes, having a hard time remembering things, and having difficulty in learning new information.

Psychomotor slow down, in the form of slow speech and movement, which are significantly different from one's usual manner.

Loss of pleasure in life's simple joys, such as play, song, humor, as well as loss of interest in sexual pleasure.

Thoughts of suicide are the hardest and the most serious sign of depression and manifest themselves with thoughts on this theme, making plans to commit suicide, and sometimes going through with these plans.

A positive answer on five of the above named symptoms almost certainly shows the presence of depression which should be treated. Of course having self-destructive thoughts is all by itself a sufficient reason to visit your physician and to seek help, on the part of the patient or on the part of their family.

Depression most often manifests itself in people who are over 60 years of age. Depression is also more frequent among males, most often men who are unmarried or divorced and people who are unemployed. However, depression can appear among all age groups including very young children.

■ **How to help a depressed person?**

Depression is treated with the application of several basic therapeutic models, such as psychotherapy, drug therapy (pharmacotherapy) and social therapy.

- **The team of experts** used to treat depression should include a psychologist, a social worker and the patient's family.

- **The psychotherapeutic approach** begins with personal contact with the patient. The patient is encouraged to talk to members of their family and friends. We can help them to open up and share what is bothering them. An honest and confidential talk with a depressed person serves to unburden them and to find a way out of their crisis.

- **Psychotherapy** has many branches but the most important one is probably cognitive therapy, whose goal is to teach the patient how to change their negative approach and to open ways of hope, and to help them get out of a crisis. These patients need to be made aware that their subsequent failure and making mistakes are normal characteristics of all people.

It's necessary to awaken hope in a depressed person, to offer them new solutions to their problems and to make them understand that their crisis is only temporary. All these steps are the beginning of the process of healing.

- **Drug therapy** includes the use of very powerful antidepressant drugs that have a strong effect and if they are suitably chosen, can lead to full recovery (3).

- **Social therapy** implies involvement in the social life of the community, the family, friends and work environment. A person becomes humanized with personal contact with other people, when exchanging thoughts and feelings, and performing common work with them. The measure of our humanity is defined by our good treatment of ourselves and of other people. The development of one's humanity can significantly be influenced by healthy human relationships in the family and in the community where one lives and works. It can also be positively influenced by the cultural and spiritual creativity of man which includes; music, poetry, painting, philosophy and religion.

MIDDLE AGE CRISIS

- Is there such a thing as male climax?
- How does a middle age crisis among men manifest itself?
- What are the causes and changes of middle age crisis and males?
- What does modern medicine offer to postpone the aging process?

When he is about 10 years old, a little boy is impulsive, mischievous, full of energy and nothing is hard for him. When he is 15 years old, this boy is unreasonably self-confident, he believes that he can do anything and often acts in an unsuitable manner. When he is 20 years old, he is untamed, practically unshakable and is ready to make big decisions in life, such as the choice of career, life partner, society and community, in which he will work and live. When he is 30 years old, a man is at the top of his mental, emotional and physical energy level where he can offer the most to himself and to other people.

Then come the years of 40 or 50, which are years of reaching a plateau for many, but not for all, when a man reaches the top in his personal life, his profession and his community. Many men begin to stagnate and question the correctness of their decisions about the choice of career, marriage partner, friends and community in which they live and work. Not infrequently there are dilemmas about the success of the family, dissatisfaction with the behavior of their children and colleagues at work. Sometimes this is a consequence of being tired, having too many obligations and sometimes because of missed chances, inconsistencies and unrealized dreams. Then, maybe for the first time, among many men, there occur thoughts of the transitory nature of life and their own mortality.

From everything we learn at this stage of life, some things represent a true awakening and enlightenment. First a man comes to understand that life doesn't last forever and second, that some long held dreams will not be realized. Third is that many things begin to cause a lot less pleasure than they did in the past. This feeling of dissatisfaction is even more pronounced after 60 years of age. One of my friends summed this up nicely by saying, "More and more, I am less interested in trivial things."

How we approach this new found knowledge, of course, determines if we truly feel older or younger than our age. Disappointments happen at this time because many men realize that some of their life's choices were wrong. Other men are disappointed because they spend a lot more energy on less important things and their main dreams in life remain unrealized.

Today, modern medicine clearly distinguishes between **chronological age** (our actual age) and **biological age**, which is a lot more important. Biological age includes; how much vital energy we have, how we save and renew this energy, how we save our health, how powerful our motivation, creativity and willingness is to face new challenges and try new things. How much is a man prepared to continue doing good things, and to reject everything that is a diversion, and not beneficial. That's why middle age crisis occurs in some men much earlier, after they pass forty years of age. Some experience this crisis after they pass 50 or 60 years of age and some men never experience it. Men like this live with a feeling of satisfaction and a healthy spirit.

- How does a middle age crisis among men manifest itself?

Physical changes during this stage in life often manifest themselves as a feeling of sluggishness, lowered level of work energy, lowered effectiveness at work, lower level of mobility and with the appearance of obesity. Obesity is not just accumulation of fatty tissue but also includes significant loss of muscle mass, softening of the bones, lower level of growth and development of osteoporosis. To this are often tied other medical problems such as; high blood pressure, high cholesterol level, problems with the heart, stomach and a predisposition towards depression. A favorite sport that one participated in becomes less appealing with unconvincing justification to avoid physical recreation and to stay isolated from our friends, staying home in front of the television set with a fridge full of food and beer.

Biological age is more important than chronological–it may be slowed down

At the beginning, psychological changes are mild, almost unseen; they include forgetfulness, absentmindedness, and weak concentration. Much greater effort is needed to learn something than one needed before. Then confusion occurs, loss of self-confidence, apathy, being overly sensitive when talking to people who are close to them, such as family members and colleagues at work. Sometimes one gets really depressed and this manifests itself by complete withdrawal, isolation, loss of sleep, change in appetite and loss of interest in the pleasures of life. Some people simply notice that something significant is missing from their life, but are not able to fully define what this is (4).

Often, at this time of life, there occur sexual problems and there is a loss of interest in sex, accompanied, on occasion, by impotence. Studies show that over 50% of men between the ages of 40 to 70 years in Canada have partial or complete impotence, which is now called erectile dysfunction. Today, there is much talk about this and medical conditions for finding solutions to this problem are much more favorable than they were a few years ago. Today it's considered that the cause of male impotence in 80% of cases is due to problems of a medical nature, such as high blood pressure, high cholesterol, diabetes, nerve disease, operations, psychological problems, drugs and many other causes. Less is known about the negative side-effects of many drugs used to treat high blood pressure, stomach disorders, and psychological disorders, which can cause a loss of libido. Some of these drugs can cause loss of desire for sex (libido) and can also cause erectile dysfunction. Emotional and psychological problems can also be a cause of impotence. These problems can include disagreements and intolerance with one's spouse, cooling down of emotional relationships, and unfulfilled expectations.

New motives and new content in the mutual relationship between two partners are the basic regenerative mechanism of a healthy emotional relationship.

■ **What are the causes and changes of middle age crisis and males?**

There are many factors that bring about the appearance of premature aging. Feeling the passage of time, the burden of years and the stress that modern man lives with, along with many obligations, and lack of time to fulfill them, are perhaps only a partial answer. Larger factors include a pessimistic approach to lifestyle, unrealistic expectations and one-sided division of energy. All these factors certainly play a significant role in determining if one is able to achieve a happy and successful life. Good health and lifestyle implies the establishment of proper balance between one's personal life and professional career, and balance between one's emotional and mental needs, and needs of the family, friends and the community. The world's greatest scientists, artists, sportsmen and businessmen often lead an unhappy life only because they are unprepared, or are unable to find a true measure to establish a balance between all of their basic needs and obligations. A grown up, mature man functions best when he is constantly active and creative in all major fields of his needs and possibilities. People who are constantly engaged in doing things they love to do, will continue to remain active and creative for a long time. These active people don't have time to think about the passage of time.

The concept of "andropause" (andro=man) is equivalent to female menopause. And just like in women after they pass 40 years of age and there is a reduction in the main female hormone (estrogen), so in men there is a reduction in the production of the male hormone (testosterone). Testosterone is responsible for primary characteristics of masculinity, including the development of sexual organs, and for creation of healthy male sperm cells, as well as for the creation of a secondary nature of masculinity, like development of muscles and bones, body hair, deep tone of voice, male type of body and many other things.

Modern medical studies have discovered that there is a significant reduction in the production of testosterone among middle-aged men and that this is one of the possible causes of the so-called middle age crisis or andropause.

A loss of balance has many consequences–a frequent cause of crisis

■ **What does modern medicine offer to postpone the aging process?**

There are some common characteristics of all men who live a long and productive life. They all have a healthy and a good sense of humor, all are very active, they always find something that interests them and in which they find pleasure, they have new ideas and try to realize them, they are always ready to participate in sport or some type of recreational activity, and they have several good friends who have similar traits. Besides that, these people are more willing to orient themselves toward the future and to face new challenges, rather than looking back and lamenting about all that they could have done but didn't do. Men who live a long life see the meaning of their life and they know why they get out of bed every morning.

How to make a turn-around in one's life?

- In order to feel young and vital, **become an important part in the lives of others,** be understanding, loving and supportive, in the true sense of the word.

- **Discover the world through curiosity!** There must have been a lot of things that you wanted to do as a child but were unable to do. Now is the time to return to those things and to realize your dreams. Awakening your "inner child" means that you are inspired and childish, which is normal, but don't act in an infantile manner because that is being immature.

- **Advance your lifestyle.** A healthy lifestyle implies healthy nutrition, regular sleep, regular participation in physical activity or exercise and being engaged in interesting work or hobbies, which keep up your motivation and self-confidence. The main components of this type of lifestyle approach are to avoid the harmful effects of tobacco and to use a moderate amount of alcohol.

- **Develop your optimism.** The glass is always half full and not half empty. This is the essence of optimism. You now have more experience and more knowledge and this can help you to learn new things and new skills.

- **Become a role model to young people.** Teach them what you have learned, give them good lessons about life that you have learned, go to sports events with them and establish a good relationship with them.

- **Share your thoughts and feelings** with good friends. Having good friends is a powerful motivation for new demands and actions.

- **Consult with a good physician.** Have a medical check-up in order to make sure that you don't have high blood pressure, high cholesterol, diabetes, an enlarged prostate or some other medical problem. Consult with your physician if you have problems with sexual potency, even though this is a sensitive topic, it can easily be solved (5).

- **Consult with a psychologist** for detailed information about possible mental problems, such as being dissatisfied, having marital difficulties with your spouse, problems with your children and colleagues at work. A psychologist can help you to tap into new sources of energy in yourself and can help you to resolve misunderstandings you have with other people.

A man only lives his life once, and he should try to offer the most to himself and to others. There is no greater consolation in your old age than knowing that you have invested your time and energy in building up things that will last. There is a great satisfaction in knowing that you are leaving behind a spiritual inheritance.

INSOMNIA: GOOD MORNING, HOW DID YOU SLEEP?

- Good sleep is a basic need and a necessary condition for health
- Your biological clock was created through millions of years of evolution
- Sleep is an active process in the brain structures
- Why and who is robbing us of sleep?
- What are the most frequent causes of insomnia and how to remove them

An adult person needs an average of 7 to 8 hours of sleep per day. Of course, some people need more sleep and some people need less. Sleep is necessary for every organism in order for the body and soul to rest from daily chores, to refresh its energy and to prepare itself for a new day. The need for sleep arose as a result of natural daily cycles of day and night, light and darkness. Life awakens in the morning and all functions begin their daily cycle with the sun and with light. The sun is the basic source of everything that is alive, and night is reserved for rest and renewal of the organism.

Electric power offers many advantages–but night work and lack of sleep may lead to day-night rhythm disturbances with unhealthy results

This phenomenon is well known to all travelers who go from one end of the globe to another. Such a trip causes "jet lag" and disturbs a person's biological clock and rhythm. Several weeks are needed for the biological clock to get back to normal. Time used up on sleep is not wasted but serves to renew all the necessary vital processes in the human body.

- **Sleep is an active process in the brain structures**

Very significant vital processes occur during sleep. These processes take place in brain structures or the brain stem and in the reticulated mass of the brain and include; breathing, which deepens and slows down, the heart rate, which also slows down and eases with lower blood pressure. Both breathing and the work of the heart are controlled by special centers of the brain which are responsible for these most important functions in the body. Besides all this, there are particular hormones of wakefulness and hormones of sleep. During sleep the biggest part of the body mass such as muscles, bones and fat tissue are resting, while the liver, kidneys and lungs remove toxic and unnecessary materials and purify and renew the whole body. During sleep, human consciousness goes through five phases of which the first three phases are preparatory or superficial, while the last stages of sleep are the deepest. These last stages of sleep are characterized by complete relaxation of muscles and with deep breathing. The third phase of sleep usually produces the most varied and vivid dreams and can be recognized by rapid eye movement. The fourth and fifth phases of sleep are particularly important regarding preservation and regeneration of central mental functions such as learning, memory, understanding and creativity.

During sleep there is the greatest secretion of growth hormone and this is why it's so important for young people to get regular and sufficient sleep.

■ Why and who is robbing us of sleep?

With the development of civilization and especially with the discovery of practically limitless sources of electrical energy, night has been converted into day and sleep can be postponed late into the night. In this manner, not only the length of sleep is shortened but its quality has become endangered. Work continues throughout the night in many institutions and on factory floors. Medicine has proven that night work or the so-called night shift has a harmful effect on health. This type of work can cause conditions for chronic, long-term tiredness, lowers work and emotional energy, lowers work capability and immunity, and makes the body susceptible to other diseases. Not only that, lack of adequate sleep can also cause preconditions like tiredness, depression, irritability and high blood pressure which can lead to disease. In such a way, of course, the quality and longevity of life is lowered. In order to remain awake, a person often resorts to means which keep him or her awake. These include coffee, cigarettes, alcohol and sometimes drugs like cocaine, amphetamines and many other drugs. It is well known that coffee can keep one awake but leads to an increase of production of stomach acids. Coffee does not improve one's concentration and it doesn't improve one's ability to learn. Coffee also increases one's irritability and only postpones being tired. Alcohol and tobacco definitely have harmful consequences, which also applies in large measure to drugs.

A cup of coffee should be avoided 4-6 hours before sleep

■ The most frequent causes of insomnia and how to remove them?

Insomnia appears in more than one third of people in the general population. It occurs more frequently among older people. The most frequent causes of insomnia are psychological problems such as irritability, dissatisfaction, worry, fear, anxiety, tension, depression, emotional problems, family problems, problems at work and long-term stress. People who are employed have the above named problems because they are overburdened and tired, and those who are unemployed have the same psychological problems, as well as a fear of uncertainty and the struggle for existence. Other causes of insomnia are physical illness, such as back pain, bone and joint pain due to rheumatism, pain due to injury or tumors and cancers, or even pain caused by nerve disease. Many drugs which are used to treat pain, depression and high blood pressure can also cause insomnia (7).

An unhealthy lifestyle can also cause insomnia. Such a lifestyle would include; lack of physical activity, irregular, unhealthy and abundant food (especially meals taken later on in the day), and immoderate use of alcohol, tobacco or other stimulating substances.

How to regain healthy sleep?

- **Establish a regular rhythm.** In order to establish a regular day-night cycle it's necessary to have a regular routine, such as always going to sleep around the same time, which includes weekends. The establishment of a proper rhythm can enable a person to fall asleep easier and to have a deep and healthy sleep so that he or she will wake up rested and refreshed. The biological clock of the day-night rhythm weakens as one gets older and that's why older people often have problems going to sleep. Sometimes older people completely reverse their sleep pattern: they sleep during the day and at night they suffer from insomnia.

- **Avoid working at night or working a night shift.** Many people are not in a position to chose their work or to determine what hours they will spend working. However, if you have this choice, avoid working at night. Not all people are suitable to work at night. Some people tolerate such work easier and some people are not able to tolerate it. If you have a hard time working at night, either change your job or change your work hours. Your health comes first!

- **Regular and healthy nutrition.** It's necessary to take smaller meals of more easily digested foods. Avoid big meals and avoid eating anything for at least three or four hours before you go to sleep. One of the problems of contemporary man is that he takes the main meal later on during the day. So after a hard day at work, one's body continues to work hard, in order to digest food eaten during unnecessarily big dinner. An old Chinese proverb wisely says, "If you wish to live a long life, eat your breakfast alone, share your lunch with your friend and give your dinner to your enemy."

- **Stay physically active!** It has been proven that people who are in good physical condition, who exercise regularly or do some kind of physical work, have a much healthier sleep. The greatest physical effort should be performed during the day, and only take easy walks and participate in light recreational activity before going to sleep.

- **Set aside a time for relaxation.** After a hard day at work it's pleasant to relax for one or one and a half hours listening to good music, reading a book or watching a TV program (if you can find such a program that doesn't contain gun play, murder or brutal violence which will only serve to worsen your insomnia!). Such a period of relaxation is necessary in order to forget problems at work, your bills, misbehaving children, wars, floods and other disasters.

- **Establish an evening routine.** Relaxation, listening to music while brushing your teeth, taking a shower, or reading several pages of a good book, and then turning off the lights and going to sleep. If you are in an inspired and emotionally healthy relationship, of course, having good sex is often a good way to obtain pleasure and satisfaction, and this will also help you to fall asleep.

- **Avoid late afternoon and evening coffees** and taking in too much liquid, because this can increase your insomnia and can cause you to go to the bathroom, have a more difficult sleep and wake up more frequently. Certainly you should avoid sleeping pills, they serve to upset your natural sleep pattern and you can become overly dependent on them, which can become a disease all by itself. If you have to take sleeping pills, don't take them on a regular basis and don't take them for a long time. It's necessary to be under the care of your physician in regard to this.

- **Afternoon nap–yes or no?** There are people to whom a short nap in the afternoon is very pleasant, however, such a nap can often disrupt your night sleep. If you can refresh yourself with a 30 to 45 minute afternoon nap, which doesn't interfere with your regular work and night sleep, then everything is OK. There are people who don't need such a nap and they don't need to get used to such a nap. If you have taken a nap before you have reached the end of this article, then evidently you don't have insomnia. If you have managed to stay awake, then perhaps you will be able to learn something useful.

- **Anecdote at the expense of sleep:** A patient says to his physician, "Physician, I can't go to sleep, what should I do? "When do you usually try to go to sleep?" asks the physician. "In the evening and in the afternoon, I have no problem falling asleep, but in the morning, I can't even keep one eye shut!"

QUALITY OF LIFE, HEALTHY MIND AND MUSCLES

- A healthy mind gives us an advantage in questions of survival
- Health awareness implies a culture of nutrition and lifestyle
- How to obtain vitamins from the B group: B6, B12, Folic Acid and Vitamin D?
- Strong muscles and the ability to move are key factors of health

The latest findings confirm an ancient common wisdom: "The mind is king and strength rolls the log." Healthy nutrition and regular physical activity is necessary in order to preserve a healthy mind and strong muscles.

- **Health awareness implies a culture of nutrition and lifestyle**

The modern fast food industry has an interest in producing food faster and easier in order to earn more money. However, this means that they don't always take enough care about people's health. Food that is easy to obtain and is tasty isn't always the best or the healthiest type of food. Fast food is attractive to many people because it is widely advertised and attractively packaged, so that people, by taking the line of least resistance and without thinking about the consequences, continue to consume this unhealthy and harmful type of food.

Wheat, rye and rice are good source of B6 and B12 vitamins

Keeping in mind one's own health, many people should change their stance toward nutrition. This means cutting out fast and unhealthy meals and seeking out healthy food, which enables better functioning of the brain cells and contributes to stronger muscles.

- **How to obtain vitamins from the B group: B6, B12, Folic Acid and Vitamin D?**

Vitamin B6, B12 and folic acid are necessary substances for brain cells!

Besides a moderate amount of calories from sugar, protein and some fats, the brain needs vitamins from group B such as vitamin B6, B12 and folic acid. These vitamins are of essential importance for proper functioning of the brain, including learning, memorization and thinking. These vitamins are built into nerve cells and into cell borders known a synapses. Synapses connect together brain cells, one cell with another cell, and are continuously renewed if the brain is made to work or they deteriorate if the brain is in a passive state. It has been discovered that nutrition that does not contain these substances harms the brain so that the thinking process stops. When the brain stops functioning properly then conditions for manipulation and misuse are created. The ability to make judgments is lessened and a person easily comes to adopt the thoughts of others that are not always beneficial. If one doesn't get a sufficient amount of B12 it is more difficult to recognize and to solve different geometric shapes, such as triangles and squares. It is also more difficult to orient oneself properly in space and to estimate distances. These observations have a huge significance, not only in everyday life and in one's resourcefulness at home, but also when one is outside or driving a car.

In the absence of sufficient amounts of vitamin B6, test subjects had a lowered capability of listening to words and numbers, and in remembering them. Brain cells are constantly dying, and this is a normal process of aging, but this process can be postponed with active brain functioning, healthy nutrition and physical activity.

Vitamin B6 and B12 are found in abundance in grain based foods like wheat, oats, barley, brown rice, and in beans (good old beans!), lentils, millet, sea algae, fish and shellfish. These vitamins are also found in somewhat of a reduced quantity in chicken and beef. Folic acid is the main component of vegetables and green salads.

People who suffer from chronic gastritis and people over 60 years of age can suffer from inadequate amounts of vitamin B12, even if they are taking it in sufficient amounts because their body is unable to absorb this vitamin in their intestines. That's why it's important to take a sufficient amount of supplemental vitamins from group B in the form a multivitamin pill. Also consult with your physician in order to confirm the state of your health, before reaching this decision to take supplements.

- **Strong muscles and the ability to move are key factors of health**

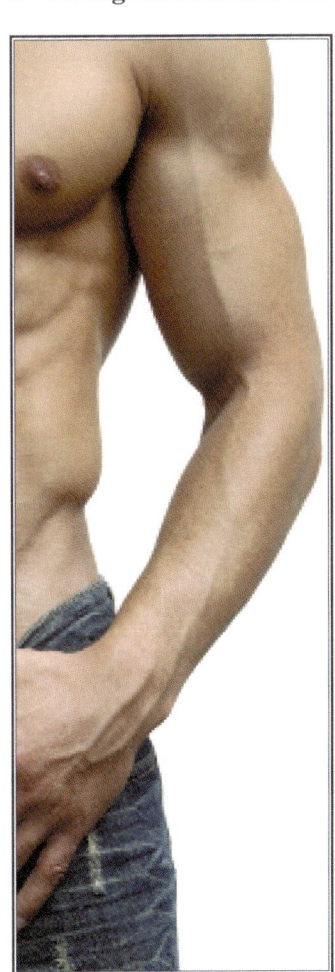

The human body is composed of about 25% to 30% of muscle mass. Muscle mass can be increased or maintained through exercise but can also be reduced with inactivity. Keeping one's muscle mass and muscle tone is of great significance in life because it enables better movement, better functionality, and ensures a better quality of life and greater longevity.

Have you saved your muscle reserve?

The muscle system in a healthy person needs to have a so-called functional reserve. This is the power and capacity to do 4 to 6 times heavier work than everyday activity. This physiological reserve is reduced as we age, but this process can be postponed, and your muscle reserve can be kept through regular activity and exercise, deep into your old age. If you are inactive, the number and thickness of muscle fibers is reduced. Fatty tissue accumulates between muscle fibers and this condition is called muscle degeneration.

How to strengthen muscle mass?

There are several types of exercise in order to strengthen your muscle mass. These exercises include; endurance training, flexibility exercises, aerobic exercise and weight training.

Studies were published recently which once again show that weight training is the best form of exercise to use in order to maintain muscle mass. By increasing muscle strength you can slow down or prevent deterioration of muscle mass. In many cases, weight training can help you to regain muscle tone to its previous size and strength in muscles that have atrophied due to inactivity.

Muscle build up and strong bones–essential health conditions

These studies were conducted with subjects who were older than 80 years. It was discovered that even people who were bedridden or who were confined to a wheelchair, were able to regain their movement and muscle strength by undertaking a systematic program of exercise. These people were then able to perform all everyday tasks such as; getting dressed, taking a bath, preparing their food, taking walks to the grocery store, and many other activities. The findings of these studies are of exceptional significance, as they show that with continuous, systematic activity and exercise, the quality of life of an individual (especially of an older person) can be significantly improved. This, in turn, serves to unburden and to ease the life of family members or the community. Of particular significance is the fact that strengthened muscle activity can greatly contribute to a lower cost of healing, and in such a manner can also greatly unburden the family and the wider social community.

Vitamin D for strong muscles and bones

Vitamin D is a complex substance which is created when skin is exposed to bright sunshine. In the upper regions of the globe and particularly in parts of the north, the amount of sunshine can be inadequate in order to synthesize sufficient amounts of Vitamin D. This particularly applies during the coldest winter months from November to February. Vitamin D is necessary for the normal functioning of muscles, the heart, nerves and bones. It enables the storage and binding of calcium in the bones, in a similar fashion that mortar binds bricks and gives it strength. It's particularly interesting that it was recently discovered that an adequate quantity of vitamin D lowers the risk of breast cancer in women and of prostate cancer in men.

Sources of Vitamin D

Vitamin D is contained in milk, because milk is enriched with this vitamin and it's also contained in some juices. The daily needs of vitamin D for the average person are about 200 units. These needs are greater for people over 40 years of age: 400 units. For people older than 50 years of age: 600 units. Women going through a post-menopausal period should take 800 units of vitamin D daily.

It's advisable for all adults to take supplements of vitamin D, especially during dark, cold winter months, and also to take a multivitamin supplement pill, which contains calcium, magnesium, iron, zinc and other minerals.

It's important to consult with your physician at this point because many people also suffer from other medical problems, such as high blood pressure, heart disease, diabetes, arthritis and rheumatic disease, and are taking other drugs at the same time.

The road to good health is not simple nor is it easy, but it always pays off in the end! Health is the basic need of every person and needs to be preserved.

Today, at a time of expensive drugs and inaccessible physicians, old wisdom is once again becoming paramount: A man or a woman is their own best physician. They need to educate themselves about health and to continuously work at this. Their reward will be a healthy body and a healthy soul from which come all other achievements.

THE HEALING POWER OF FORGIVENESS

- **Science is in agreement with the common wisdom of the people**
- **Anger is undesirable for both the body and the soul**
- **Anger harms the heart and the blood vessels**
- **Control of negative emotions through agreement and respect**

It is well known today that the most frequent causes of blood circulation problems such as a heart attack or myocardial infarct and strokes are high blood pressure, high fat content in the tissues, diabetes, obesity and stress.

- **Anger is undesirable for both the body and the soul**

Recently, the university clinic in London, England published their findings that clearly show that anger has very harmful consequences for health. This is the case both for healthy people and for people who already suffer from diseases of blood vessels, especially in the heart and in the brain. This study is of particular significance because it represents a meta-analysis (a study which encompasses many other studies on the same topic or problem). It was discovered that there were 25 studies done in various clinical centers in the world with healthy subjects, as well as an additional 19 studies with subjects who had signs of damage to their blood circulation.

Anger is often an introduction to aggression and violence

- **Anger harms the heart and the blood vessels**

By analyzing these studies, it was discovered that anger is a big cause in the worsening of diseases of blood circulation and more often leads to the appearance of heart attacks or strokes. To make things more interesting, it was discovered that this effect of anger is more pronounced in men than it is in women. It was not certain if women possessed a greater biological defense against anger or maybe have an easier time to forgive. Anger is a negative form of stress that leads to a long-term increase in the production of hormones, such as cortisone and adrenaline, in the blood. These hormones lead to a prolonged spasm of blood vessels. This impairs blood circulation and lowers the amount of oxygen that is supplied to vital organs such as; the brain, the heart, kidneys and the liver. The authors of these studies recommend that patients be under regular care of a physician and consult with a psychiatrist in order to help them solve problems they have with other people who have different opinions, without resorting to anger. It would be abnormal if everyone thought the same about important things. This difference of opinion is the cause of many disagreements in personal relations, in the family, in marriage, with friends or in the wider arena of international relations. This difference of opinion is often the cause of conflict, starting with quarrels of little children. It leads to misunderstandings between friends and causes marriage break ups, and can even lead to outright war between countries. All you need to confirm this is to look at people around you and look at the current state of international and economic relations between different countries today!

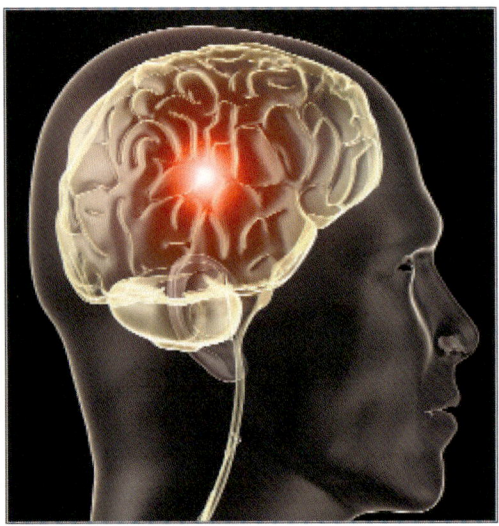

With hindsight as experience, common wisdom concludes that anger is not good for either the person that is angry or for the person that this anger is directed against. There is a good saying among the people, "If you want to solve a problem, you should approach it with a warm heart and a cool head." This means that one treats problems with a feeling of love and wisdom. (For those who wish to read the original article: Chida, Y. and Steptoe, A. "The association of anger and hostility with future coronary heart disease; a meta-analytic review of prospective evidence." *J. Am. Coll. Cardiol. 2009, 53:936-946*).

Where does anger come from? Anger, rage, being upset and fearful, come from the same group of defensive reactions that originate in the lower parts of the brain. These reactions have a biological usefulness of defense in conflicts. This is described in physiology as a basic reaction of stress, or fight or flight syndrome. Biologically, it's expected that this state doesn't last very long. It can last from several minutes to several hours. In modern man, unfortunately, stress can often last for a very long time, and produces negative consequences both for physical health and for spiritual life (8).

Humans have a well developed greater brain, with a pronounced brain cortex, which enables the development of consciousness and control of primitive reflexes of anger, and what is extremely important, the development of the possibility of agreement, such as verbal, emotional and social agreement. Thus, a mature person with his or her culture, humanity, nobility, empathy and respect of other people, looks for solutions to disagreements without anger and without conflict. In this manner, he or she avoids their own stress and avoids the negative consequences of this stress. This person avoids exposing others to unpleasant things that they themselves don't wish to be exposed to. Common wisdom says, "Don't do to someone what you don't want done to you." Forgiveness is a very significant psychological category. A person forgives other people for his or her own sake but also for the sake of other people. According to the Bible, Christ said while he was on the cross being crucified, "Forgive them Father, for they know not what they do!"

- **Control of negative emotions through agreement and respect**

What makes human beings human and what makes them happy is establishing good relations with those with whom they live, through understanding, respect, love, cooperation at home, at work, and in the community in which they live. It's well known, from history and psychology that people draw much closer to each other during times of suffering, crisis and wars, than they do in time of material abundance and peace.

Getting close to people and the development of spirituality begins at home. This is the best medicine against unhealthy relationships and constant anger. Pay attention to your children, ask for their opinion before you command what and how to do things. See what they are doing and with whom, and how they are spending their time. Every day I see children that have become strangers to their own parents that are unable to deny themselves momentary pleasures, who are poor students, who use alcohol and drugs, and unfortunate girls who become pregnant when they are 13 or 14 years old. The most frequent cause of this situation is that these children are not receiving proper love and care from their own parents, who are too busy, and this only serves to produce even bigger problems.

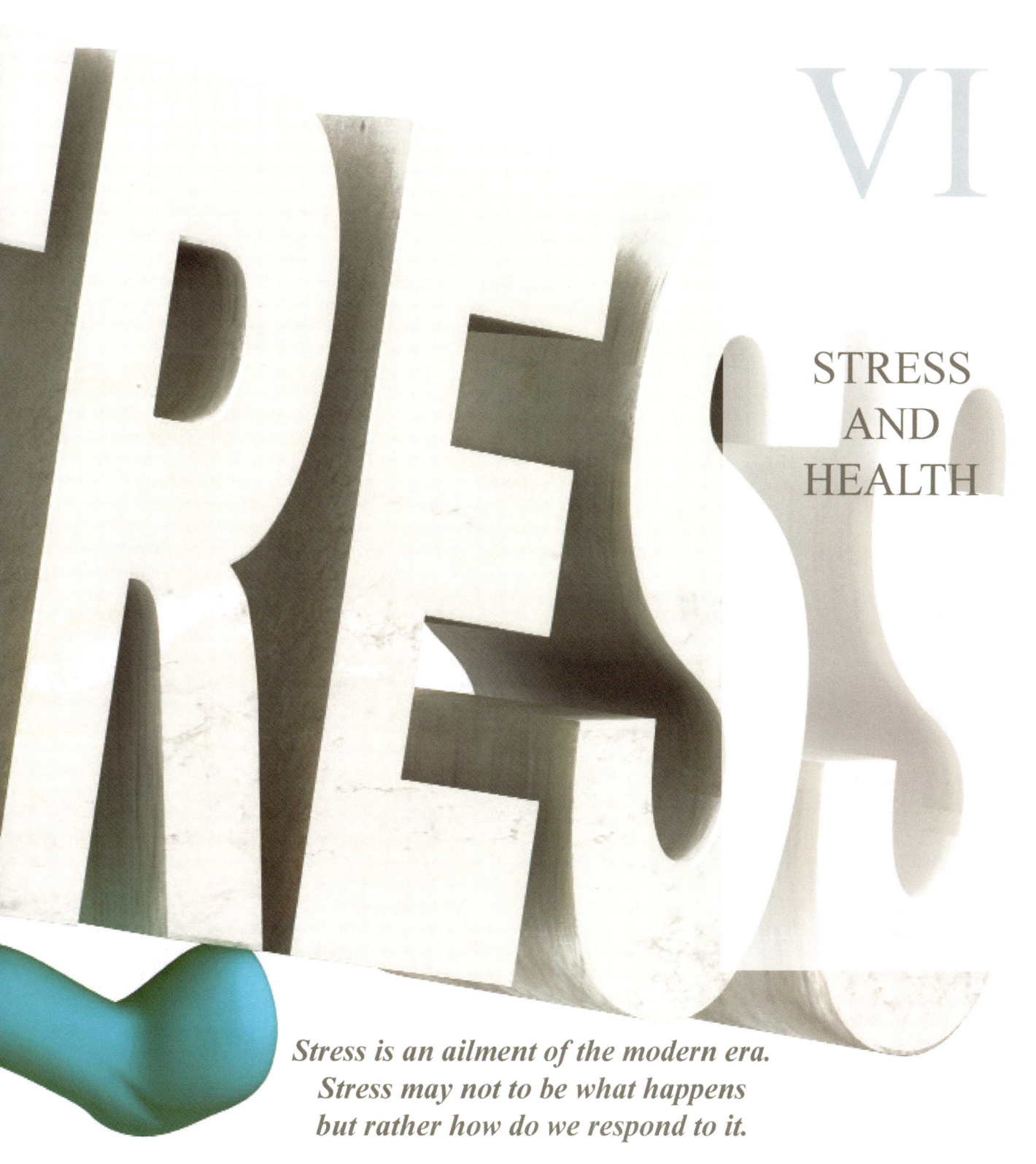

VI

STRESS AND HEALTH

*Stress is an ailment of the modern era.
Stress may not to be what happens
but rather how do we respond to it.*

STRESS AND CHRONIC STRESS–THE MODERN AGE DISEASE

- How does science define stress?
- The race for money, career, material goods, is endless
- Testing the level of your stress
- Chronic stress harms both psychological and physical health
- How to recognize chronic stress in oneself and in others?

Every day I see people who are tired, exhausted, dissatisfied, and people who complain that they are too busy and don't have enough time. No one is satisfied, neither the people who work nor the people who wait for them at home. One professional truck driver says, "I don't know how long I can last. I am on the road constantly in my truck and either I am sleeping or I am driving. I have to pay my bills, to pay my debts, my children are still in school." His wife stays alone at home with the children. She is busy doing house chores but is not happy. She is depressed, as she doesn't see where it will all end and she has lost the sense of it all. She says with a deep sigh, "I feel like an empty toothpaste tube, there is nothing left to squeeze out of me." Both the husband and the wife need help.

Lengthy time sitting at a computer is stressful to the eyes, neck and back muscles

How does science define stress?

What is stress really? Stress is an approach or an attitude toward things, life and problems. For one person, something can be a challenge or even an inspiration, and for someone else this same thing is a problem. Stress begins when you consider something to be a problem. Probably the best definition of stress is: stress is not something that is happening around us or inside us but is defined by how we react to it. Stress is the answer of the body to our perception and our observation of reality, as we want it to be and not as it really is. If a person feels that his or her duties are greater than his or her momentary ability to fulfill them, then that person will experience stress. If stress continues for a long time, it can have harmful consequences on health.

Every person perceives things differently and the same person can react to the same situation at different times in a different manner. Stress is the feeling of anxiety that we develop when demands are placed on us that go above our ability to solve them or to complete them on time. Stress is a signpost of adaptability. The more stress there is, the less is our ability to adapt. With a wise effort and learning, this ability to cope with stress can be successfully rewarded.

The race for money, career, material goods, is endless

The human organism is a perfect creation. It's very complex, but it's flexible and very adaptable. In other words, when body and soul are in balance, there are great possibilities, but there are also limitations. These limitations need to be recognized and respected. Humans are created so that they can function for a very long time if they work at a moderate rate, if they eat a moderate amount of food, if they take time to rest and take care of other aspects of their life (9).

A person will function at an optimal level if he or she works at a reduced capacity. It's been estimated that this ideal rate is about one quarter or 25% of one's full potential and work capacity. The energy reserve that is left is needed for other activities which life demands, especially when one needs to make exceptionally hard efforts like a fight for survival under a lot of stress. Such a stressful situation shouldn't last for a long time: the most it should last for is several minutes or several hours. After this, it is necessary to take a serious, long rest and recovery period.

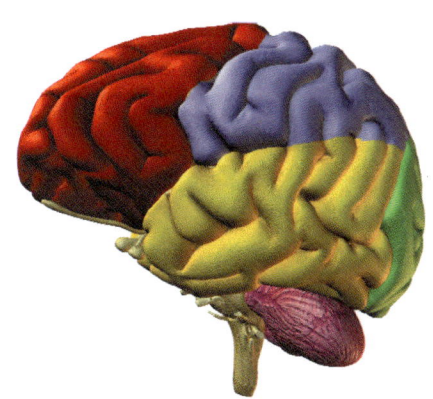

However, in the economically developed countries, which include Canada, there are a lot of demands placed on time of people who work. They need to work a lot, for a long time and to work hard (10). This means that one is under stress, one gets tired and one doesn't have a lot of time to do other, often more important things. Such things as satisfying personal emotional and spiritual needs, spending time with one's family and friends, participating in sport, recreation, music, art and some interesting hobby.

Stress is an intense emotion and it may reduce the reasoning and memorizing

What types of changes in the body are produced with stress?

The feeling of stress increases sympaticus system tone, a part of the autonomic nervous system that directly, or through the hormone of adrenaline, controls the work of the heart, blood pressure, pulse, increases the amount of sugar in the blood, and also increases the tension in the muscles, controls our state of being awake, controls the number of white blood cells in the blood, speeds up breathing and expands the breathing passages. With all these functions, the body gets ready for greater effort, for a "fight or flight" reaction, which doesn't always have a literal meaning in the modern world but certainly has a figurative meaning. If you don't finish your task, if you don't perform your duties, if you drive over the speed limit, you will soon see the consequences. At your job, you will complain to your boss or get fired, you will argue with your spouse, and you will receive a warning or a fine if you break the rules of traffic.

With what symptoms does stress manifest itself?

The effects of stress can be recognized by various signs they leave on different organs and systems in the body, including:

- **the nervous system;** headache, insomnia, irritability, weakness, absentmindedness and exhaustion. There is a psychological feeling of tension, worry, insecurity, fear, emotional instability, loss of interest in sex and loss of self-respect.

- **the heart;** chest pains, speeding up of heart rate, arrhythmia and numbness in arms and legs (11).

- **the digestive organs;** dry mouth, nausea, bloated stomach, poor digestion of food, diarrhea or constipation and loss or an increase of body weight. There can also be a frequent urge to urinate, muscle tension, sweaty palms and many other symptoms.

It's always wise to consult with your physician to rule out the presence of other diseases.

Young, employed mothers are frequently stressed out

■ Chronic stress harms both psychological and physical health

If you live under stress for a long time, the consequences are many. Here are just a few of these consequences: high blood pressure; disturbed heart rhythm; heart attacks; strokes; headaches; insomnia; tiredness; exhaustion; lowered capacity for work; choking for breath; asthma; pains in the muscles; loss of menstruation; infertility; reduction of immunity; and a predisposition to catch infections.

Stress can also lead to a predisposition to developing malignant diseases and cancers, as well as many other diseases. Everything depends on the type of personality you have. A person with A-type personality is overly ambitious and is often called a "workaholic". A lot also depends on your genes and many other factors. A small amount of neuroticism is useful and stimulating but too much neuroticism leads to disease. According to the opinions of some psychologists, all great scientists, artists, writers, philosophers, theologians and other brilliant people, were slightly neurotic. They were dissatisfied with existing reality, so they tried and often succeeded, in improving and changing reality for the better.

Chronic stress, tiredness and exhaustion are harmful for one's health. They produce tenseness, irritability, depression, isolation and dissatisfaction. Because of this, there is a cooling down of relationships between one's spouse and children, and one becomes withdrawn from one's own family.

Chronic stress leads to high blood pressure, clogging up of the blood vessels and can cause heart attacks or strokes. This is not the end of the matter. Tiredness and stress lead to exceptionally lowered immunity, which means that one is more prone to get infected, to develop auto-immune diseases such as rheumatic disease, and what is even worse, to develop malignant diseases in the form of different types of cancer.

By not finding good solutions to their stress, people often succumb to drinking too much alcohol, smoking cigarettes and sometimes using recreational drugs, which only serves to harm their health even more.

It appears that women who are employed experience more stress than men who are employed. The cause of this is very simple. Despite working outside the home, a woman is not freed from having to do all her chores when she returns home such as; cooking, cleaning and taking care of the children.

■ **How to recognize chronic stress in oneself and in others?**

- Are you too tired and busy to regularly play with your friends?
- Are you afraid or do you feel afraid to go to work?
- Do you feel uninspired to solve problems at work?
- Do you feel as if nothing special is waiting for you in your life?
- Has someone told you that you are sarcastic and cynical?
- Do you lack true inner self-confidence?
- Do you often think that all this is meaningless?

If your answers are "yes" to only two or more of these questions, then psychologists would consider that you are under a great deal of stress, that you are practically burned-up and exhausted and that you need help.

How not to burn up and how to save one's health?

- *Take a few days off from work to rest up and get lots of sleep.*

- *Go somewhere where you can be alone with your family for several days. Have a good talk with your family. Come to a decision about what is most important in your life and what you have to do, and what you can postpone doing. What are the priorities in your life that you need to be devoted to; your health and your whole family's health and having good communication with members of your family? It's vital that you maintain good relationships with members of your family and that your relationship is based on mutual agreement, respect, love and understanding.*

- *If your work is the problem, then work only as much as you can, and do work that is most suitable for you. Tailor your work to your capabilities and needs so that work doesn't become burdensome. If you are not able to perform all the work that is required of you, then you should look for a new job, because there are a lot of other jobs and there will always be someone who will value what you do.*

- *Talk to your friends or to your physician, psychologist, advisor and to someone you trust. Psychological studies have proven that networks of family and friends play a determining role in helping you to avoid burn-out.*

- *Introduce something new into your life, such as a new hobby, new interest and play with your children or your friends. Try to maintain a regular level of recreational activity at least 2 to 3 times per week.*

- *Make short and long-term plans. Inform your family members about this and seek their help, because you will also help them with their plans. Doing something together, especially if it's creative, serves to bring people closer, and gives them self-confidence, feelings of achievement, and a sense of purpose.*

- *Be realistic in taking stock of your energy reserves. As you age, you will have less energy, so you should adjust your obligations in order not to be frustrated if you are not able to complete everything that you planned to do. Be ready to say: "Sorry, but I can't do it, because I have to do things that have a greater priority."*

- *It's particularly important to be kind to yourself and to other people. You need to love yourself! If you don't love yourself, how will you be able to love other people? This same principle applies to trust and respect. Express your thankfulness to people who have helped you and who have helped to teach you something. Write a short letter expressing your thanks to these people and you will feel a lot better.*

- *Save yourself from stress and from having tense relationships with others. You can celebrate various holidays but control how much food and drink you have during these celebrations!*

HOW TO SURVIVE PSYCHOLOGICAL STRESS AFTER TRAUMA?

- Mass destruction during war can leave long-lasting psychological consequences
- Normal reactions to personal suffering, loss of family, destruction and expulsion?
- How to save one's own integrity, help oneself and others?
- Who to consult about healing and how to find help?

A lot has been said in public and medical literature in the last few years about post-traumatic stress that surrounded about 10 million Americans at the time of the terrorist attacks in New York. Medicine has been aware since ancient time about serious psychological traumas that people experience during wars, earthquakes and other mass destructions.

Destruction caused by wars in Yugoslavia during the 1990's destroyed thousands of innocent people, families and homes. If we just ignore massive financial losses, people's suffering and trauma will be felt for many years to come. Many people will carry this trauma all their lives.

One of the many exiles from Yugoslavia came to my office to seek help. He was about 50 years old but looked much older. He had a deeply wrinkled dark face with dried up eyes without any gleam or happiness in them. He was gray-haired. His teeth were mostly missing. He was skinny, bony and he was twiddling his hands and fingers, with a far off look on his face. His voice was filled with sadness and pain as he said, "Half my family was wiped out, my property was robbed and my home was burned. I was in a concentration camp for six months. I can't describe how I suffered there. These pictures of the past are always before my eyes. I can't sleep, I have nightmares, it's like I am in some kind of delirium. I can't find rest, I can't eat and I can't do anything. I don't know if it was better to survive my suffering there or to run away from there. Now I find myself in a completely strange country, unusual and foreign. People don't understand me here, even when I find the right words."

Why people choose war instead of peaceful solutions?

There are a lot of stories like this. Every story is true and every story describes the fate of innocent men, women, children and old people.

■ **Normal reactions to personal suffering, loss of family, destruction and expulsion?**

What are normal reactions to this type of stress? Intensive psychological stress caused by misfortune or traumatic events begins a whole series of reactions; including fear, anger, intense revolt, deep pain, confusion and worry. Different people react in different ways. Some people are possessed by paralyzing panic filled fear, some people are motivated to defend themselves and people closest to them. After these initial reactions come depression, sadness and sorrow, as well as:

- Shock–characterized by unbelief and rejection of what had happened;
- Anger–with a strong explosion of emotions, crying and a feeling of guilt (wasn't there something that could have been done?);
- Sadness and grief–for losing loved ones, friends and properties that one worked extremely hard in order to obtain;
- Depression–with a feeling of despair, helplessness and hopelessness; and
- Reconciliation and acceptance of reality and a gradual resumption of normal activities as much as is possible.

Every one of the above named phases can last different lengths of time and can manifest in different ways among different individuals with different personality types. Many people become overly sensitive, nervous, have a lower level of concentration and work capability. They also experience exhaustion. Feelings of loss of self-confidence, insecurity, meaninglessness and hopelessness become long-term, and sometimes life-long, followers and barriers.

The main characteristics of post-traumatic psychological stress: remembering tragic events in vivid pictures and scenes, nightmares with flashbacks from the past and hallucinations. This can occur in waves and can be a trigger for remembering people, objects, scenes from the past, or appearance of typical sounds, noises, voices or even the same type of weather. Re-living these scenes can be followed by an exceptional feeling of unease, rapid breathing and pulse, sweating or feeling of pressure in the chest or in the stomach.

Many people with this type of experience and psycho-trauma lose trust in people, have a hard time making long-term relationships, become overly sensitive, easily upset and often retreat and isolate themselves (they want to be left alone).

■ **How to save one's own integrity, help oneself and others?**

How to help oneself and other people? Express your feelings freely, expose them to the light of day, talk to a good friend or a reliable person like your physician, who has time to hear you out and to understand you. By recognizing and freeing your emotions, you reduce inner tension and will feel better.

Take care of yourself by taking good nutrition, ensuring that you get enough rest and healthy sleep, and enough recreation and exercise. Good food supplies us with energy and serves to renew the body. Sleep regenerates the body, and exercise and recreation help one to relax and to release tension.

Establish new contact with members of the family and friends. They can offer you understanding, support and advice. With good support and understanding, a person will feel better and will be able to carry the problems of stress with greater ease.

The establishment of regular activity and obligations. Seek out a path into an active life and open new ways into the future. Activity offers a new feeling of meaning and value. It helps to create new hope.

Postpone making important decisions. The ability to make good judgments can be lowered under the influence of stress and under the influence of intense negative emotions. By re-energizing yourself with new energy and new hope, you will be able to make better decisions.

Avoid harmful habits and unhealthy forms of solutions for stress, such as alcohol, tobacco, drugs, passivity and idleness. Harmful habits not only harm one's health but also lead into a dead end and new depression.

The innocent are frequently exposed to undeserved suffering

- **Who to consult about healing and how to find help?**

Who needs a special type of help? Persons who have both physical and psychological injuries, who have already had problems with health, and emotionally unstable persons. Persons who are preoccupied with depression or thoughts of suicide should seek professional help. A physician, psychiatrist or a psychologist can offer, in the course of several sessions, understanding, support and treatment. A majority of people can be helped when they learn about psychotherapy, or are educated how to resolve stress and can sometimes be helped through the use of moderate amounts of medications. Techniques of relaxation, change in mental approach and seeking new motives, can all lead to a real regeneration. People who refuse help should receive special care from their relatives and from people with whom they live. The first step forward is always the hardest.

The mental approach is the way we look at life, how we look at ourselves and how we view our community around us. A person will be able to more easily tolerate their own suffering if they understand it. Grief can mean something if we know what its causes are, if we can see the end to this suffering, and if we are able to learn something from it. Suffering teaches us to be able to forgive and in such a way, to become better people, more ennobled. The meaning of life consists in how it's lived, through activity, work, happiness, creativity, love and by establishing healthy relationships with people around us.

Childhood: priceless treasury of the mature adult

The psychological health of an adult person continuously uses up its motives which can be derived from different sources. These motives are most frequently derived from one's childhood, both from positive and negative experiences in our earliest period of life, especially the first ten years of our life. When they asked one poet where he found his inspiration for the magnificent poetry that he wrote, he said, "All my inspiration, motives, happiness and ideas come from my earliest childhood. My childhood was full of happiness, joy, spontaneity, full of play, understanding, love and creative responsibility."

This knowledge is often confirmed by many long-term psychological studies. The roots of the personality of the child and of the future man or woman, including their curiosity, creative play, approach to life, learning through trial and error, and responsibilities–with the support and supervision of parents, are built during these first years of life. All motives from our early childhood remain in our subconscious and tend to be repeated in the life of an adult (12).

Sadly, the same principle applies to negative experiences we have in early childhood. Recently, there was a large multi-year study conducted by pediatricians, psychologists and whole teams of experts who used a large number of children to conduct this study. The team of experts reached a conclusion that children who grow up in unhealthy and dysfunctional families with emotional, verbal or physical abuse, or in families of alcoholics or where there was abuse of drugs, have many more problems when they grow up. Children who were exposed to just one type of abuse have an 80% chance to be exposed to another form of abuse. From this group of children, later appear antisocial and asocial types of behavior, such as rejection of responsibility, running away from school, abuse of alcohol, tobacco and drugs, stealing and criminality. The early appearance of dissatisfaction turns into depression and depression becomes the cause of a new cycle of health problems such as social isolation, high blood pressure, and often leads to obesity, diabetes, high levels of cholesterol, heart disease and serious diseases of the bones and joints.

Recommendations for parents: your child should be your highest priority in life and deserves to have your full care, time, concern and love, which should help them to become responsible for themselves and for other people later on in life.

Recommendation for physicians: if you have a middle aged man or woman in front of you who is suffering from depression, has high blood pressure, is obese or has diabetes, isn't the main cause of their current problems a common cause of trauma they received in their early childhood? If you have in front of you a parent with a child, ask them how and how much time they spend with their child? The way to truth is long and hard, but usually pays off in the end and people will be grateful for it.

STRESS AND TIREDNESS: PATIENT'S AND PHYSICIAN'S RIGHTS

- The modern lifestyle imposes great obligations on patients and physicians
- Stress is the main component of many professions
- Physicians belong to a profession with the greatest level professional responsibility
- Tiredness of physicians not only harm their health but also their patients' health

The fast pace of time that we are living in imposes big duties on every individual. There are duties which we owe to our self and to our profession, duties we owe to our children and our family, and duties which we owe to our society and community. All the present forms of modern technology in medicine have not served to lower the complexity of a physician's calling and profession, but have only served to make his/her work more complex. Today, it is much harder to be a physician, their duties are much greater than they were 20 to 30 years ago. There has been a great increase in new scientific medical knowledge and there are many more complex technological innovations and medical equipment that is used today. The number and type of medical procedures used to establish a diagnosis or treatment is much greater. The number and type of drugs has also increased tenfold.

What is ironic is the health of the general population in some aspects is better, but in other aspects many people are still ill and more people make physician's visits. The problem of infectious diseases and lack of adequate food are significantly less but, despite this, there are other problems of health which have appeared such as: eating too much; obesity; diabetes; malignant diseases; traffic accident injuries; depression; anxiety; and the state of chronic stress. These above named facts have served to increase the scope of a physician's work and responsibilities.

However, personal contact, a warm human word, understanding and comforting words can't be replaced with any type of new technology.

- Stress is the main component of many professions

To be a physician is stressful all by itself. According to psychological criteria the most important personality traits of physicians are:

- Continuous learning and staying up to date about new medical knowledge from books, journals, of professional conferences, symposiums, the internet and other sources of information;

- Self-discipline and renunciation of pleasures, long hours of work, night shifts, irregular nutrition, lack of adequate sleep and rest, and rare and irregular exercise. This list can be extended with renunciation of emotional, cultural and other needs;

Physicians are frequently stressed out

- Conscientiousness, diligence, persistence, even obsessive behavior, which are classically recognized personality traits and allow them to become physicians and to maintain their calling but, at the same time, these traits are a cause of excessive stress;

- A strong motive to satisfy the needs of the patients and not requiring to be praised or thanked for this are the sign of the usual approach of physicians;

- An exceptional feeling of responsibility toward one's work and a feeling of guilt if their own expectations are not fulfilled;

- The need for self-control and to be under control, and have insight about every patient and his or her medical history, diagnosis, and treatment, as well as to have insight about the system in which he or she is functioning during every moment, can also produce stress; and.

- An occasional feeling of insecurity (Have I learned everything that I need to know?) from which comes the conclusion that one needs to work even harder and to learn even more.

- Physicians belong to a profession with the greatest level professional responsibility

Exceptional professional responsibility, long and exhausting hours of work leave little time and energy to perform other obligations and needs like personal, emotional, physical, psychological, family and socializing needs. At the same time, this situation creates conditions for misunderstandings with one's spouse, children, friends and community.

The nature of a physician's calling, which consists of persistence, endurance, the long-term ability to tolerate tiredness and suffering, enables a physician not to admit to themselves and to others that he or she is not feeling well. In such a way, he/she postpones the prompt taking of rest and looking for help and his or her stress just gets worse.

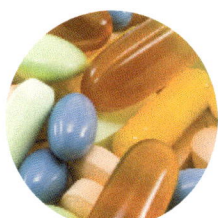  

Pills, alcohol, cigarettes and drugs–unhealthy stress solutions

Physicians are just like other people who are prone to get tired, stressed out, to get ill and to experience other weaknesses. A substantial number of physicians rush to use drugs and alcohol, which only temporarily postpones their stress and complicates it even more and can lead to disease. The most frequent diseases that these stressed out physicians succumb to are where they are most overburdened; their psychological and nervous systems, and as a result they experience depression and anxiety.

■ Tiredness of physicians not only harm their health but also their patients' health

What are the signs of being exhausted or "burned-out" among physicians:

- Emotional exhaustion: a person somehow manages to finish their work day, but when they return home they don't want to do anything, they are very irritable and they feel too tired;

- Social isolation: a physician who is too tired often doesn't have strength for social gatherings, and thus withdraws and isolates himself or herself; and

- A feeling of lowered level of achievement because of lack of satisfaction, and lack of appreciation and recognition for their good work. Because of this, many physicians are seriously considering leaving their profession and finding some other type of work.

What are the warning signs?

Feeling tired, being in a bad mood, appearance of diseases, and pains and negative thoughts are usually the first signs that a physician is too tired and over-worked. Such signs also occur in other people who are exposed to similar conditions at work.

Problems at work, less contact with colleagues, not attending important professional meetings, and problems in the family and with close friends.

Often there is a significant increase of bad habits with the intention to lower levels of stress. These bad habits include: immoderate use of alcohol, painkillers, and tranquilizers.

How to resolve stress?

A key factor is to re-establish a balance between all one's obligations and needs. In order to unburden themselves of stress, physicians, like other people, must find a proper balance between their personal, professional, family and social needs and obligations. How to achieve this (13)?

- Rationally arrange one's time and energy, and develop a daily, weekly, monthly and long-term program of activity, which includes; work, learning, family time, time to be spent with colleagues, friends and time spent on rest and relaxation.

- Satisfy one's basic personal needs on a regular basis. Taking regular healthy nutrition, set aside time for good sleep, participate in a regular program of physical activity and meet one's emotional needs.

- Make a list of priorities. It's definitely clear that not all things are of equal priority. Things on this list of priorities should be arranged according to what is most important so that we will be able to complete things that are most important first.

- Planning. Most important events can be foreseen and planned for, so that solving these things can be less stressful.

- You must learn to say, "No" to things that are unrealistic and that go outside the bounds of normal behavior.

- Create regular short periods of rest, change of activity and location at least 2 to 3 times per year.

- Adopt and apply techniques of relaxation, and release of tension through music, reading a good book, sport, meditation or religious ritual. These activities serve not only to provide rest but also to regenerate both the body and the soul.

- Consult your own personal family physician, approach him or her as a patient and explain to them what health problems and complaints you are having. Attempting to heal yourself and members of your own family is not recommended.

- Free yourself of the feeling of perfectionism. Many physicians are overburdened by the need to do everything perfectly. Perfection may not be possible to achieve, nor is it necessary. "We don't need to be perfect, we just need to be good enough!" according to modern psychology. One needs to have realistic expectations.

- It's very important to achieve financial effectiveness and balance. Being able to properly handle money is a significant aspect of a healthy life. There is a common saying which says, "It's harder to save money than it is to earn it." A person needs to invest in their basic needs, above all else, in their own education and education of their own children. This is something that brings happiness and satisfaction, and particularly benefits us in the long-term.

- The race for money often consists of a desire to obtain material goods and material riches which can be its own goal. The best, most beautiful and most important things in life can not be bought for money. They include good mental and physical health, self-respect, dignity, honor, understanding and love.

- Taking care of all the above named things is a stress all by itself!!! That's why it's important to remember one more way to get rid of stress–LAUGHTER! Have the courage and skill to laugh at oneself, and at one's own weaknesses, and to laugh at many funny characteristics of people around us. Laughter is healthy and has a relaxation effect.

BIBLIOGRAPHY

CHAPTER I

1. Recognizing and Addressing Healthcare Disparities in Medication Prescribing Among Racial and Ethnic Minorities With Acute and Chronic Pain CME Medscape CME Family Medicine. Didier Demesmin, MD, CME Released: 12/30/2009;

2. Metabolic Syndrome Increases CV Risk by Twofold Medscape CME News Author: Sue Hughes.CME Author: Laurie Barclay, MD Brande Nicole Martin, CME Clinical Editor, Medscape, LLC Laurie Barclay, MD Freelance writer and reviewer, Medscape, LLC, Sarah Fleischman, CME Program Manager, Medscape, LLC

3. Healthier Life Steps: A Clinician-Patient Guide From the AMA Carlo C. Di Clemente, PhD Professor, University of Maryland, Baltimore, et al.

4. Authentic Happiness: Using the New Positive Psychology to Realize Your Potential for Lasting Fulfillment by Martin E P Seligman, Ph.D. Free Press, ISBN: 0743222970, ISBN-13: 9780743222976

5. Fredrickson, B. L. (2001). The role of positive emotions in positive psychology: The broaden-and-build theory of positive emotions. American Psychologist, 56, 218-226.

6. Myers David. The American Paradox: Spiritual Hunger in an Age of Plenty (Yale University Press, 2000) explores our post-1960 material prosperity and social recession, and suggests a road to renewal.

7. Exercise and Well-Being: A Review of Mental and Physical Health Benefits Associated With Physical Activity, Frank J. Penedo; Jason R. Dahn Posted: 04/15/2005; Curr Opin Psychiatry. 2005;18(2):189-193.

8. Physical Activity and Public Health: Updated Recommendation for Adults From the American College of Sports Medicine and the American Heart Association William L. Haskell et All; Medicine and Science in Sports and Exercise®. 2007;39(8):1423-1434. © 2007 American College of Sports Medicine

CHAPTER II

1. Exercise and Well-Being: A Review of Mental and Physical Health Benefits Associated With Physical Activity, Frank J. Penedo; Jason R. Dahn Posted: 04/15/2005; Curr Opin Psychiatry. 2005;18(2):189-193.

2. Dean Ornish's Program for Reversing Heart Disease, Ballantine, 1992

3. A Randomized, Placebo-controlled Trial of the Effects of Physical Exercises and Estrogen Therapy on Health-related Quality of Life in Postmenopausal Women Carolina Kimie Moriyama et al.. 2008;15(4):613-618. © 2008

4. Heart Failure in the Elderly: Advances and Challenges, Bodh I Jugdutt , Expert Rev Cardiovasc Ther. 2010;8(5):695-715.

5. Alcohol Consumption in Young Adults and Incident Hypertension: 20-year Follow-up from the Coronary Artery Risk Development in Young Adults Study Journal Article, American Journal of Epidemiology, March 2010

6. A Review of the Literature on the Cognitive Effects of Alcohol Hangover How does an alcohol hangover state affect performance or cognitive functioning? What pathophysiological changes or biological mechanisms give rise to ... Journal Article, Alcohol and Alcoholism (Oxford, Oxfordshire), March 2008

7. Association of Average Daily Alcohol Consumption, Binge Drinking and Alcohol-Related Social Problems: Results from the German Epidemiological Surveys of Substance Abuse Journal Article, Alcohol and Alcoholism, May 2009

8. Blood Tests Say Drunk Drivers Escaping Conviction, News, Reuters Health Information, October 2010

9. Predictors of Enrollment and Retention in a Preventive Parenting Intervention for Divorced Families Motivation Theory (Rogers 1983) and the Transtheoretical Model (Prochaska et al. 1994), overlap with those of the HBM. A large body of research . Journal Article, J Prim Prev, March 2009

10. A Computerized Smoking Cessation Intervention for High School Smokers it predicts the systematic change required to adopt a health behavior (Prochaska & Prochaska, 1999). The theory identifies five stages of change: (a) ... Journal Article, Pediatr Nurs, January 2008

11. Estimating the Short-term Clinical and Economic Benefits of Smoking Cessation: Do We Have it Right? From a short-term perspective, how cost-effective are smoking cessation products? and Introduction Abstract Smoking cessation is cost effective Journal Article, Expert Rev Pharmacoeconomics Outcomes Res, June 2009

12. Using Multiple Sources of Knowledge to Reach Clinical Understanding of Chronic Fatigue Syndrome Journal Article, Annals of Family Medicine, July 2008

13. Feeling "Numb" Today... Anyone Else? as "creating a distance from patients" and including symptoms such as chronic tiredness, irritability, lack of joy in life and destructive behaviors .Blog, In Our Own Words: Medscape Nurses, April 2009

14. Humor and Laughter May Influence Health: III. Laughter and Health Outcomes Mary Payne Bennett; Cecile Lengacher, Evid Based Complement Alternat Med. 2008;5(1):37-40. © 2008 Oxford University Press

15. Three "Shrinks" Rap About Mental Health Embracing the notion that humor is an essential ingredient in mental health, 3 psychiatrists maintain a blog that invites free-ranging personal and . Article, Medscape Med Students, May 2007

16. Effectiveness of Chlamydia Screening: Systematic ReviewAre the benefits of chlamydia screening on preventing pelvic inflammatory disease.over-estimated? about how chlamydia screening would prevent pelvic ... Journal Article, International Journal of Epidemiology, April 2009

17. Changes in Cervical Cancer Screening Guidelines Could be Cost-Effective Now that vaccines and DNA testing for human papillomavirus are available, changes to the current cervical cancer screening guidelines could be cost-effective. News, Medscape Medical News, March 2008

18. Beliefs, Risk Perceptions, and Gaps in Knowledge as Barriers to Colorectal Cancer Screening in Older Adults Are older adults aware of the risk of colorectal cancer (CRC)? How can providers better talk to their older patients about CRC screening? Journal Article, J Am Geriatr Soc, February 2008

CHAPTER III FOOD

1. Vital Signs: State-specific Obesity Prevalence among Adults — United States, 2009This report looks at the latest data on obesity across the US, and discusses the many implications for public health in general. ... Journal Article, Morbidity & Mortality Weekly Report, October 2010

2. Thought for Food, Part 2: A Great Weight-Loss Supplement? ...Americans spend over $50 billion per year on weight-loss plans, diet food, and supplements,[1] and yet obesity rates are climbing in 49 of...answer is .Experts And Viewpoint, Medscape General Medicine, November 2005

3. American Mania: When More Is Not Enough the American national obsession with materialism and overconsumption from the perspectives of economics, philosophy, psychology, and neurobiology. Article, Medscape General Medicine, September 2005
4. Lifetime Medical Costs of Obesity: Prevention No Cure for Increasing Health Expenditure study estimated the annual and lifetime medical costs attributable to obesity. Find out why obesity prevention is not a cure for increasing health . Journal Article, PLoS Med, February 2008
5. The Obesity Epidemic in the US Is Due Solely to Increased Food IntakeThe rise in obesity in the US since the 1970s is entirely due to increased food consumption, not to a lack of physical activity. If Americans truly want to .News, Heartwire, May 2009
6. Salt to Go: US Fast Food Contains Excessive Levels of Sodium Meals from fast-food chains in New York City contain excessive amounts of salt, a new study has shown. Sandwich and fried-chicken outlets and one pizza. News, Heartwire, April 2010
7. Nutrition Info on Fast-Food Menus May Influence Parent's Choices for KidsOne of the first studies of fast-food choices at chain restaurants both before and after nutritional information was required on menus has delivered a. News, Heartwire, October 2010
8. The "MacStatin": Fast Food With Some Ketchup, Salt, and a Statin to Go calling for a statin, for free, situated beside the ketchup and salt, in fast-food restaurants. The group argues that the statin would neutralize the.News, Heartwire, August 2010
9. Food Manufacturers Cutting Portion Size To Combat Obesity: Effective or Not? Range of products from biscuits to cheese spread, says it is to reduce size of the portions. It will also scrap marketing campaigns in schools, and. Blog, KuorageousMD's blog, August 2009
10. SHED-IT Trial Reveals Weight Loss Keys for MenAs their preferred weight reduction strategies, men choose smaller portion sizes, and cut down on sugary drinks and fat intake. News, Medscape Medical News, June 2010
11. Calorie Counts Increasing in Classic Recipes A study shows ballooning portion size and heftier ingredients in classic recipes. to a shift to larger serving sizes and higher-calorie ingredients. News, WebMD Health News, February 2009
12. School Drink Agreement Cuts Calories: Group out of U.S. schools has begun to work, with diet beverages and smaller portions replacing some full-size, full-calorie varieties in school vending. News, Reuters Health Information, March 2010
13. Low-Fat, Vegan Diet May Be Effective for Weight Loss, a vegan diet led to significant weight loss in overweight postmenopausal women, despite the absence of prescribed limits on portion size or energy intake. News, Medscape Medical News, September 2005
14. Heavy Alcohol Use Linked to Colon Cancer Risk Previous studies have been inconclusive about the role of alcohol as a risk factor for colorectal cancer, Dr. Sethi said. To test the. News, Medscape Medical News, October 2003
15. Cancer Incidence among Patients with Alcohol Use Disorders -- Long-Term Follow-Up Are patients with alcohol-use disorders more susceptible to developing cancer? This study was to compare the cancer morbidity in a large cohort of ... Journal Article, Alcohol and Alcoholism, September 2009
16. Cancer Risk Increased by Excess Body Fat, Red and Processed Meats, and Alcohol finds that the consumption of certain foods, excess body weight, and alcohol consumption can increase the risk for a variety of different types of . News, Medscape Medical News, October 2007
17. Most Pounds Off With Lowest CarbsA TO Z Weight Loss Study compares Atkins, Traditional, Ornish and Zone diets. Results for women enrolled are surprising Â– Atkins better than traditional. Journal Article, Journal Watch, April 2007
18. Soft Drinks and Weight Gain: How Strong Is the Link? soft drinks.[12] Soft drinks are aggressively marketed, and 2 companies -- Coca-Cola and PepsiCo -- dominate sales in the United States. In 1999,Journal Article, Medscape J Med, August 2008
19. Predictors of Overweight and Obesity in Five to Seven-year-old Children in Germany: Results From Cross-sectional Studies have shown overweight or obesity to be related to lower socioeconomic status, migration background, and an overweight mother. Which factors. Journal Article, BMC Public Health, May 2008
20. The Antibiotic Food-Chain Gang Swann principles. The Swann report, issued in 1969, recommends that antibiotics used to treat infections in humans not be used as animal-food Journal Article, Emerging Infectious Diseases, May 2001
21. Food Additives For centuries, food additives have been used for flavoring, coloring, and extension of the useful shelf-life of food, as well as the promotion of food Blog, NUTRITALK, July 2010
22. Study Shows Garlic Protects Against Some CancersA new study shows that garlic can help protect against stomach and colorectal cancer, according to researchers at the University of North Carolina at. News, Medscape Medical News, October 2000
23. Switching Protein Sources May Reduce CHD Risk Relying on fish, nuts, and poultry instead of red meat for protein significantly reduced the risk of coronary disease in the Nurses' Health Study. News, Heartwire, August 2010
24. Red Wine for the Heart: Sour Grapes or Sound Medical Advice? Could washing down dark chocolate with a glass of red wine improve one's cardiovascular health? washing down dark chocolate with a glass of red. Conference Coverage, December 2002
25. Regular Tea Consumption May Slow Cognitive Decline New research suggests regular tea consumption may help slow the rate of cognitive decline in older adults. Hawaii) — Regular tea consumption may. News, Medscape Medical News, July 2010
26. Resveratrol May Slow Aging in Humans Common food sources of resveratrol include grapes, wine, peanuts, blueberries, and cranberries. Study author Husam Ghanim, PhD, of the University of. News, WebMD Health News, August 2010
27. Eggs: Are They Really Good or Bad for You? Of work-related endeavors. Back to nutrition, over the past 5 years the Egg Nutrition Center, based in Washington, DC, has been sending me newsletters. Blog, NUTRITALK, July 20
28. Adherence to the Mediterranean Diet Moderates the Association of Aminotransferases with the Prevalence of the Metabolic Syndrome; the ATTICA Studyare markers of metabolic syndrome in healthy adults. However, for the first time, a study shows that a Mediterranean diet may alter this relationship. Journal Article, Nutr Metab, October 2009
29. New PREDIMED Data: Mediterranean Diet Halves Incidence of New-Onset Diabetes. A new study examining whether use of the Mediterranean diet prevented the onset of diabetes in individuals at high cardiovascular risk found that it did, ... News, Heartwire, October 2010
30. Improved Autonomic Function May Partly Explain Benefits of Mediterranean Diet: Twin StudyA new study linking high adherence to a Mediterranean-like diet to better heart-rate variability may get researchers one step closer to understanding just ... News, Heartwire, June 2010
31. Mediterranean Diet Linked to Lower Risk for Stomach Cancer In a prospective cohort, greater adherence to a relative Mediterranean diet was associated with a significantly lower risk for incident gastric adenocarcinoma. News, Medscape Medical News, December 2009

CHAPTER IV

1. Work Stress and Coronary Heart Disease: What Are the Mechanisms? Is the accumulation of work stress associated with higher risks of CHD? Does work stress affect CHD directly through neuroendocrine mechanisms and/or. Journal Article, European Heart Journal, March 2008

2. Depression and Stress Hit Hard on the Heart Studies find depression, stress, and general disposition affect cardiac outcomes; cardiac patients are more likely to develop depression.News, Medscape Cardiology, March 2003

3. Heart Rate and Blood Pressure Responses to Mental Stress and Clinical Cardiovascular Events in Men and Women After Coronary Artery Bypass Grafting: The Post Coronary Artery Bypass Graft (Post-CABG) Biobehavioral Study Vigorous heart rate and BP responses to mental stress testing may be markers for a lower risk of incidence of clinical cardiovascular events among patients.Journal Article, American Heart Journal, August 2003

4. Type A, Race, Anger, Forgiveness, Plus Stroke, HRT, and Hydralazine - The Bad, the Good, and the To-Be-Avoided appears to indicate that if anger at an offender can be assuaged by forgiveness, considerable blood pressure benefit can be gained by the person who. Article, Medscape Cardiology, November 2003

5. The Art of Apology: When and How to Seek Forgiveness care from another physician. Even when there seems to be genuine forgiveness, it may not be appropriate for the doctor to continue as the patient's. Journal Article, Family Practice Management, August 2007

6. Disparities in Adult Awareness of Heart Attack Warning Signs and Symptoms--14 States, 2005 Disparities in awareness were observed by race/ethnicity, sex, and level of education for awareness of heart attack warning signs. Journal Article, Morbidity & Mortality Weekly Report, February 2008

7. Receipt of Outpatient Cardiac Rehabilitation Among Heart Attack Survivors -- United States, 2005 is essential to recovery care post-myocardial infarction (MI)/heart attack. What is the prevalence of receipt of outpatient cardiac rehab among. Journal Article, Morbidity & Mortality Weekly Report, February 2008

8. Advances in the Prevention of Sudden Cardiac Death in the Young Genetic heart disorders are an important cause of sudden cardiac death (SCD) in the young. This article discusses recent advances in SCD prevention. Journal Article, Ther Adv Cardiovasc Dis, March 2009

9. MEDLINE Abstracts: Environmental Influences on Asthma - The Role of Indoor Allergens ... MEDLINE Abstracts: Environmental Influences on Asthma - The Role of Indoor Allergens What's new concerning the impact of indoor allergens on asthma? Abstract, Medscape Pulmonary Medicine, January 1998

10. Allergen Immunotherapy in the Prevention of Asthma Asthma is the most common chronic disease of childhood, and it is associated with substantial morbidity and mortality. the use of allergen. Journal Article, Curr Opin Allergy Clin Immunol, April 2004

11. Diagnosis and Management of Chronic Daily Headache Learn the differential diagnosis for the various forms of chronic daily headache, and their appropriate management. Journal Article, Semin Neurol, April 2010

12. The Headache Management Trial: A Randomized Study of Coordinated Care This trial sought to determine if patients cared for in a coordinated headache management program. Journal Article, Headache, October 2008

13. Themed Review: Lifestyle Treatment of the Metabolic Syndrome Lifestyle modification consisting of exercise and caloric restriction for treatment and prevention of the metabolic syndrome is examined.Journal Article, Am J Lifestyle Med, March 2008

14. Components of Metabolic Syndrome Linked to Plaque ProgressionA new IVUS study has found that although the metabolic syndrome is associated with accelerated plaque progression, this can be attributed to its individual News, Heartwire, March 2010

15. Diabetes Mellitus The discovery of insulin was the turning point in the management of diabetes mellitus. point in the management of diabetes mellitus. The first ... Journal Article, South Med J, January 2002

16. Diabetes Mellitus Type 2 Resource Center Review in-depth clinical information, latest medical news, and guidelines about diabetes mellitus type 2 and the major types of diabetes mellitus, such as gestational diabetes, adult-onset diabetes, and insulin-dependent diabetes mellitus. Resource Center

17. High Cholesterol in Childhood What can be done to curb cholesterol levels at an early age? and the screening for and treatment of lipid abnormalities in childhood and ... Journal Article, US Pharmacist, March 2009

18. High-Risk Patients Remain Undertreated for High LDL Cholesterol to have the highest risk of elevated low density lipoprotein (LDL)-cholesterol, according to new research published in the Journal of the American ... News, Reuters Health Information, November 2009

19. The Association of Periodontal Disease, Diabetes, and Cardiovascular Disease...associated with an increased likelihood of coronary heart disease and diabetes Scope: A consensus group...connective tissue and bone which anchor the ... Journal Article, British Journal of Diabetes and Vascular Disease, July 2008

20. Infection or Inflammation: The Link Between Periodontal and Cardiovascular Diseases...of people retaining more of their natural teeth, such that this increasingly dentate population is...bone loss, increased the odds of coronary heart . Journal Article, Future Cardiology, January 2009

21. Tooth and Periodontal Disease: A Review for the Primary-Care Physician regular professional cleanings. Figure 2. Location of pit and fissures on tooth surfaces. During office visits with patients of all ages, physicians are. Journal Article, South Med J, September 2001

22. The Epidemiology of Nonalcoholic Fatty Liver Disease: A Global Perspective Nonalcoholic fatty liver disease is an increasingly recognized cause of liver disease globally. This overview provides an epidemiological background on ... Journal Article, Semin Liver Dis, November 2008

23. Chronic Liver Disease in an Ageing Population The most common chronic liver diseases that geriatricians are likely to encounter in clinical practice are presented. of chronic liver disease. Journal Article, Age and Ageing, January 2009

24. The Role of Diet in the Prevention of Common Kidney Stones Review key dietary recommendations for people with a history of kidney stones. for patients who form kidney stones are discussed. Focusing on. Journal Article, December 2005

25. DASH-Style Diet May Help Prevent Kidney Stones shows that following a Dietary Approaches to Stop Hypertension diet may help lower kidney stone risk by increasing urinary citrate and urinary volume. ... News, Medscape Medical News, September 2010

26. Lifestyle Interventions in the Prevention and Treatment of Cancer Certain lifestyle factors continue to be causally related to certain cancers, and other cancers have lifestyle-based etiologic factors. Lifestyle changes. Journal Article, Am J Lifestyle Med, November 2009

27. A Systematic Review and Lessons Learned From Early Lung Cancer Detection Trials Using Low-Dose Computed Tomography of the Chest Lung cancer accounts for one third of cancer deaths in men and one fourth of cancer deaths in women in the United States, despite advances in the treatment ... Journal Article, Cancer Control, July 2003

28. Prevention and Management of Colorectal Cancer in Women...Abstract and Introduction Abstract Objective. To review prevention and management strategies for colorectal cancer, with an emphasis on studies. Journal Article, J Am Pharm Assoc, July 2001

29. MEDLINE Abstracts: Prevention and Treatment of Breast Cancer Read what's new in breast cancer prevention and treatment in this collection of recent MEDLINE abstract. Abstracts: Prevention and Treatment of, Abstract, Medscape Hematology-Oncology, March 2002
30. NIH Consensus Development Panel on Osteoporosis Prevention, Diagnosis, and Therapy, March 7-29, 2000: Highlights of the Conference The National Institutes of Health organized this conference to define the factors associated with prevention, diagnosis, and treatment of osteoporosis. Journal Article, South Med J, June 2001
31. Current Approaches to the Prevention and Treatment of Postmenopausal Osteoporosis Sometimes referred to as the silent thief, osteoporosis is a disease that can rob the skeleton bank of its resources. to the prevention,Journal Article, American Journal of Health-System Pharmacy, May 2003
32. Positive Associations of Serum Concentration of Polychlorinated Biphenyls or Organochlorine Pesticides with Self-Reported Arthritis, Especially Rheumatoid Type, in Women A study examining associations of background exposure to persistent organic pollutants with arthritis among the general population. Journal Article, Environmental Health Perspectives, June 2007
33. Too much red meat linked to increased risk of RAreported the first evidence of a link between excessive consumption of red meat and the development of rheumatoid arthritis. However, further work is. News, Medscape Medical News, December 2004
34. Baseline Testing Important in Glaucoma Prevention Because optic nerve damage is a sign of glaucoma, baseline documentation of the optic nerve in all patients for later comparison is important. David M. ... Medscape Ophthalmology, July 2009
35. Novel Measures of Cardiovascular Health and its Association With Prevalence and Progression of Age-Related Macular Degeneration: The CHARM StudyThis study evaluated whether cardiovascular health was associated with an increased risk of prevalent AMD and progression. Journal Article, BMC Ophthalmol, December 2008

CHAPTER V

1. Bipolar Disorders and Genetics: Clinical Implications of High Heritability the presence of early psychopathology, psychosocial stressors such as dysfunctional family environments, stressful life events, and ineffective coping ... Experts And Viewpoint, Medscape Psychiatry & Mental Health, September 2004
2. Childhood Trauma, Stress Linked to Adult Chronic Fatigue Syndrome suggest that stress early in life, during critical periods of heightened brain plasticity, may permanently affect areas of the brain involved in. News, Medscape Medical News, November 2006
3. Clinical and Pharmacologic Strategies to Achieve Remission in Depression Careful assessments, frequent follow-ups, and strategic adjustments to treatment can help patients with depression overcome their symptoms. Clinical Review, Medscape CME Psychiatry & Mental Health, October 2010
4. Vardenafil May Improve Both Erectile Dysfunction and Mild DepressionIn a placebo-controlled, randomized study, vardenafil was well-tolerated and highly efficacious in men with erectile dysfunction and untreated mild depression. News, Medscape Medical News, January 2006
5. Men Over 50: An Endangered Species impairs quality of life. , Testosterone Decline in Aging Men: Does "Andropause" Exist? For healthy adult men, testosterone is associated with the. Clinical Review, October 2001
6. Vardenafil May Improve Both Erectile Dysfunction and Mild DepressionIn a placebo-controlled, randomized study, vardenafil was well-tolerated and highly efficacious in men with erectile dysfunction and untreated mild depression. News, Medscape Medical News, January 2006
7. Advances in Understanding the Nature of Insomnia studies that link poor sleep to a variety of comorbid disorders and reviews research that clarifies the pathophysiology and heritability of insomnia. Conference Coverage, July 2005
8. Depression: Lifestyle and Complementary Therapies to Promote Healthy Moods in Teens Health Strength Confidence and courage Faith Flexibility Adaptability Forgiveness Endurance Cheerfulness Hope Focus Focus/ Attention Love Coordination .Clinical Review, Medscape Pediatrics, November 2007
9. Work Stress Ups Risk of CHD via Biologic MechanismsNew research confirms that stress at work can increase the risk for coronary heart disease and shows for the first time that such stress mediates its. News, Medscape Medical News, January 2008
10. Workplace Stress Management Program Reduces Heart-Rate Variability and BPA workplace stress-management program based on cognitive restructuring and relaxation training reduced heart-rate variability and decreased blood pressure ... News, Medscape Medical News, January 2007
11. Posttraumatic Stress Disorder Symptoms May Increase Coronary Heart Disease Risk In a prospective study, a higher level of symptoms of posttraumatic stress disorder was associated with increased risk for coronary heart disease in older men.News, Medscape Medical News, January 2007
12. Childhood Trauma, Stress Linked to Adult Chronic Fatigue Syndrome Two studies suggest that stress early in life, during critical periods of heightened brain plasticity, may permanently affect areas of the brain involved. News, Medscape Medical News, November 2006
13. Mindful Communication Education May Help Prevent Burnout in Primary Care Physicians...September 28, 2009 — Mindful communication education may help prevent burnout in primary care physicians, according to the results of a before-after. News, Medscape Medical News CME, September 2009

CPSIA information can be obtained
at www.ICGtesting.com
Printed in the USA
LVIC04n1157130716
496072LV00006B/11